WELFARE POLICY UNDER NEW LABOUR

Views from inside Westminster

Hugh Bochel and Andrew Defty

First published in Great Britain in 2007 by

The Policy Press
University of Bristol
Fourth Floor
Beacon House
Queen's Road
Bristol BS8 1QU
UK

Tel +44 (0)117 331 4054
Fax +44 (0)117 331 4093
e-mail tpp-info@bristol.ac.uk
www.policypress.org.uk

British Library Cataloguing in Publication Data
A catalogue record for this book is available from the British Library.

Library of Congress Cataloging-in-Publication Data
A catalog record for this book has been requested.

ISBN 978 1 86134 790 9 hardcover

Hugh Bochel is Professor of Public Policy, **Andrew Defty** is a Research Fellow, both at the University of Lincoln.

Cover design by Qube Design Associates, Bristol.
Printed and bound in Great Britain by Hobbs the Printers, Southampton.

For Alistair and Isobel
and
Matthew, Isobel and Michael

Contents

List of tables

Tables

Acknowledgements

This work draws extensively on a series of interviews with 76 Members of Parliament (MPs) and 10 Peers, undertaken between November 2004 and January 2006. We owe a great debt of gratitude to these parliamentarians without whom this work would not have been written. All were generous with their time, submitting themselves to lengthy face-to-face interviews on a subject on which some claimed little detailed knowledge, while others clearly had a great deal. Yet, without exception, they made valuable observations either about the nature of state welfare or the role of Parliament or more often both, and answered our questions with intelligence, insight and good humour. We would also like to thank the army of MPs' assistants who willingly arranged these interviews and helpfully rearranged them when unforeseen events, key parliamentary debates and a general election, understandably forced MPs to cancel appointments.

Several individuals offered advice and comments at various stages of this project and we are particularly grateful to Peter Taylor-Gooby, Philip Norton, Philip Cowley and the staff of the Department of Policy Studies at the University of Lincoln. We are grateful to the University of Lincoln for generously funding this research, and to Philip de Bary and Emily Watt at The Policy Press for their encouragement and their patience.

ONE

Introduction

Welfare reform is a central part of the modernisation programme adopted by the Labour governments since 1997. Demographic pressures generated by expansive patterns of demand for pensions and healthcare for an ageing population, coupled with the pressures of globalisation to drive down taxes and regulation, have led to a fundamental shift in Labour Party thinking regarding the principle of universal welfare provision. Despite a commitment to increased public expenditure on some areas of welfare provision, in office New Labour followed many of the policies of the previous Conservative government, including spending restraint, the use of market principles in the state sector, an emphasis on selectivity, and a more modest approach to the direct delivery of services, targeted at those who can demonstrate the most need. The government's policy priorities and Labour's attempt to steer a 'Third Way' between traditional concepts of universal welfare provision and the New Right commitment to the market, has led some to identify the emergence of a new political consensus on approaches to welfare. However, the extent of support for such a consensus within parliament and among the public is at present far from clear.

Recent years have also seen renewed debate about the role of parliament in the scrutiny of government policy. Successive governments have presided over a shift of responsibility for significant areas of policy away from Westminster to the European Union and quasi-independent bodies such as utility regulators and the Bank of England. Since 1997, the Labour governments have pursued an extensive programme of constitutional reform that has seen the devolution of power, including large areas of social policy, to the Scottish Parliament and the Welsh Assembly. There have also been significant changes in the operation and composition of the Westminster Parliament, with reform of parliamentary procedure designed to 'modernise' the House of Commons; and substantive reform of the House of Lords, in an effort to make the upper House more representative and legitimate. The removal of the hereditary peers has for the first time led to Labour being the largest party in the Lords, and also prompted an influx of new life peers, from a range of backgrounds and experience, including a number with backgrounds in social policy. There have also been significant changes to the composition of the House of Commons since 1997, with a surge in the number of women elected to parliament in 1997, up from 60 to 120, and a less significant rise in the number of non-white Members of Parliament (MPs), up from 6 to 9. These constitutional and compositional changes have led to considerable debate about the effectiveness of parliament as a body for scrutinising the executive and renewed debate about the representative function of parliament.

This book focuses on the perceptions and activities of MPs in relation to welfare policy since 1997, and seeks to assess their influence on policy and legislation. Based on interviews with 76 MPs from across the House of Commons, it examines the extent of cross-party consensus on approaches to the role of the state in welfare, and the level of intra-party debate about welfare policy. It also examines the relationship between MPs' attitudes to welfare and those of the general public, in order to determine the extent to which any shifts in the political consensus on welfare is reflected in public opinion, and raising important questions about the nature of representation at Westminster. Drawing on additional interviews with 10 peers from each of the main parties, and from the crossbenches, the book also assesses the role of the reconstituted House of Lords in the scrutiny of welfare.

This book follows from an earlier study, *Parliament and welfare policy* (1992), by Hugh Bochel, which examined MPs' attitudes to welfare during the 1980s. That study drew on a series of interviews with 96 MPs undertaken by Bochel and Peter Taylor-Gooby in 1986 and 1987 (Taylor-Gooby and Bochel, 1988). The timing of Taylor-Gooby and Bochel's survey was propitious. The broad postwar consensus on the welfare state was challenged in the 1980s by the Conservative governments of Margaret Thatcher. A deteriorating economic situation, consequent rises in unemployment, and an ageing population had led to new and expansive patterns of demand for welfare provision. These economic and demographic pressures, coupled with the ideological imperatives of the New Right that were driving the Thatcher government's commitment to reducing the role of the state, led to successive cuts in welfare spending and an expansion in private provision. At the time of Taylor-Gooby and Bochel's survey, the Thatcher government was nearing the end of its second term, and apparently unassailable in the polls. Interest in social policy had been aroused by the Thatcher governments' attempts to rein in the welfare state, and the survey coincided with two pieces of welfare legislation – the 1986 Social Security Act and the 1986 Disabled Persons (Services,

Consultation and Representation) Act, both of which were the subject of detailed case studies in *Parliament and welfare policy* (Bochel, 1992).

Taylor-Gooby and Bochel's survey confirmed the widely held view that in the 1980s there was a distinct absence of consensus in parliament about welfare policy. MPs interviewed by Taylor-Gooby and Bochel were clearly divided on party lines. This, they found, was particularly the case at the broad philosophical level, with Conservative MPs generally in favour of a minimal 'safety net' role for the state, while Labour MPs wanted a high standard of state provision and universal social services. While the parties were ideologically divided, intra-party divisions were not pronounced, and Taylor-Gooby and Bochel found that, in general, MPs' responses to questions about welfare were well within the parameters of their parties' policies, and closely reflected the views of the party leadership. In general, they concluded, the potential for consensus was slight, although there was some broad cross-party agreement on the existence of some groups who were particularly in need, or 'deserving' of state support, most notably older people and people with disabilities. Interestingly, they also discovered that MPs from all parties were concerned about the 'presentational' aspects of their policies, most notably in relation to the public perception of the Conservatives as a party of cuts, and Labour as profligate (Bochel, 1992).

The survey on which this book is based is similarly timely. Undertaken between October 2005 and January 2006, it examined parliamentary attitudes at a similar point in the lifetime of the second Blair government. At the time of most of the interviews, the Blair government was in a strong position in the polls, and had a larger majority in parliament than the second Thatcher government. Like Thatcher, Blair has sought a fundamental reform of the postwar consensus on welfare. Blair's welfare reforms have generated considerable interest among the public, academics and public sector workers. However, the response to Labour's welfare reforms, particularly within parliament, suggests that in some respects consensus may be more evident between the parties than within them. Intra-party debate about the role of the state in welfare provision has been considerable, not least within the parliamentary Labour Party. The largest government rebellions of the 1997-2001 Parliament were generated by cuts in Lone Parent Benefit (1997), and proposed reform of Incapacity Benefit (1999). Welfare reform continued to be the cause of disquiet on Labour benches throughout Labour's second and third terms, with substantial revolts on foundation hospitals (2003), tuition fees for higher education (2004), and access to schools (2006), and further controversial proposals to reform Incapacity Benefit (2006). The survey also coincided in part with leadership contests in both the Conservative and Liberal Democrat Parties. These contests served to highlight significant divisions within both parties, not least over approaches to welfare and the role of the public services.

Taylor-Gooby and Bochel's earlier work not only provides a model for this research but also provides a body of data with which to compare MPs' attitudes today, and those of MPs sitting in the 1980s, at a time when a different party was in power, and the welfare environment was markedly different. This is particularly important in determining whether any shift in MPs' attitudes is indicative of a movement towards a consensus in political attitudes to welfare. Taylor-Gooby and Bochel were not so fortunate in being able to compare their findings, which suggested the decline of consensus, with similar data from earlier periods said to be characterised by a greater degree of consensus, such as the 1960s. Studies of the attitudes, beliefs and values of MPs were, and remain, relatively sparse. Among such studies as have emerged there exists great variation in the aims and objectives and in the concepts and methodologies employed. Many studies focus in particular on the attitudes of MPs from one party. Moreover, welfare-related issues have figured only in minor or rather general ways in the existing studies.

A number of studies have surveyed MPs' attitudes using interviews and postal questionnaires. Several of these preceded and informed Bochel's earlier study. In 1969 Kornberg and Frasure measured differences between the parties on a range of issues during the period of Harold Wilson's second Labour government (Kornberg and Frasure, 1971). Their objective was to put to empirical test two existing views about the ideological distinctiveness of the parties. Information was collected by postal questionnaire from 197 Labour and 126 Conservative MPs. Of the 10 issues used to test difference, only five were found significantly to discriminate between Labour and Conservative respondents. One of these was comprehensive education, the only social policy issue included by the researchers. Also in the 1960s Putnam (1971 and 1973) collected data by interview from 93 British backbench MPs to compare with that obtained from 83 Italian deputies. Putnam's interest was in investigating aspects of 'elite political culture', and particularly the 'political style' of respondents, to establish whether and what differences existed between the two countries. While he asked respondents to discuss issues including one or two related to social policy, Putnam's interest was in how they conceptualised these and in their values in relation to their democratic political systems.

For a study of ideological variations within The Labour Party,

Whiteley (1983) analysed responses to a number of postal surveys carried out between 1975 and 1978, one of which was directed to MPs. Using reactions to 25 Likert-scaled statements related to 'all controversial political issues' within the party, Whiteley compared the attitudes of 51 MPs with those of parliamentary candidates, local councillors and conference delegates. His results indicated the existence of a distinct left–right continuum of attitudes in the party, the conference delegates and parliamentary candidates being further to the left than MPs and councillors. Among his 25 statements Whiteley included two relating to welfare policy, both on the public private issue in health and education. Both figured among the seven issues attracting the highest degree of consensus among the pool of respondents.

More recently, Donald Searing's (1994) monumental study of MPs' roles was based on lengthy interviews with 521 MPs in the early 1970s (83% of the then House of Commons). Searing sought to assess the various political roles adopted by MPs, both as backbenchers and ministers, identifying distinctive roles developed by MPs themselves such as constituency members, policy advocates and 'parliament men', and the manner in which MPs adapted to established roles such as those of whips, parliamentary private secretaries and ministers. This research included some investigation of MPs' values. Using a ranking technique for 36 values, Searing found that those most sharply separating Conservative from Labour MPs were social equality, freedom, socialism, social planning and public order. However, Searing found little evidence that values played an important part in the roles adopted by MPs, and his focus on political roles precluded detailed assessment of MPs' attitudes towards specific policy areas such as welfare.

Between 1994 and 1996, the MPs Project assessed the attitudes of Conservative and Labour MPs towards European integration using postal questionnaires, to which 33% of both Conservative and Labour MPs responded (Baker et al, 1995, 1996; Baker, 1997). While dealing with an issue that has caused major faultlines in British politics, within the main parties as much as between them, the survey included questions on the social dimension of European integration. Despite the overall intra-party divisions on Europe, on the social dimension they found some level of agreement, with overwhelming Conservative backbench support for opting-out of the social chapter of the Maastricht Treaty (Baker et al, 1995), and near-unanimity among Labour MPs in support of harmonisation of social policy in general, and working standards in particular (Baker et al, 1996).

More comprehensive evidence of the divisions between the parties has been revealed by the British Representation Survey (BRS). At successive general elections since 1992, the British Candidate Survey in 1992, and the BRS 1997, 2001 and 2005, have collected quantitative data on attitudes by a postal survey sent to all parliamentary candidates and MPs standing in the general elections, with the response rate generally consisting of around one third of sitting MPs. The BRS is designed to collect information on the selection process of parliamentary candidates, their political attitudes and personal backgrounds, and includes scalar questions to assess respondents' ideological positions on issues such as nationalisation versus privatisation, the redistribution of wealth, European integration and gender equality.

The BRS has been used in particular to assess the impact of women on parliament in terms of representation (Norris and Lovenduski, 1995; Lovenduski and Norris, 2003). Since 1997, this work has been augmented by a number of studies that have used interviews to examine the experiences of women MPs (Bochel and Briggs, 2000; Childs, 2004), and also MPs from minority ethnic groups (Puwar, 2004). Although these studies did not look in particular at social policy, their conclusions inform research on MPs' attitudes in terms of understanding the operation of parliament and the development of the public policy agenda. Bochel and Briggs interviewed 39 female politicians from across the UK, including 24 MPs. They found that women politicians often feel that they operate in a different manner to their male counterparts, being less confrontational and more willing to cooperate, and that they may bring different perspectives to the political arena (Bochel and Briggs, 2000). These findings were supported by Childs who interviewed 34 of the 65 newly elected Labour women MPs in 1997, and re-interviewed 23 of them three years on (Childs, 2004). Childs found that while some new Labour women MPs believed that women would employ a new 'feminised' style of politics, in practice they felt pressurised to conform with the masculine style of the Commons. Perhaps most importantly, while many women MPs claimed that their presence in parliament was important for the representation of women, Childs concluded that the reality was more complex than this, and that in questions of policy preference other factors such as party identification are at least as important as the gender of MPs. Puwar (2004) argues that the model into which black and Asian MPs are pressurised to conform is not only defined by established male-dominated parties, but the "hegemonic culture of upper/middle class whiteness" (Puwar, 2004, p 77).

Interviews and questionnaires are not, of course, the only means of determining the values and attitudes of MPs. An alternative approach is to make use of the established instruments for recording parliamentary opinion, such as early day motions (EDMs), and voting records. EDMs are resolutions tabled by MPs to express views about topical issues and signed by any other MP wishing to indicate agreement. The attraction of EDMs as a tool for researching MPs' attitudes is that these resolutions are initiated and signed by MPs without interference from the whips – "spontaneous unwhipped backbench manifestos" (Finer et al, 1961, p 7). The analysis of EDMs, as indicators of backbench opinion, was pioneered in the 1960s and 1970s by Finer et al (1961), Berrington (1973) and Berrington and Leece (1977). The aims of these studies included the investigation, for both the main political parties, of the relationship between the political attitudes of backbench MPs and their social backgrounds, and of the existence of different 'opinion blocs' within the parties. While only a small part of their study considered attitudes to social policy, on the basis of their analysis they were able to allocate Labour MPs to distinct 'wings' of the party, but this was not possible in the case of the Conservatives who were generally more homogeneous, and among whom divisions on social policy were more attributable to constituency concerns, or the "variegated nature of electoral support", rather than any coherent social philosophy (Finer et al, 1961, p 102).

More recently, Childs and Withey (2004) studied sex differences in the signing of EDMs by Labour MPs in the 1997 Parliament, in order to test whether Labour's women MPs were acting for women. They concluded that while women were less likely to sign EDMs in general, Labour's women MPs were more likely than Labour men to sign EDMs that related to 'women's' and especially 'feminist women's' issues, adding weight to the arguments made elsewhere (Bochel and Briggs, 2000; Lovenduski and Norris, 2003; Childs, 2004) that male and female MPs behave differently, and that the gender of representatives in parliament is therefore important.

Researchers' enthusiasm about the potential value of EDMs as a "splendid mine of information on backbench opinion" is understandable (Finer et al, 1961, p 8). However, there are methodological problems connected with its use as an indicator of attitudes: not every potential supporter signs EDMs – there are always absentees from the House, some MPs may be too busy, some will be apathetic about the particular topic, and the motions show only those in favour and not those indifferent or opposed. Moreover, while this may not have been the case in the 1960s, these motions are today neither solely backbench, unwhipped or spontaneous.

A number of studies have sought to assess MPs' attitudes through analysis of voting behaviour. Studies of parliamentary rebellions, by Norton, and more recently Cowley, have respectively sought to assess the level of cohesion in the parliamentary Conservative and Labour Parties (Norton, 1975, 1978; Cowley, 2002, 2005). Cowley's studies of Labour rebellions in the first two Blair governments are particularly relevant to this study. Based on analysis of voting records coupled with interviews with Labour rebels and whips, Cowley has shown that there has been significant and growing discontent within the parliamentary Labour Party about various aspects of policy since 1997. Contrary to frequent claims that Labour MPs have been overwhelmingly loyal and supine, he has demonstrated that Labour MPs are prepared to rebel, and rebel in large numbers, when sufficiently exercised by the issue in question, and moreover, that the government has been prepared to respond to such discontent by making significant concessions on policy (Cowley, 2002, 2005).

However, while it is clear that a significant proportion of Labour MPs have been sufficiently exercised by various aspects of welfare policy to set aside party loyalty to vote against the government, what is not clear is the extent to which such backbench rebellions are indicative of a wider disquiet on Labour benches. As Norton (1978) has observed, voting against the whip is just one means by which MPs may express dissent about their party policy, but it is merely the tip of the iceberg. There are numerous other fora in which intra-party dissent may be expressed, both preceding and succeeding its expression in the division lobbies. Verbal or written dissent may be expressed privately at party meetings, in meetings with ministers and whips, or publicly in the House, constituency, or in the media. Such dissent or concerns are of course much more difficult to measure than the quantifiable data provided by voting records. Scrutiny of parliamentary debates, speeches and MPs' statements in the media may provide a useful indicator of opinion within the party. Beyond these public expressions of dissent, Norton suggests, interviews with MPs can provide a much broader and deeper analysis of the extent of parliamentary dissent, and more importantly the reasons for that dissent (Norton, 1978, pp 27-8).

Moreover, while analysis of rebellions has served to highlight opposition to Labour policies, it is less helpful in explaining the extent of parliamentary support for the government's reform agenda. As analysts of parliamentary dissent such as Norton and Cowley are at pains to stress, voting against one's own party remains a minority pastime in Westminster, and party cohesion is the norm. However, explaining cohesion is perhaps more difficult than identifying the causes of dissent. Critics of party government will argue that MPs are effectively restrained by a combination of threats and rewards orchestrated by the whips office. However, as Cowley has argued in relation to Labour MPs, cohesion since 1997 is evidently not the result of any lack of backbone, as many have been prepared to rebel when the issue warranted. Rather, he suggests, cohesion may be explained by a broad agreement on the part of many Labour MPs with the government's programme. Agreement, which may be explained at least in part by a shift in political attitudes in The Labour Party (Cowley, 2002, p 231).

However, the evidence for such a change in MPs' attitudes is not clear, and certainly cannot be deduced from voting behaviour alone. In order to determine whether there has been a genuine shift in the political attitudes of MPs one must make a more forensic analysis of their attitudes and the extent to which they correspond with party policy, and moreover, whether these views are noticeably different from those expressed by MPs in the past.

Methodology

Detailed research on MPs' attitudes and opinions is notoriously difficult to conduct. Any attempt to construct a representative sample of parliamentary opinion is dependent on the willingness of MPs to agree to lengthy face-to-face interviews. Nevertheless, this research is based on a substantial sample of MPs that is broadly representative of the House of Commons as a whole, according to a number of criteria. Seventy-six MPs were interviewed between October 2004 and January 2006, a sample comprising at least 10% of each of the main parties in the Commons, balanced to reflect the balance of the parties: 35 Labour, 22 Conservative, 14 Liberal Democrat, 2 SNP, 2 Plaid Cymru, 1 Independent.

Those interviewed reflected a broad range of parliamentary experience, including MPs first elected to parliament between 1970 and 2005. While the relatively small numbers involved make cohort analysis difficult, the sample is broadly representative of the balance of experience in the Commons: 54% of the sample were elected at the time of the 1997 General Election or since, a group which comprises 61% of the House as a whole. The survey also included a number of MPs elected to parliament for the first time in the General Election of May 2005. The 2005 General Election saw 122 new MPs enter parliament: 40 Labour, 54 Conservative, 20 Liberal Democrat and 8 from other parties. The newly elected MPs comprise 19% of the current House of Commons and 20% of the sample, once again balanced to reflect the balance of the parties, with no less than 10% of each of the main parties' new intake interviewed: 7 Labour, 5 Conservative, and 3 Liberal Democrat.

Another marked feature of the House of Commons since 1997 has been the relative growth in the representation of women in parliament, and this is reflected in the sample. In the 2005 Parliament, 20% of MPs were women, compared to 24% in the sample.

The sample also reflects a broad spectrum of parliamentary experience and opinion. MPs interviewed included current and former MPs, parliamentary private secretaries, current and former whips, and new and long-serving backbenchers. Members of both the Conservative and Liberal Democrat Shadow Cabinet were interviewed. Although the highest ranking Labour MPs interviewed were junior ministers, several former secretaries of state were interviewed. Given the nature of the research, a particular effort was made to interview members of the relevant select committees, and as a result the sample includes interviews with members of the Commons select committees for Work and Pensions, Health, Education and Skills, and the Office of the Deputy Prime Minister, including serving or former chairs of these committees.

There is a danger with surveying parliamentary opinion that the only MPs prepared to take part in such a survey will be those with a particular interest in the subject matter; consequently, any results may exaggerate the level of parliamentary interest and knowledge of a particular policy area. So, while it was considered important to interview those MPs with a particular expertise in social policy, or a particular responsibility for scrutinising this area of policy, the research also sought to interview MPs with no apparent interest or expertise in the field. Once again, the representative nature of the sample in this regard was dependent on the number of MPs prepared to be subjected to a detailed interview on a subject of which they had little experience. Nevertheless, a number of those MPs interviewed had little apparent interest or experience of social policy, had not held a ministerial post related to welfare, or served on any of the relevant select committees, and in some cases openly confessed their relative ignorance. These MPs displayed a wide variety of expertise in other areas, including former government and shadow ministers with briefs including defence and the environment, and members of a diverse range of select committees including Science and Technology and Foreign Affairs. One

Conservative MP, a recognised expert on defence, admitted to limited knowledge of welfare but took great delight in using the work of the military strategist Carl von Clausewitz to illustrate the failings of the NHS!

A more problematic question relates to whether the sample comprises a balance of opinion within the parties. Many MPs are reluctant to classify themselves as sitting on the right or left wings of their parties, and consequently determining the range of opinion within the parties was one of the objects of the research. However, in drawing conclusions about the state of opinion within the parties the research may fairly be criticised for over-representing the opinions of small groups of MPs who may be disproportionately represented in the sample. This problem is difficult to overcome, but some factors may be used to suggest a broad spectrum of opinion has been represented. Firstly, the larger the sample involved the greater the likelihood that the opinions expressed represent the range and balance of opinion within the parties. This sample, which included at least 10% of the MPs from each of the main parties, comprises a significant number of MPs. It is also possible to determine whether particular groups are over-represented according to other indicators such as cohort (see above), or indicators of opinion such as voting behaviour. Thus, for example, one of the broad conclusions of this research relates to the level of dissent within the parliamentary Labour Party, about government policy on welfare. Of course, dissent on such issues is well known, as indicated by parliamentary revolts on welfare legislation. However, the number of well-known Labour rebels, the so-called 'usual suspects' included in this survey, represents a small proportion of those Labour MPs who expressed concern about government policy. Of the 30 most rebellious Labour MPs from 2001-05 identified by Philip Cowley (2005), only three were interviewed as part of this research. This suggests that the level of dissent revealed in this research is not the result of many interviews with a small group of well-known Labour rebels, but is indicative of concerns expressed by a broader range of Labour MPs.

Another problem relates to the extent to which MPs are candid in responding to surveys such as this. This is particularly important when seeking to assess the level of support for party policies. Short of using a lie detector, there is no way of ensuring that the MPs interviewed were not offering their own considered opinion but simply reciting the party line. Studies of MPs' attitudes, including Bochel's earlier study, have often employed anonymous surveys in an attempt to overcome MPs' propensity to toe the party line and their natural desire not to upset party managers and colleagues (for example, Bochel, 1992;

Childs, 2004). This is a model that has been followed with this study, and which it was hoped would allow MPs to speak with candour about their values and attitudes. Interviews were conducted on a confidential basis; MPs were reminded of this at the time of the interview, and encouraged to articulate their personal attitudes and beliefs. They were also reassured that the study was not primarily intended to determine the opinions of particular individuals, but how MPs as a group view welfare policy, and how such policy is developed and scrutinised by parliament as an institution. Reference to party affiliation and status may be used in the final text, but has been kept vague enough not to identify the MP concerned (for example, 'Labour backbencher', 'former minister').

Moreover, while it may be anticipated that many MPs will use the opportunity of an interview to highlight the achievements of their particular party or the failures of the rest, in practice it was rare for MPs interviewed to express unequivocal support for their party's policies. Examples of unwavering support, such as the Labour MP who declared tax credits to be "the best thing ever invented" were mercifully rare. Similarly, many MPs expressed begrudging admiration or support for a number of policies pursued by the other parties that their party did not support. Indeed, the success of the interviews may be indicated by the number of MPs from all parties who were prepared to express opinions at variance from party policy. However, as Cowley (2002) reminds us, we should not be surprised if MPs express strong support for party policy. It should be recognised that MPs within the same party tend to share the same beliefs and values. Those who express support for party policy should not be dismissed as toeing the party line. MPs should be expected to support the party line more often than not, not because they feel they have to but because it coincides with their personal beliefs.

Candour was also encouraged by the format of the interviews. The survey was conducted through face-to-face interviews with MPs. These interviews generally lasted between half an hour and an hour, and took place in a range of locations across Westminster, generally in MPs' offices; a small number of interviews took place in constituency offices, and one was conducted on the telephone. The interviews were semi-structured. In general, interviews in social research have been divided into structured and unstructured types (Fontana and Frey, 2000). The structured approach, usually associated with survey research, seeks to ask each person the same question in the same way so that both questions and responses follow a closely worded and strictly sequenced schedule. This method permits close comparability between responses, and is particularly advantageous when surveying large groups. Unstructured interviews are more open-ended in character, and allow the interviewee the freedom to range across a given subject, only loosely guided by prompts and probes from the interviewer. These formats are not, however, intended to be rigidly applied and a semi-structured interview that combines structured and unstructured questions allows interviewees the freedom to answer questions on their own terms, while providing a degree of structure that allows comparability between interviews (May, 2001).

For this research a questionnaire was designed that combined both structured and unstructured aspects aimed at eliciting both general and specific responses regarding MPs' attitudes to welfare and welfare policies. The questionnaire comprised three sections. The first section sought to elicit MPs' general attitudes towards welfare, what might loosely be described as their 'philosophy of welfare'. In this unstructured section prompts were used to introduce or amplify several broad themes such as selectivity or universality. Having outlined their broad views, MPs were asked a series of more structured questions about specific areas of welfare policy. In consideration of time constraints it was decided to ask questions on just four specific policy areas: healthcare, pensions, the benefits system and income maintenance. These areas, it was felt, were currently the subject of some concern and debate in parliament, scholarship and indeed, among the public. MPs were not, however, discouraged from straying into areas not covered by the questionnaire, and indeed were encouraged to identify areas of welfare provision they felt were neglected. Finally, MPs were asked about the role of parliament, and about their own perceived role in the formulation of welfare policy. This section sought to address two broad questions: what factors influence MPs in their thinking about welfare? And what influence do MPs have on welfare policy? The former sought to determine in general what factors influenced MPs thinking about welfare, with prompts on such issues as personal experience, party policy, and key thinkers. In addition specific questions were asked about the influence of lobbying, the media and constituents. The latter section dealt with internal and external limits on policy formulation, with questions on parliamentary scrutiny and the perceived decline in parliamentary power, and the impact of the European Union on the formulation of welfare policy. In this section in particular, respondents were encouraged to be reflective, to think about their own position in the policy process, the power they wield as MPs, and any potential conflicts between their values and attitudes and their party and parliamentary position.

A significant factor in the drafting of the questionnaire was to construct the survey in such a way as to allow comparisons to be made with Taylor-Gooby and Bochel's survey of MPs' attitudes in the 1980s (1988), and with public attitudes to welfare as indicated in the annual *British Social Attitudes* survey and other indicators of public opinion such as opinion polls. While it was not intended that the present research should simply repeat Taylor-Gooby and Bochel's survey, it was designed to allow some comparability, and to enable the identification of shifts in MPs' attitudes since the 1980s. Consequently, some of the questions asked by Taylor-Gooby and Bochel were repeated directly in the current survey, most notably those on the broad philosophical level, such as what MPs felt should be the role of state in welfare, and how welfare should be financed.

Some of the more detailed questions on specific policy areas were designed to reflect the kind of questions asked in the *British Social Attitudes* survey. The *British Social Attitudes* survey provides a particularly useful database for tracing public attitudes to welfare from the 1980s to the present day. Since the first survey was undertaken in 1983, this annual national survey with a stratified random sample of about 3,500, has been widely regarded as having high methodological standards. The annual survey asks a number of questions relating to welfare, most notably about people's priorities for welfare spending, their attitudes to taxation and the financing of welfare, and the relationship between state and private welfare services. In addition, in recent years individual surveys have asked a number of more specific questions about such issues as pensions, the process of getting people off welfare into work, and the impact of New Labour policies on standards in various sectors of welfare provision (Jowell et al, 1999; Park et al, 2003, 2004, 2005). In order to allow some comparisons between public and parliamentary attitudes, MPs were asked a number of questions that reflected those posed in the *British Social Attitudes* surveys, most notably: when asked to identify their priorities for welfare spending; to identify which parts of the National Health Service (NHS) are particularly effective; and which are not; whether they considered benefit fraud to be a significant problem; and whether they would support an increase in taxation to pay for increased welfare provision. Although MPs, unlike the public, were not asked to choose between a selection of prepared responses, and their responses were therefore more varied, and invariably longer, they nevertheless provided a useful body of data with which to compare public and parliamentary attitudes.

Through this detailed assessment of parliamentary opinion, and its relationship both to government policy, and public opinion, this study of parliament and welfare policy aims to provide a comprehensive examination of the role of parliament in the scrutiny and formulation of welfare policy. Moreover, by offering a detailed assessment of the current state of opinion within the main parties it has a clear bearing on the future development of welfare policy by whatever party is in power. Chapters Two and Three provide contextual background to the substantive research on the role and attitudes of MPs and peers. Chapter Two examines the welfare policies pursued by the New Labour governments since 1997, and policies advocated by the main opposition parties. Chapter Three provides the parliamentary context for the study of MPs' attitudes. It examines the role and functions of the Westminster Parliament, and the manner in which the Blair government has sought to reform parliament as part of its programme of modernisation and constitutional reform. In doing so, this chapter addresses the sustained debate about the perceived decline of parliament, and focuses in detail on the fate of Labour's welfare legislation within parliament. The substantive examination of MPs' attitudes to welfare is provided in Chapter Four, in which MPs' attitudes towards the role of the state are considered alongside attitudes to specific policy areas. The question of political representation is considered in Chapter Five, as MPs' attitudes are compared with public attitudes to welfare. Chapter Six takes the analysis of the role of parliament one stage further by examining the role of the House of Lords in relation to welfare policy. Chapter Seven seeks to examine the extent to which MPs are able to scrutinise welfare legislation and policy, and whether MPs as a group or as individuals have an influence on policy. Finally, Chapter Eight concludes this study by summarising the key points of this research and drawing out the implications about the continued relevance of MPs in the policy process in the field of welfare.

TWO

Continuity and change: the politics of welfare under New Labour

In terms of the politics of welfare, from the start of the first Labour term considerable attention has been devoted to the extent to which New Labour's policies have deviated from or been consistent with those of the preceding Conservative government, including the extent to which the government had accepted New Right arguments, such as over the centrality of the market and the shortcomings of attempts to achieve greater equality. Given that The Labour Party, prior to the 1997 General Election, seeking to reduce the danger of portrayal as a 'tax and spend' party, had committed itself to abiding by the Conservatives' public expenditure plans for the first two years of government, it was perhaps unsurprising that the new government was characterised by some as cautious and lacking radicalism. Although levels of public expenditure increased substantially from 1999, particularly on areas such as public order, health and education (see Table 2.1), critics of New Labour were also able to highlight examples of policy where there had been significant continuity from the approaches of the Conservatives, such as the continued commitment to a significant role for the private sector in the provision of welfare, including parts of the work of the NHS, cuts in entitlements to some social security benefits, the frequently managerialist approach, and the use of targets and performance measures. On the other hand, it is possible to point to initiatives such as the commitment to eradicate child poverty, the expansion of childcare, and the increases in expenditure on some areas of welfare, notably the NHS, to argue that there has been a significant degree of redistribution of wealth from the rich to at least some of the poorer parts of the population (for example, Gregg et al, 2005), although this is something that few Labour politicians have emphasised publicly. One of the features of the Labour governments was the acceptance of social exclusion as a major factor in society, with, for example, the establishment of the Social Exclusion Unit in late 1997, an initiative that also reflected the government's attempts to create a new approach to policy making, including greater use of 'evidence' and 'joined-up' policy (for example, Cabinet Office, 1999a).

Table 2.1: Public expenditure on services (1996-97 and 2004-05, £ billion)

	1996-97	2004-05[a]
Public order and safety	16.3	29.1
Employment policies	2.8	3.2
Housing and community amenities	4.9	7.3
Health	42.8	82.6
Education and training	37.8	65.8
Social protection	111.9	162.9

Note: [a] Figures for 2004-05 are estimates.

Source: HM Treasury (2005)

New Labour has clearly been firmly committed to a significant degree of welfare reform, believing that the traditional welfare state has been flawed, for example in relation to the encouragement of dependency, bureaucracy and fraud (Giddens, 2000), that earlier assumptions about the egalitarian potential of state welfare were misleading, and that the welfare state is unable to meet the challenges of globalisation, labour market change, increased consumerism and greater diversity of family formations. Labour's policies have also been affected by the desire to stay broadly in tune with the party's perception of public opinion rather than leading opinion, and this has resulted in the development of policies designed to encourage the middle classes to continue to use state services, such as education and health, while at the same time rejecting any increases in Income Tax.

New Labour have also reinterpreted the goal of equality, favouring equality of opportunity rather than equality of outcome (see, for example, Lund, 2002), so that attempts to improve the education system or to tackle child poverty have been designed to equalise opportunities.

Employment

Employment and work have been key features of Labour's approach to social policy since 1997, with initiatives intended not only to increase employment or reduce unemployment, but also to use employment to help to tackle poverty and social exclusion. The first Labour government saw considerable emphasis on welfare to work, and attempts to devise a more active system that would offer unemployed people "a hand-up, not just cash payments that give them a hand-out" (Mandelson and Liddle, 1996), increasing the conditionality of benefit payments. To that end the government introduced the statutory National Minimum Wage in April 1999, and has also used mechanisms such as tax credits to supplement wages for some workers, and changes to Income Tax and National Insurance to reduce the tax burden for low-wage workers. In addition there have been changes such as the introduction of the Working Time Directive and improved rights to maternity and paternity leave, as well as greater provision of childcare aimed at helping some parents to work.

However, arguably the flagship of the government's approach has been the New Deal programme, including the New Deal for Young People, which has sought to improve young people's long-term job prospects through early intervention and the options of subsidised employment, environmental work, voluntary work or full-time education, but with no 'fifth-option' of non-participation. Over time the government extended the New Deal to cover other target groups, such as lone parents and sick and disabled people.

Employment has also been a significant component of the government's attempts to reduce poverty among future pensioners, including the New Deal 50 plus, intended to help raise participation rates in the labour market for workers aged over 50, and changes to pensions provision such as the introduction of the Stakeholder Pension.

The government has frequently claimed employment as a major area of success, with the numbers of unemployed people falling for much of the period since 1997, and with the government claiming that around two million new jobs were created between 1997 and 2005. What is not clear is the extent to which these changes can be attributed to Labour's management of the economy or to its welfare-to-work initiatives. In addition, one of the features of many of Labour's welfare-to-work initiatives has been a new emphasis on compulsion, with receipt of benefits being conditional on participation for claimants within the eligible groups and sanctions for those who do not participate, and this remains an area which many critics feel can be both counter-productive and inappropriate.

Social security

Where social security is concerned, Labour's policies have arguably been substantially guided by the phrase 'work for those who can, security for those who cannot'.

Using the taxation and social security systems, largely without publicising it the government has undertaken a significant degree of redistribution from those in the top half of the income distribution to those in the bottom half. More specifically, there has also been a redistribution of wealth from working-age families without children to pensioners and working-age families with children. However, people without children receiving benefits have been a much lower priority for additional support.

One of the significant new developments under New Labour has been the increased use of tax credits, with April 2003 seeing the introduction of Child Tax Credit and Working Tax Credit. The use of tax credits has served to blur the divisions between the taxation and social security systems, and it has also been accused of adding to the already substantial level of complexity in the systems. Indeed, there have been significant criticisms of the administrative operation of tax credits. In 2003 the government admitted that around 800,000 families had not received Child Tax Credit on time, and it later became apparent that up to 1.8 million claimants had not only been overpaid in 2003/04 but were subsequently being required to repay money that they had already spent, while the National Audit Office (2005) estimated that for the same year fraud and error cost the Inland Revenue £460 million.

In 1999 Blair announced that the government was committed to ending child poverty. While a variety of explanations were put forward for this decision, it arguably reflected the government's view that in order to achieve greater opportunities for all adults it was important to tackle poverty during childhood, an explanation that has been echoed in the government's refusal to countenance 'failing schools' as these impact not just on children at that time but also on their opportunities at adulthood.

In October 2003 the government also announced its proposals for the child trust fund ('baby bond'), to take effect from 2005, with each baby receiving a payment of £250 (up to £500 for babies from low-income families) to be invested for its future. Critics, however, pointed out that this was unlikely to provide a significant sum by the time that children reach 18, and also that allowing families to add further contributions might exacerbate rather than reduce inequality.

In response to the ageing population and the 'pensions crisis', New Labour have introduced a number of reforms attempting to encourage people to save for their retirement. Following the 1998 Green Paper *A new contract for welfare: Partnership in pensions* (DSS, 1998), the government established the Pensions Commission, chaired by Adair Turner, to review and make recommendations on private pensions and long-term savings, with the Commission's second report, published in late 2005, making proposals for reform including the creation of a National Pensions Saving Scheme (Pensions Commission, 2005). Where public sector pensions were concerned the government sought to reduce the rising costs of pensions, including through increasing the normal retirement age for new entrants, and reached agreement on this with a number of trades unions in 2005, although this did not extend to local government employees.

Another potentially difficult challenge facing Labour has been reform of Incapacity Benefit, prompted by the increase in the number of people claiming the benefit to over two million, and the consequent cost to the public purse. One attempt to tackle this was made through the New Deal for Disabled People and later the Pathways to Work pilot scheme, with the gradual extension of the latter to more of the country. However, the government continued to face the challenge of how to deal with the large number of claimants of Incapacity Benefit and in 2005 published proposals for change (DWP, 2005). As with other initiatives such as the New Deal, these again linked training, support and advice with a degree of conditionality, particularly for those deemed able to work. Nevertheless many organisations representing people with disabilities gave the proposals a cautious welcome, although there remained the possibility of significant opposition, including among Labour MPs.

Health

Following the ending of Labour's commitment to honour the Conservatives' plans for public expenditure and the Comprehensive Spending Review, from 1999 the government undertook to increase spending on the NHS by £21 billion over the next three years, an annual increase of 4.7% in real terms. In 2002 the government took this further with a pledge to increase spending by an average of 7.4% a year for five years to bring the proportion of GDP spent on the NHS to more than the EU average expenditure on health care (see Table 2.1).

However, while there has been a significant rise in public expenditure on healthcare, one of Labour's approaches to funding the NHS has been more controversial. The use of the Private Finance Initiative (PFI) to fund a programme of hospital building was viewed with suspicion by many of the party's MPs and by others including the trades unions. Similarly, the creation of foundation hospitals, with freedom from central control and the ability to borrow money from private sources, did not sit easily with many traditional Labour supporters, including those concerned that this would lead to a 'two-tier' health service.

As with other aspects of social policy, Labour have sought to use targets, regulation and inspection to improve the quality of healthcare provision, for example through creating bodies such as the National Institute for Clinical Excellence and the Healthcare Commission.

In the field of public health Labour's 1999 Green Paper *Saving lives: Our healthier nation* (DH, 1999) did place greater emphasis on economic, environmental and social causes of ill health than had been the case under the Conservatives. However, critics were still able to point out that the emphasis appeared to be on reducing mortality rather than morbidity, and that there was a lack of national targets for reducing health inequalities.

Personal social services

Shortly after coming to power the Labour government established a Royal Commission on Long-term Care for the Elderly, but following the Commission's report in 1999 (RCLTC, 1999), the government rejected the recommendation that personal care should be paid for from general taxation, favouring the use of means testing of both personal care and living costs. In Scotland, however, the newly established Scottish Executive decided that long-term personal care should be paid for by the state.

As with other areas of social policy, modernisation and 'performance' have been key to much of Labour's approach to the personal social services. Concerns with regulation have been a significant feature of developments in this area, with the 2000 Care Standards Act leading to the creation of the General Social Care Council to regulate the social care workforce in England. In 2004, a new Commission for Social Care Inspection was established to undertake inspection of local authorities and social care providers.

The government has sought to develop its commitment to 'what works' and 'joined-up government' in relation to social care, including the development of evidence-based practice covering research and literature reviews, and the creation of care trusts that bridge health and social services for children and for adults, as well as encouraging partnership across public, private and voluntary sectors.

Labour have also sought to tackle youth crime using a variety of approaches. For example, the introduction of Youth Inclusion Programmes in 1999, targeted at urban estates with high crime levels, was intended to achieve a 70% fall in arrest rates for 13- to 16-year-olds at risk, while the 2000 Criminal Justice and Police Act extended curfews to children under 16.

Crime and criminal justice

As noted above, some elements of Labour's programme sought to link crime and social exclusion, frequently linked with other New Labour notions such as 'joined-up' approaches and 'partnership', for example through the 1998 Crime and Disorder Act, which placed a statutory duty on chief police officers and local authorities, together with police authorities, probation committees and health authorities, to produce strategies to reduce crime and disorder in their areas. Similarly the 'modernisation' agenda has seen an emphasis on efficiency, effectiveness and the measurement and management of performance for criminal justice agencies.

On the other hand, other strands of Labour's approach have been grounded in traditional approaches to crime and punishment, with a dramatic rise in the prison population to over 76,000 in July 2005, largely as a result of policies that have led to longer sentences rather than to changing patterns of crime and offending. In addition there have been changes such as the extension of stop and search powers for the police and the possibilities of trials without juries, albeit only in cases that are likely to be long and complex or where the defendant requests it. There has been an increase in police numbers by around 13,000 to 141,000, together with the introduction of more than 6,000 community support officers, who can be viewed as providing policing 'on the cheap' or as providing support for the police and a visible presence on the streets.

Following the attacks in the US of 11 September 2001 it was perhaps unsurprising that there was a significant shift in the law and order agenda, with the government seeking to emphasise measures that it claimed would help reduce the risk of terrorist attacks on the UK, a message that it sought to reinforce further following the suicide bombings in London on 7 July 2005. The government also sought to link its proposals for ID cards to both the prevention of terrorism and attempts to reduce other forms of crime, as well as to tackling benefit fraud.

From 2002 the government has paid considerable attention to the notion of 'anti-social behaviour', an agenda given additional impetus by the inclusion of 'respect' as a significant part of Labour's 2005 General Election manifesto. Louise Casey was appointed as the 'respect tsar' responsible for implementing plans ranging from the greater use of parenting orders, requiring people to attend counselling or guidance, as well as potentially imposing conditions, a failure to abide by which could ultimately lead to a criminal offence, to more positive proposals such as mentoring or rewarding young people for participating in voluntary work. Critics have pointed out that there are a variety of problems with the government's proposals, such as the risks of attempts at 'quick fixes', the dangers of portraying young people as 'yobs', their implications for human rights and the increasing scale of government intervention in family life.

Housing

In 1997 Labour's manifesto had included a pledge to release the capital receipts from the sale of council housing, but while the government did implement this, it did so on a phased basis and with a reduction in approval for other borrowing, so that in the early years of the government the reality was a fall in expenditure on housing (Lund, 2002).

The continued government support for the transfer of local authority housing stock to registered social landlords, combined with this lack of public expenditure in social housing during the first Labour term, prompted many more local authorities to opt for the transfer of their housing stock to registered social landlords, while at the same time there was a decline in the number of new building starts.

Labour's acceptance of the dominance of the market in housing was reflected in its approaches to the private landlord sector, where it made very limited changes, and to home ownership. However, the continued growth in house prices under Labour made it difficult for the public sector to recruit staff in certain areas and the government was forced to introduce the Starter Home Initiative to assist specified groups of key workers to buy homes in areas with high prices where they would otherwise be unable to live or to be near the communities that they served.

In other respects the government has demonstrated a greater willingness to intervene, for example through the introduction of the Bed and Breakfast and Rough Sleeping Units. The shortage of housing in London and the South East led to four areas being identified for the growth of 'sustainable communities', including through the creation of development agencies to be supported by public funds. In *Quality and choice: A decent home for all: The way forward for housing* (DETR, 2000), the government undertook to bring all social housing up to a 'decent standard' by 2010, but with an estimated repair bill of £19 billion in the local authority sector much of the financing required to achieve this would have to be through stock transfer and the use of the PFI.

Education

As with work, in the early years of the Labour governments, education was highlighted as vital to the task of tackling social exclusion and creating an 'opportunity society'. Since 1997 it is therefore not surprising that there have been significant developments at different age levels. One of the most noticeable, and arguably the most successful, initiatives has been the expansion of pre-school provision, with 65% of three- and four-year-olds making use of pre-school provision by 2002/03 and a government commitment to provide free nursery places for all who wanted one by September 2004.

In addition, the government launched the cross-cutting Sure Start programme to work across the responsibilities of different government departments to provide families with young children in disadvantaged areas with improved access to services and opportunities as a means of combating social exclusion and as part of the commitment to eradicate child poverty by 2020.

In relation to school-age education the first two Labour terms were frequently characterised as dominated by flows of initiatives from central government, particularly in relation to 'standards' and 'performance', with widespread use of targets together with the use of Ofsted to place pressure on schools to meet them. Labour largely accepted the Conservatives' attempts to diversify the variety of educational establishments and, following the 2001 Green and White Papers, *Schools: Building on success* (DfEE, 2001) and *Schools achieving success* (DfES, 2001), continued to extend diversity among secondary schools through the creation of more specialist schools, faith schools and city academies.

Labour's key target for higher education was to achieve a participation rate of 50% of young people by 2010, but this in turn was closely linked to debates over the funding of higher education and the introduction of 'top-up' fees of £3,000 per year from 2006.

However, many of Labour's educational reforms were controversial, with significant criticism from the teaching profession. Similarly, the introduction of 'top-up' fees for higher education resulted in one of the biggest parliamentary rebellions since 1997, and a number of concessions by the government.

New Labour, old thinking

As noted above, and perhaps inevitably, there have been debates around the extent to which Labour have drawn on the ideas of the preceding Conservative governments and whether the government's policies have continued to reflect any commitment to socialism or social democracy, been significantly influenced by New Right thinking, or reflect an acceptance of many of the more liberal interpretations of the impact of globalisation. Similarly there has been considerable debate over whether there is an identifiable Third Way, and if there is, the extent to which it draws on neoliberalism or traditional Labour themes. It is certainly true that New Labour's thinking on social policy has been different from that of large parts of The Labour Party in the late 1980s and 1990s, and some would therefore argue that it departs significantly from traditional patterns of democratic socialism and social democracy. However, others suggest that even with a diminished stress on equality, with its attempts to create a more inclusive, more entrepreneurial society, and an emphasis on opportunities for all and rights and responsibilities, there are in places significant strong resonances with previous visions of social democracy.

Government of social policy

Despite the inevitable attention paid to developments in policies and the politics of welfare, in some respects perhaps equally as important have been the changes made to the processes and methods of policy implementation of social policies.

Prior to 1979 the traditional approach of governments to social policy could adequately be described as being based on a public administration approach, with a focus on state provision and the five core social services (education, health, housing, the personal social services and social security) being delivered by different combinations of national and local governmental organisations. However, under the Conservative governments of 1979 to 1997, this changed significantly. From 1979 to 1988 the Conservatives arguably took a 'managerialist' approach, seeking to reflect what the government believed to be private sector values and attempts to transfer business performance tools from the private sector to the public sector as a means of increasing the efficiency and effectiveness of both central and local government. This was followed by a second phase, termed by Hood (1991) 'the new institutional economics', with initiatives such as the use of markets and an emphasis on consumer choice being central to this. The Conservatives also sought to encourage a greater range of service providers across the public, private and voluntary sectors, thus creating a wider network of organisations and a more complex system for the planning and delivery of services. Many of these changes were encapsulated in the term the 'new public management', encompassing a variety of features such as an emphasis on performance management, devolved financial and personnel management, greater responsiveness to users and other customers, increased use of market-type mechanisms and the privatisation of parts of the public sector (OECD, 1993).

Many of the features of the reforms introduced under the Thatcher governments are well known, resulting in significant changes to both the structures and styles of governmental involvement in the social policy process. They reflected much of the 'new public management' and included initiatives such as the development of internal markets, such as those in the NHS and in education, privatisation, the greater use of performance measures and monitoring, the increased use of 'arm's-length' government in the form of agencies and quangos, the centralisation of power (and frequently a decentralisation of responsibility), mechanisms to enhance consumer voice and choice, and the reform and residualisation of local government.

Developments under New Labour

While the 18 years of Conservative government saw significant changes to the mechanisms of social policy formulation, implementation and evaluation, the pace of change accelerated further under New Labour from 1997. The first New Labour government saw some degree of continuity of mechanisms, such as the use of performance 'league tables', including for hospitals and schools, but at the same time significant change, such as the creation of devolved administrations for Scotland and Wales, and new emphases on partnership, 'joined-up government' and 'what works'.

One of the features of the Labour governments since 1997 has been their commitment to improving the quality of policy making, with a plethora of documentation and guidance being published, including, for example, *Professional policymaking for the 21st century* (Cabinet Office, 1999a), which set out nine core 'competencies' including 'using evidence', 'inclusive' and 'joined-up'. Concepts such as 'joined-up', 'evidence-based' and 'what works' became familiar as the government sought to introduce them into all tiers and forms of policy making and implementation.

It is possible to identify a variety of mechanisms that have been used by Labour. One of these has been the widespread use of performance measurement, often against targets, accompanied by audit and inspection to ensure that services are meeting their objectives and providing efficient and effective provision. While under the Conservatives much of the concern was on making information available, in part to fit with market models of consumer choice, under Labour an additional dimension has been the attempts to measure 'quality', whether through the use of star systems, as applied to local authorities for education and social care and to NHS trusts, or whether certain organisations are 'failing', such as schools. However, critics have argued both that too many targets and insufficient funding can create problems (Appleby and Coote, 2002), and that organisations' work and priorities will be affected by the need to meet the requirements of these activities (Clarke et al, 2002; Clarke, 2004).

Labour have also sought to place greater emphasis on 'partnership' than the Conservatives, with attempts to encourage partnerships across the public, private and voluntary sectors in a variety of fields, including crime prevention, education, health and housing. This may in part be a response to the complexity that arose from fragmentation of welfare provision in the Conservative years, in part due to a view that more holistic and comprehensive responses are needed to many policy problems, and in part due to a view that the whole policy process is more integrated and dynamic and that joined-up-ness is a means by which governments can more successfully respond. It also reflects the view that in this complex society public sector bodies find it difficult to deliver their responsibilities without collaborating not only with other parts of the public sector but also with private and voluntary agencies (Rouse and Smith, 2002); indeed it is arguable that for New Labour the entire concept of partnership has implied a significant role for the non-state sector. However, it might also be possible to suggest that there is also some underlying notion of seeking to empower citizens and involving people in developing responses to social problems.

In the early years of the Labour government this approach to partnership was reflected in a range of area-based initiatives, which emphasised tackling problems in particular geographic areas through 'partnership' and 'collaboration' across the public, voluntary and private sectors rather than 'competition', together with the continued use of mechanisms such as targets, external audit and inspection as a means of seeking to drive forward change and improve standards, and a view that continued to see local government in particular as an enabler rather than a provider of services. However, as Newman (2001) has argued, Labour's attempts to encourage collaborative forms of governance have been restricted by the same government's attempts to centralise and manage through the use of goals, targets, performance measurement and audit and inspection. These inevitably create constraints on the ability to successfully draw on more bottom-up initiatives, including participation and collaboration (Rouse and Smith, 2002).

Like the Conservatives, Labour have made use of arm's length organisations for the delivery of their policies. However, while the Conservatives used these as they viewed state bureaucracies as inefficient, self-interested and unresponsive and saw central government bureaucracy as unlikely to deliver government goals, in contrast, under New Labour, there has been a view that (central) government action can be effective in delivering desired social and economic outcomes, reflected in further strengthening of control and coordination mechanisms. To some extent, therefore, agencies have been brought back into line with government departments, being directed towards corporate goals and managed through the same mechanisms of public service agreements and targets (Gains, 2003). Bache and Flinders (2004) have argued that for New Labour's particular vision of reformed social democracy these are a particularly useful governance mechanism.

Another significant development under Labour was the role of the Treasury under Gordon Brown as Chancellor of the Exchequer. This saw the Treasury playing a much greater role in directing social policy through mechanisms such as the Comprehensive Spending Reviews, which fixed departmental spending over three-year cycles and Public Service Agreements and Service Delivery Agreements, which have involved setting targets for government departments and establishing who is responsible for delivering them, as well as through the use of the tax system to deliver credits such as Child Tax Credit and Working Tax Credit. More controversially, the government used the Private Finance Initiative (PFI) to encourage the private sector to build schools and hospitals that are then leased back to local authorities and the NHS. Critics have claimed variously that over time PFIs are more expensive than traditional models of public sector capital investment, that in reality the government has continued to bear the risk, and that many schemes have not provided good value for money. The government's response has been that PFI has been a way of enabling a massive programme of investment in the public sector without this showing as part of public borrowing, and as such has provided a remedy to years of under-investment.

However, there have been limits to the government's willingness to modernise the mechanisms of policy making and scrutiny, and as Chapters Two, Six and Seven make clear, the government's commitment to improving the quality of policy making has not extended as far as increasing the powers and abilities of the House of Commons or the

House of Lords to influence or even scrutinise the policies and actions of the executive.

Multilevel governance

One of the potentially most important changes for social policy has been the introduction of devolved administrations for Scotland and Wales (and for Northern Ireland, although the implementation for the latter has been affected by the on–off nature of the peace process). While the constituent parts of the UK have always had economic, social, legal and cultural features that have distinguished them from each other, and these have been recognised by the existence of the Northern Ireland Office, Scottish Office and Welsh Office, until recently these had not been reflected in the existence of elected legislative bodies.

However, following referenda in the autumn of 1997, the Scottish Parliament and the National Assembly for Wales came into being 1 July 1999, followed by the Northern Ireland Assembly on 2 December 1999. Each of the new administrations has some powers over social policy, arguably greatest for the Scottish Parliament and least for the National Assembly for Wales. While some have criticised the lack of radicalism in the approaches of the new bodies (see, for example, the debates in Mooney and Scott, 2005), it is perhaps not surprising, particularly given that Labour has been in power at national and devolved level (albeit in coalition in Scotland) that in their early years they have largely followed the lead from Westminster. However, there have been some areas where each has chosen to diverge from the position taken at Westminster. In Scotland the Scottish Parliament took an early decision to repeal Section 28 of the 1988 Local Government Act, which banned the promotion of homosexuality by local authorities, three years before a similar move was successful at Westminster, and, in contrast to the government at Westminster, also accepted the recommendation of the Royal Commission on Long-term Care for the Elderly that long-term care should be free. Another notable area of policy divergence has been the lack of introduction of tuition fees for higher education in Scotland while in Wales they were pegged at £1,150 until 2007/08. In some instances, key areas of government policy in England, such as foundation hospitals, have not been developed at all in Scotland and Wales.

Labour set out their thinking on local government in the Green Paper *Modernising local government: Local democracy and community leadership* (DETR, 1998a) and the White Paper *Modern local government:*

In touch with the people (DETR, 1998b), which argued that councils were not effectively engaging with their communities. Reforms have arguably been focused around electoral participation and accountability ('democratic renewal'), new decision-making structures and the introduction of Best Value, while areas such as possible reforms to loosen the constraints on local government finance have been largely neglected (for example, Game, 2002). Barnett (2003) has argued that "New Labour's approach to local government is now consistent with a move to an 'active welfare' state, in line with Third Way ideas which stress responsibilities and duty along with rights as welfare principles. These require the individual behaviour of citizens to be re-shaped and the relationship with government to be re-thought. Increasingly, however, they are being applied to public agencies on an organisation-wide scale" (p 29).

One of the most notable aspects of Labour's reforms of local government has been the introduction of new models of decision making, including directly elected mayors in a few areas, but a much more general shift towards a cabinet model, with in most authorities a cabinet and a leader, with other 'backbench' councillors having responsibility for scrutinising the decisions of the cabinet. Labour also replaced the system of compulsory competitive tendering (CCT), introduced by the Conservatives, with a new scheme called Best Value. While critics claim that there has been little difference, the government has argued that while CCT was concerned only with the cost of a service, Best Value also emphasises quality, public consultation and continuous improvement, making it a more sophisticated and comprehensive system. However, should a council be deemed to be failing in its duty to secure Best Value, the secretary of state has the power to intervene and even to impose an outsider provider.

Indeed, it is the degree of central control and the plethora of directives and targets emanating from Whitehall, particularly during the early years of the New Labour governments, which many have argued reflected a lack of faith in local level agencies. The Conservatives' development of performance measurement has therefore been utilised by Labour in an attempt to drive forward partnership and cooperation in policy making and implementation, including initiatives at central and sub-central government levels. In contrast, despite occasional rhetoric, local government finance has been tightly controlled and little freedom granted to authorities in either raising or spending of revenues.

Participation

Finally, one of the other features of politics during this period has been low electoral turnout: for general elections the figures were 71.4% in 1997, 59.4% in 2001 and 61.2% in 2005. These were mirrored in low levels of turnout for local government and European Parliament elections. While some have argued that non-voting may reflect contentment on the part of the electorate, for others, including many politicians and commentators, it is a cause for some degree of anxiety, and for New Labour, with its initial emphases on participation and democratic renewal, this form of non-participation has been a matter for particular concern. A variety of explanations for low levels of turnout have been put forward, including disillusionment with party politics and the mechanisms and processes of representative democracy, perceptions of a lack of 'real' choice, a lack of confidence that voting changes anything, ignorance of politics and government among electors, and election results since 1997 being seen as foregone conclusions. The Labour governments have sought to tackle some of these, including by making it easier to vote, by trials of postal voting, telephone voting and Internet voting (although these have been accompanied by increases in allegations of electoral fraud), experimenting with polling stations in supermarkets, attempts to introduce directly elected mayors for local government, the use of more proportional electoral systems in elections for the European Parliament, the National Assembly for Wales and the Scottish Parliament, and the introduction of citizenship into the National Curriculum.

However, while participation has often been characterised by voting, it has never been limited to this. People also participate through joining pressure and action groups, engaging in debates, being co-opted onto working groups for statutory and other bodies, becoming members of citizens' juries or panels, responding to consultations, campaigning, volunteering and a wide range of other activities. Like the Conservatives before them, New Labour have been seeking to encourage other forms of citizen participation, albeit to some extent with different motives and priorities, including a belief that participation can contribute to social capital, a continued commitment to choice in public services, and also arguably in part because of a belief that participation in decision making can lead to improved policies and thus to better outcomes. In addition there may also be a belief that there are financial benefits in encouraging some forms of participation, such as volunteering; for example, a survey carried out by the Home Office (2004) suggested that informal volunteering was worth £22.6 billion to the economy in 2003.

On the other hand, it is possible to argue that there are less positive reasons for such enthusiasm for citizen involvement, and for example Newman (2001) suggests that "Labour's drive to enhance public participation and involvement, then, may have been more about sharpening the accountability of the public sector downwards to citizens and users, eliciting pressure to drive up standards, than about new ways of engaging citizens in decision making as a form of co or self-governance" (p 130).

Pressure groups

Pressure groups have long been an important factor in social policy, including those that not only campaign but also those that provide services. However, after a period during the 1960s and 1970s when the activities of pressure groups grew rapidly, including in welfare politics, with the emergence of a variety of groups such as the Child Poverty Action Group and Shelter, the election of the Conservative government of Margaret Thatcher in 1979 saw a significant change. Under the Thatcher governments many pressure groups felt sidelined in relation to policy making. This was in part due to Thatcher being a conviction politician who was not particularly amenable to open discussion or to persuasion from groups, and many were largely excluded from policy formulation. This approach was underpinned by the influence of New Right thinking that meant that under the Conservatives there was a considerable degree of suspicion of interest groups, who were seen as encouraging overload and un-governability, and as a result there was "an attempt to reduce the role of groups and undermine existing policy networks" (Richards and Smith, 2002, p 179). Richards and Smith argue that the Conservatives did this in four ways: firstly, they attempted to change the terms of debates, with markets rather than governments being presented as the source of solutions, and as a result there was no need for groups to be involved in the policy process; secondly, they argued that intermediate organisations, such as pressure groups, local authorities or churches, were a barrier to direct contact between government and voters; thirdly, although suspicious of many groups, such as many interest groups, trades unions and professional groups associated with the development of the welfare state, other organisations, such as the Institute of Directors, were allowed greater access to government; and fourthly, they made significant use of right-wing think tanks, both in producing ideas and in introducing them to the media and the public.

Richards and Smith (2002) also claim that "In the area of social security policy, the government almost completely excluded pressure groups". They referred to one official as saying that Peter Lilley, Secretary of State from 1992 to 1997, "had no interest in consulting pressure groups and did not really care about the relationship with them" (p 180). Indeed, the Thatcher government's attitude to some groups, including those representing professionals such as doctors or teachers, was almost confrontational, as these organisations were viewed by many Conservatives as representing the worst elements of interest articulation, being self-interested and supporting both high levels of public expenditure and large welfare bureaucracies.

The Conservatives took a similar approach to many policy networks, for example in education, health and local government, where they were seen as conservative forces opposing attempts at reforms, so that government frequently attempted to bypass existing networks, to create new ones, or chose to override them. This was apparent, for example, in relation to education where the government sought to create more direct relationships between schools and the Secretary of State, bypassing local authorities.

When Labour took office in 1997 they appeared to offer greater possibilities for consultation and partnership with many pressure groups, with more widespread use of consultations, producing numerous consultation papers and inviting responses from a wide range of bodies. In addition the use of a more rational and 'inclusive' approach to policy making also appeared to offer greater possibilities for input from organised interests. Marsh et al (2001) have suggested that in contrast to the Conservative years, following Labour's return to office in 1997 there was a significant increase in the level of consultation, citing interviews with both civil servants and representatives of interest groups. They suggest that reasons for this included the relationships that Labour had built up with many groups in its 18 years in opposition, and the consequent debts that it owed to many of them, and the different policy objectives from the Conservatives that meant that Labour was more committed to consultation. In addition, in their initiatives aimed at 'modernising' policy making, Labour have called for a more inclusive process that involves a range of interests and stakeholders (for example, Cabinet Office, 1999b). Newman (2001) also recognised the scale of involvement in the early years of the Labour government, including, for example, the Policy Action Teams established by the Social Exclusion Unit, which included members from a range of public, voluntary and private sector organisations.

In 2000 the government produced a code of practice on consultation, revised in 2004, with the stated intention of making consultation more effective, opening up decision making to as wide a range of people as possible, with the use of electronic means as an important tool in this process. According to the government's figures, for each year from 2001 to 2004, between 70 and 80% of 'national, public consultations' complied with the objective of running consultations for periods of 12 weeks or more.

However, Richards and Smith (2002) suggest that while the Labour governments might initially have been more open to pressure groups, they soon became less amenable to their influence. They also note that New Labour had better contacts with business than previous Labour governments, and this, in some policy areas at least, might have enabled opposing inputs into the policy process to those coming from many interest groups. Similarly Newman (2001) notes the potential dangers associated with such developments, including questions about the transparency, accountability and the representativeness of those involved. Grant (2004) points out that there is also a risk that consultation acts as a substitute for genuine dialogue, and that while the electronic provision of information might work for many, it may not work as well for socially excluded groups.

Parties, personalities and politics

The Labour Party

Tony Blair described welfare reform as Labour's 'Big Idea'. Labour's manifesto for the 1997 General Election declared that Labour would be the party of welfare reform. It promised that Labour would create a modern welfare state based on "duties and responsibilities", designed to get people off benefit and into work. This emphasis on welfare-to-work was partly motivated by a desire to combat the poverty and deprivation that often accompanied unemployment but was also motivated by more practical concerns about the cost of welfare provision. The government's workfare proposals, it asserted, were designed to "break the spiral of escalating spending on social security" (The Labour Party, 1997). In Labour's first term the principal targets for welfare-to-work programmes were the young, the long-term unemployed, including those on Incapacity Benefit, and lone parents. The manifesto also promised to "crack down" on benefit fraud.

The task of creating a modern welfare state ostensibly resided with the Department of Social Security. However, the administration of welfare reform was dogged by misfortune, either by accident or design, almost from the moment of Labour's election in 1997. Prior to the election Blair had given the impression to Frank Field, a veteran Labour MP and a recognised expert on welfare, that he would be offered the post of Secretary of State for Social Security. Field seemed an ideal candidate to push through the government's programme of welfare reform. Formerly Director of the Child Poverty Action Group, and Chair of the Social Security Select Committee for 10 years prior to Labour's 1997 victory, Field was widely recognised and respected for his knowledge and experience of welfare. Described by Toynbee and Walker as "a charismatic man with many admirers, most of them in the Tory Party" (Toynbee and Walker, 2001, p 17), Field's views also increasingly reflected those of the Prime Minister. Field was harshly critical of the perverse incentives created by a welfare system that encouraged dependency, the avoidance of work and fraud. He was also acutely aware of the problems created by the public's desire for modern public services and low taxes. In an article published shortly before Labour's victory in 1997 he had declared that the only way to meet public expectations of low taxes was to cut expenditure on welfare (Powell, 1999).

Unfortunately, Field probably had more admirers on the opposition benches than in his own party and following the 1997 Election the Prime Minister was prevailed on by Gordon Brown and Peter Mandelson to offer the post of Secretary of State to Harriet Harman (Rawnsley, 2001). Field was offered the position of Minister for Welfare Reform, and by way of compensation a place on the Privy Council. According to several observers he was also led to believe that his elevation to the Cabinet had merely been postponed (Rawnsley, 2001; Bower, 2004). However, the relationship between Field and Harman was fractious to say the least, and ultimately unworkable. Andrew Rawnsley, Chief Political Editor for *The Observer* (Rawnsley, 2001, pp 106-10) has described the poisonous relationship between Harman and Field in lurid detail. Turf wars inevitably broke out in the Department of Social Security as Field and Harman wrangled over control of welfare reform and both parties took their complaints to the Prime Minister. Although Blair was clearly reluctant to lose key personnel who were central to the government's reform agenda both Harman and Field lost their jobs by the time of the first reshuffle in July 1998, although Field left of his own volition.

While providing much of interest for seasoned Westminster watchers, the real story behind Labour's early difficulties in the Department of Social Security was the evident power of the Chancellor of the Exchequer and the Treasury over key aspects of welfare policy. While Harman and Field grappled for control of welfare reform, the real architect of Labour's welfare strategy was the Chancellor, Gordon Brown. As was noted earlier, unlike previous Chancellors, Brown was not simply concerned with scrutinising expenditure, but also played a much greater role in directing social policy. Brown wielded considerable power through mechanisms such as the Comprehensive Spending Review, while policy units were established in the Treasury for health, education, transport and social security (Bower, 2004), which mirrored government departments, and also similar structures in the Cabinet Office.

The power of the Chancellor to direct social security policy was illustrated by the cuts to Lone Parent Benefit that precipitated Harman's difficulties as Secretary of State for Social Security. In order to maintain the spending freeze that allowed the government to follow Conservative spending plans Harman had been forced by Brown to push through unpopular Conservative plans for cuts to Lone Parent Benefit, despite the fact that she had spoken out against such cuts in opposition.

Social security policy was also developed in the Treasury with little consultation with the Department of Social Security. Brown launched his plans for providing assistance to poorer families through the tax rather than the benefits system, without consulting the Department of Social Security, and earned the ire of Field. Field's unswerving opposition to means-tested assistance inevitably led him into a conflict with the Chancellor. At the first meeting of the Cabinet's welfare-to-work sub-committee, Field, who was apparently unaware of the Chancellor's commitment to the use of tax credits, dismissed the plans as unworkable (Bower, 2004, p 235). Inevitably, it was Brown, supported by Harman, who prevailed while Field was forced to rail against the iniquities of means testing from the backbenches.

If the Chancellor had flexed his muscles in 1997 to ensure that Harriet Harman got the social security brief in place of Frank Field, he further consolidated his control over welfare policy following the departure of Harman and Field. The next two secretaries of state to hold the social security brief were Alistair Darling (1998-2002) and Andrew Smith (2002-04). Both were loyal Brownites who came to the post directly after serving alongside Brown as Chief Secretary to the Treasury.

However, by 2004, with Labour nearing the end of its third term, the internecine warfare between the Chancellor and the Prime Minister was beginning to inflict casualties on the Labour benches. In September 2004, Smith resigned shortly before an expected reshuffle. While the stated reason for his departure was the familiar wish to spend more time with his family, observers suggested that he had been a casualty of the conflict between Blair and Brown. In particular it was suggested that disagreements had emerged with Number 10 over the future of Incapacity Benefit, an expensive benefit claimed by almost three million people ('Minister "forced out" by power struggle,' *The Guardian*, 7 September 2004). As discussed in Chapter Three, previous attempts to reform Incapacity Benefit had been deeply unpopular among Labour backbenchers. Smith had sought to combat the problem by slowing the flow of people onto the benefit, and luring individuals back into work through a pilot scheme entitled Pathways to Work, which offered a mixture of a weekly back-to-work credit with mandatory monthly interviews for those still claiming benefit. Pathways to Work was popular on the Labour backbenches and was widely praised by MPs interviewed for this research. However, it was suggested by some that Number 10 was sceptical about the success of the pilot and was looking for a more radical solution including benefit cuts.

Smith's departure provided the Prime Minister with the opportunity to reassert control over welfare policy. Smith was replaced by Alan Johnson, a moderate former trade unionist from the Blairite wing of the party in his first Cabinet post, and following the 2005 General Election Johnson was replaced by David Blunkett. While the government had always been chary about seeking to gain political capital out of Blunkett's disability, his appointment was clearly designed to help in selling further reform of Incapacity Benefit to the parliamentary Labour Party, as well as the public at large. The 2005 manifesto promised "opportunity for all – the modern definition of full employment", with the most significant welfare reform being the replacement of Incapacity Benefit with a new benefit regime whereby even those with the most severe conditions would be encouraged to engage in activity, for which they would receive more money (The Labour Party, 2005). Blunkett was central to these plans, as one former parliamentary private secretary from the Department for Work and Pensions observed, "here is a man [Blunkett] who could be on Incapacity Benefit, yet holds down a very demanding job, it makes it very hard to argue that others couldn't do the same".

Blunkett's resignation was undoubtedly a blow for Blair's welfare reform agenda, and the proposed plans to overhaul Incapacity Benefit were postponed until July 2006, to allow time for Blunkett's replacement, another Blairite, John Hutton, to establish himself.

Hutton's appointment marked the end of another unsettled period for the Department for Work and Pensions in which four secretaries of state had led the department in a little over a year, Smith, Johnson, Blunkett and Hutton. But perhaps the most significant figure had remained in place throughout, the Chancellor Gordon Brown.

Conservative Party

For much of the period of the first two Labour governments the Conservatives found themselves struggling for direction. Between 1997 and 2006 the Conservatives suffered three general election defeats and four leadership contests. Between the resignation of John Major in 1997 and 2006 the Conservatives had four leaders – William Hague, Iain Duncan Smith, Michael Howard and David Cameron. It was therefore unsurprising that there was some lack of focus in their approach to social policy as each leader sought to develop their own policies.

However, even before the election of David Cameron as leader in December 2005, this period did see a revival of something like 'one-nation' Conservatism, with the Left of the party becoming somewhat more assertive than had been the case for most of the period since the 1970s. For some this was epitomised by Michael Portillo's conversion from an apparent devotee of New Right ideas to a leading spokesperson for a form of 'caring Conservatism', albeit with a failed bid for the leadership in 2001. It was further highlighted in the 2005 leadership election. In a prominent speech at the 2005 party conference Malcolm Rifkind, an early casualty of the leadership contest, called for a return to 'one-nation' Conservatism, while the remaining candidates in the contest included two candidates from the Left of the party, Ken Clarke and David Cameron, and two from the Right, David Davis and Liam Fox, with significant divisions emerging over their approach to social policies and to taxation.

In terms of social policy, the Conservatives fought the 1997 General Election arguing for tax cuts and a low tax economy, promising to ensure that they would increase public expenditure by less than the rate of growth in the economy, although at the same time promising to spend more on hospitals, schools and the police. The 1997 Election manifesto also placed significant emphasis on the family, both in terms of taxation and savings and reducing state interference in families, while also recognising that there was some role for the state in helping some families. In terms of social security the primary emphasis was on tackling social security fraud. In education the Conservatives promised to continue their previous policies of testing, inspection and extending choice and diversity of schools. Law and order was also emphasised in the manifesto, and in particular tackling juvenile crime, including the use of parental control orders and speedier punishment of offenders, and tougher sentences for persistent house burglars, dealers in hard drugs and people convicted of a second serious sexual or violent crime.

Following the 1997 Election defeat, William Hague was elected party leader in a contest in which he defeated the Left-leaning pro-European Ken Clarke. Although Hague initially sought to reach out to potential supporters, apologising for the party's failure to listen to voters in the final years of the Major government, and taking a liberal line on gender and 'race', his period as leader was ultimately characterised by an attempt to consolidate the Conservatives' core support.

One notable attempt to refashion the party under Hague illustrates the problems facing the Conservatives in seeking to move the party towards the electorally profitable centre ground. Peter Lilley, who had been Social Security Minister under Major, had been made Deputy Leader by Hague and charged with a major policy review. In April 1999, Lilley made a speech that marked a significant breach with Thatcherism. In response to research that showed that the party was not trusted by the voters on the core public services of health and education, Lilley declared that under the Conservatives these services would continue to be provided by the state and the party had no plans to extend privatisation of them. Lilley's speech caused some consternation in the party particularly among Thatcherites, including members of the Shadow Cabinet, and shortly afterwards Lilley was moved in a reshuffle (Kavanagh, 2004).

By the time of the 2001 General Election, with press speculation rife about who was likely to succeed Hague, the Conservatives had produced few new significant policy initiatives, in part because they found it difficult to deal with New Labour's shift to the centre ground, in part because those issues on which they were potentially electorally strongest were those of least salience to voters, and in part because the primary emphasis was on maintaining the party's 'core vote', rather than reaching out to potential new supporters. The 2001 General Election manifesto therefore again called for a smaller state and "welfare without the state" and emphasised the party's support for the family, including tax cuts, 'freeing' schools from local authority control, increasing police numbers, tougher sentencing for criminals and increased expenditure on the health service.

Following the 2001 Election defeat William Hague was succeeded by Iain Duncan Smith, after a leadership contest that saw Michael Portillo defeated in the first round of voting by MPs, after campaigning on a platform calling for a softer, more tolerant Conservative Party. Duncan Smith was from the Right of the party, a prominent Eurosceptic, described by Ken Clarke, a rival in the leadership contest, as a "hang 'em and flog 'em Tory" (*The Guardian*, 27 April 2002). While commentators frequently characterised Duncan Smith by his military service and his experience as Shadow Secretary of State for Defence that immediately preceded his leadership, he also had a particular interest in welfare and social justice, which stemmed in part from his religious faith, and he had also served as Shadow Secretary of State for Social Security from 1997-99.

Despite his much publicised Euroscepticism, following his election as party leader Duncan Smith sought to close down debate about Europe and refocus the party onto issues with appeal beyond the core voters targeted by Hague, such as health, education and transport. In February 2002, he set out his vision of 'Compassionate Conservatism' in a speech delivered on a Glasgow housing estate in which he pledged his commitment to public service reform and helping 'the vulnerable' (Seldon and Snowdon, 2005).

Duncan Smith failed to convince the party, not least elements of the Shadow Cabinet, of the merits of 'Compassionate Conservatism', and his performances in parliament and at conference quickly led to questions about his leadership. Nevertheless, Duncan Smith's interest in social justice and advocacy of 'Compassionate Conservatism' was influential, particularly among a group of young Conservative MPs who would eventually come to prominence when David Cameron became leader in 2005. In interviews for this research, while those on the Right of the party continued to extol the virtues of Thatcherism, a number of younger MPs prominent in the Cameron team went out of their way to distance themselves from the Thatcherite wing of the party, and pointed to the influence of Iain Duncan Smith in setting an agenda that has subsequently been taken up by David Cameron. Cameron's intellectual debt to Duncan Smith paid off in December 2005 when he asked the former leader to chair a policy review group on social justice.

Another prominent figure on the Conservative benches in terms of welfare in this period was Duncan Smith's successor as Shadow Secretary of State for Social Security, David Willetts. Willetts was appointed to the post by William Hague in June 1999, and retained the brief (which became Work and Pensions following departmental changes in 2001), until 2005. The length of time Willetts held the social security brief provided an important element of continuity in an insecure period for the party, and gave the Conservatives an advantage over Labour who had six secretaries of state responsible for social security between 1997 and 2006. Although a prospective leadership contender in 2005, Willetts has often appeared more comfortable in the intellectual engine room of the party. He is widely respected as an expert on welfare, and is one of a small group of MPs with a particular expertise in this area (including Labour's Frank Field and the Liberal Democrat Steve Webb), whose views are valued by MPs from other parties. As one of the few MPs to understand the complexities of the tax credit system, Willetts orchestrated the Conservative opposition to Gordon Brown's commitment to targeting support through means testing (Willetts, 2000), and was largely responsible for the Conservatives' pensions policies. Willetts was also a strong advocate of 'Compassionate Conservatism' (Willetts, 2005a). In the run-up to the Conservative leadership contest in 2005, while older figures such as Rifkind called for a return to 'one-nation' Conservatism, Willetts argued that it was not sufficient for the Conservatives to be "a bunch of backward looking people who want to recreate British society as it was in the 1950s", and instead advocated a 'new Conservatism' that combined a commitment to a strong economy with social justice (Willetts, 2005b).

Duncan Smith was replaced by Michael Howard in 2003. Under yet another leader the Conservatives again fought the 2005 General Election on a platform that promised lower taxes, although at the same time promising to "spend the same as Labour would on the NHS, schools, transport and international development, and more than Labour on police, defence and pensions" (Conservative Party, 2005, p 3). The Conservatives undertook to reverse the policy introduced under Margaret Thatcher and in future to increase the basic state pension in line with earnings rather than prices. For education the Conservatives emphasised a need for greater discipline in schools, again promised to free schools for local authority bureaucracy, and undertook to scrap fees for higher education. On the NHS, the party's manifesto promised to increase expenditure by at least as much as Labour during the next parliament, to cut waiting times and to reduce bureaucracy. Crime and law and order again figured prominently, with policies to recruit more police officers and to increase prison places, together with providing more treatment places for drug addicts. Controversially the 2005 manifesto also argued that "It's not racist to impose limits on immigration" (p 18), and proposed major reforms of the asylum system, including withdrawing from the 1951 Geneva Convention.

However, in a campaign dominated by negative campaigning the Conservatives once again failed to convince the electorate that the party was ready for government. The Conservative campaign was partly undermined when the party Deputy Chair Howard Flight, who had been partly responsible for the party's tax and spend policies, made a number of unguarded comments at a private meeting suggesting that the party's stated plans for tax cuts might be expanded by making spending cuts beyond the proposed efficiency savings. Although Flight's indiscretion was quickly followed by his resignation and deselection as a candidate, the impression that there was a secret agenda to make drastic cuts in public spending crystallised the fears of some voters and was exploited by Labour whose campaign had sought to highlight £35 billion of Conservative cuts.

When David Cameron replaced Michael Howard as leader in December 2005 he moved quickly to try to change the image of the party, particularly on social issues, effectively ruling out substantial radical reform of the welfare system, including committing the Conservatives to maintaining an NHS free at the point of delivery, saying that he would not reintroduce a grammar school system and dropping the Conservatives' opposition to tuition fees for university students. In April 2006, Oliver Letwin, a member of the Shadow Cabinet, committed the Conservatives to achieving Labour's target of abolishing child poverty by 2020, although the key to achieving this appeared to be largely seen as through voluntary initiatives rather than the state (Letwin, 2006).

However, the extent to which ideas such as these were likely to become accepted by the bulk of the Conservative Party will take time to become apparent. The unguarded comments of Howard Flight, and the reaction among some Conservatives to his dismissal suggested a reluctance on the part of some senior figures to move away from a commitment to substantive cuts in taxes and public spending, and several have publicly expressed reservations about Cameron's refusal to countenance tax cuts. Moreover, the plethora of commissions set up by Cameron, such as those on social inclusion, chaired by Iain Duncan Smith and on public service improvement, chaired by Baroness Pauline Perry and Stephen Dorrell, meant that it was likely that in many key policy areas any new Conservative approach would not be clear until 2008.

Liberal Democrats

In contrast to the Conservatives, the Liberal Democrats' electoral performance improved at each of the 1997 (46 MPs), 2001 (52 MPs) and 2005 (62 MPs) General Elections so that the pressures on the leadership and the party were significantly different from those experienced by the Conservative Party.

In 1997 with Paddy Ashdown as leader, the Liberal Democrat manifesto, *Making a difference* (Liberal Democrat Party, 1997), made education a central focus including a pledge to increase expenditure by £2 billion a year, reducing class sizes in primary schools, spending more on books and equipment and tackling the backlog of repairs and maintenance to school buildings. The party claimed that its policies had been fully costed and could be met by an increase of 1 pence on Income Tax and 5 pence on a packet of cigarettes. The party committed itself to increasing the number of police officers, tackling youth crime and setting up a Royal Commission to identify policies on drug abuse. Where housing was concerned the Liberal Democrats promised to use partnerships between the public sector, private sector and housing associations to build more homes, and to end rough sleeping by requiring local authorities to provide schemes to enable homeless people to take up private tenancies and by providing more short-stay hostel places. The NHS was promised additional spending of at least £540 million per year and patients were to be given greater choice. A new top rate of Income Tax of 50 pence on taxable income over £100,000 was to be used to raise tax thresholds for low earners, while a new top-up pension was to be introduced for pensioners with incomes below the Income Support level.

In 1999 Paddy Ashdown was succeeded by Charles Kennedy as party leader, following a contest in which he easily defeated Simon Hughes. While under Ashdown the party had arguably moved closer to Labour, especially once Tony Blair had become leader, one of the major challenges for the party now was whether to present itself as a party of the Centre or one that was to the Left of Labour. Under Kennedy's leadership and in the 2001 General Election education and health were clearly identified as priority areas for the Liberal Democrats. The 2001 manifesto therefore promised the recruitment of additional staff to the NHS and the provision of an additional 10,000 beds, as well as an acceptance of the Royal Commission on Long-term Care's recommendations from 1999 that long-term personal care costs should be met by the state. Whereas the 1997 manifesto had proposed cuts in primary class sizes to 30, in 2001 the party went further pledging average class sizes of 25 for 5- to 11-year-olds. It also undertook to recruit 5,000 additional secondary school teachers and to abolish tuition fees for university education. Crime and law and order were also a priority in 2001, with promises to recruit 6,000 more police officers and a promise to focus on crime prevention rather than building more prisons. For those on low wages and dependent on benefits the Liberal Democrats promised lower taxation, additional money for families on long-term Income Support, and an increase in pensions, particularly for people aged over 75 (up by £10 for a single person and £18 for a couple).

Responsibility for much of the Liberal Democrats' policy on tax and benefits in this period fell to Steve Webb, a former professor of social policy who became Liberal Democrat spokesperson for social security on his election to parliament in 1997, and Shadow Secretary of State for Work and Pensions from 2001-05. Like Willetts, Webb is widely viewed as the custodian of the party's knowledge on welfare, whose views are respected across the House. Under Webb's direction the party presented more generous policies than Labour, designed in particular to combat pensioner and child poverty and funded by increases in the basic and the top rate of Income Tax. Webb was a prominent critic of Labour's commitment to maintaining Conservative spending plans in their first term, and tabled the motion opposing cuts to Lone Parent Benefit in 1997, which was supported by a large group of Labour rebels. He was also largely responsible for the Liberal Democrats' pensions plans that included improvements in the basic state pension for the over-75s and the introduction of a citizens' pension based on entitlement rather than contributions.

However, while the party had been presenting itself as close to, or to the Left of, The Labour Party, there remained divisions in the party over its future direction and this was demonstrated prior to the 2004 party conference, the last one before the 2005 General Election. A number of prominent Liberal Democrats published *The orange book: Reclaiming liberalism* (Marshall and Laws, 2004), which, among other things, called for more competition and choice in public services, a social insurance-based approach to healthcare, and took a generally more market-oriented approach to policies. However, the 2005 Election manifesto continued to show a commitment to removing poorer people from the tax system, the scrapping of university tuition fees, the recruitment of more teachers and the achievement of lower class sizes, 10,000 additional police officers and a further 20,000 new community support officers, free personal care for older people and increased pensions for those aged 75 and over. These were to be funded by a shift to a 50% top rate on tax for people earning over £100,000 per year and the replacement of the Council Tax by a Local Income Tax.

Following Charles Kennedy's departure as leader of the party at the beginning of 2006 there were three candidates for the leadership – Sir Menzies Campbell, seen as an 'elder statesman', not closely linked with any particular section of the party, with an expertise in foreign affairs rather than domestic policy, Chris Huhne, who was generally viewed as being on the more economically Liberal wing of the party, and Simon Hughes, the party's president who was widely seen as being on the Left of the party.

As with the election of Charles Kennedy, the party chose a compromise candidate in Menzies Campbell, a safe choice as an experienced and tested MP with no firm affiliation to either wing of the party. However, in a short period Campbell presided over a significant shift in party thinking. Campbell's first reshuffle brought a number of prominent MPs from the Right of the party into significant posts, such as Chris Huhne who took the environment brief despite only having been elected in 2005, and Ed Davey who moved from shadowing the Office of the Deputy Prime Minister to Trade and Industry, and most notably David Laws, a former investment banker who co-edited the *The orange book* and epitomised the free market liberalism of a new generation of Liberal Democrat MPs, who replaced Webb as Shadow Secretary of State for Work and Pensions. This was followed in June 2006 by a significant shift in policy, as Campbell announced that the Liberal Democrats were dropping their long-standing policy of higher overall taxes, and would instead introduce a 2 pence cut in the basic rate of Income Tax, financed in part by increasing taxes for those who pollute the environment, and by increasing the tax burden of the very wealthy by, for example, ending capital gains tax breaks for people with second homes.

Conclusions

Since the demise of the postwar 'consensus' on the mixed economy and the welfare state there has been a constant questioning of the future direction of social policy and the role of the state in relation to the provision of welfare services. With the economic problems of the 1970s and the election of Margaret Thatcher in 1979 came a new emphasis on individualism, economy and the role of the market, rather than collectivism, universalism and continued growth in expenditure funded through taxation. Nevertheless, despite extensive reforms by the Conservatives in many areas, substantial parts of the welfare state remained in place when Labour returned to power in 1997.

The extent to which the Labour governments' approach to social policy has been underpinned by different ideological perspectives and other pressures has been widely debated in the period since 1997, including in parliament, as reflected in the discussions in Chapters Four and Five. The Labour governments' shift towards the centre ground, and their acceptance of many of the changes introduced by the Conservative governments, including a wider role for the private sector within the public provision of welfare, together with the significant increases in public expenditure in areas such as education and health, as well as the changes to the government (or governance) of social policy including devolution to Scotland and Wales and the use of a broad range of new public management techniques, have provided fertile ground for these debates. They have also impacted on the other main political parties who have had to respond to New Labour's relatively flexible and pragmatic approach to social policy. As noted earlier in this chapter, for the Conservatives in particular this has been difficult, as the government shifted towards their traditional standpoint in some areas, such as aspects of law and order and the role of the market, while the public's desire for tax cuts also appeared to have waned since the 1980s. Successive Conservative leaders therefore found it difficult to develop a distinctive and potentially popular approach to social policy. The Liberal Democrats have also had to seek to develop policies that are acceptable to both the more economically liberal and more social inclusive wings of the party.

Given these developments it is perhaps not surprising that there have been suggestions that there has been the emergence of something like a new consensus on welfare between the main parties. Williams (2000) has argued that the 1990s saw a new consensus on the role of the state. He suggested that this consensus was nowhere captured better than in approaches to welfare, largely driven by the perceived need for national competitiveness in the global economy, with the two main parties seeking to achieve this in part through fundamental reform of the welfare state aimed at containing public spending; shifting the balance towards those services that are used by most of the electorate; controlling demands on welfare by encouraging claimants to enter the labour market; and modernising public services to raise productivity.

Focusing in detail on welfare, Taylor-Gooby (2001) also argued that there has been the development of a new 'liberal' consensus on welfare. Like Williams, he explains welfare reform in the UK largely as a response to labour market change, demography and globalisation, but also emphasises the electoral imperatives of Britain's two-party system in which parties may diverge when seeking an electorally viable solution to problems but then converge on the 'middle-ground' when such a solution appears to attract support. Taylor-Gooby suggests that the perceived 'solution' involves widespread agreement on the retrenchment of spending, the promotion of privatisation in key areas, notably pensions, the targeting of benefits through means testing and other restrictions, and the importance of labour market activation through incentives, training and welfare-to-work.

In contrast, Lowe (2005) highlights the continued tensions within the main political parties, noting that there has been a sustained debate within the Conservative Party over the extent to which the welfare state should be dismantled, and that The Labour Party has been split by a more fractious debate over the extent to which the role of the market should be enhanced in a range of welfare policy areas. Lowe recognises that such internal tensions, arising from the fact that the two main parties have converged from very different ideological positions, are not sufficient to invalidate the concept of consensus, but argues that they are nevertheless significant and suggests that the shifts towards consensus remain a source for debate within, as well as between, the main parties. While Lowe's argument focuses on the Conservative and Labour Parties, to these could be added the continuing debate within the Liberal Democrats about future policy directions, as evidenced by the publication of *The orange book*, including contributions from several leading MPs, in 2004.

These debates over the directions of welfare policy and the extent of their impact and acceptance within the political parties at Westminster are explored further in Chapter Four, while their relationship with public opinion and representative democracy, as well as the ability of parliament and parliamentarians to influence the policies of governments, form key themes for the remainder of this book.

THREE

A declining force?
Parliament under Blair

Role and functions of Parliament

Under the Westminster model of parliamentary government the British Parliament does not play a significant role in the formulation of policy. Responsibility for the formulation of public policy resides almost exclusively with the executive – the Prime Minister and the Cabinet. It is the role of Parliament to scrutinise proposals for new legislation, to examine government policy and administration, and more broadly to provide a forum within which the major issues of the day may be debated. Many attempts have been made to outline the role and functions of the British Parliament. Studies of the Westminster model often begin with Walter Bagehot's lucid description of the five functions of the House of Commons in 1867. The main function of the Commons, Bagehot asserted, was elective, to provide an assembly from which the executive is drawn, and to maintain that executive as long as it is deemed fit to govern. Secondly, Bagehot described an expressive function, whereby parliament should "express the mind of the English people on all matters which come before it". Bagehot also placed particular emphasis on the teaching function of parliament, arguing that "a great and open council" placed in the middle of society, ought to "teach the nation what it does not know" and alter society "for the better". In addition, the House of Commons, Bagehot stated, had long had an "informing function", that is, to inform the executive of the grievances of the people. Finally, Bagehot identified the legislative function, which, while undoubtedly important, and at times supremely important, was not, he suggested, as important as other functions, most notably the educative function (Bagehot, 1867, pp 152-5).

It has become customary in works on British parliamentary government to enhance Bagehot's assessment with modifications or additional functions. Some have highlighted long-standing functions of parliament neglected by Bagehot, most notably a financial function. The granting of supply was one of the original functions of the English

Parliament, and the role of parliament in approving government expenditure and taxation features prominently in recent attempts to summarise parliament's functions (Hennessy, 1995; Tyrie, 2000; Wright, 2000; Rush, 2005). Others have suggested that societal and political developments since the 19th century have served to undermine some of Bagehot's functions and led to the creation of new roles for parliament. The political scientist and Labour MP, Tony Wright, questions whether parliament any longer serves an important educative function, "now that informed discussion about the issues of the day is more easily accessible elsewhere" (Wright, 2000, p 211). Similarly the creation of other legislative assemblies, both within and beyond the UK, has transferred some decision-making power from Westminster and thereby undermined parliament's legislative function. At the same time however, as Riddell observes, the creation of new legislative assemblies has also served to create new roles for parliament, most notably in the scrutiny of European legislation (Riddell, 2000).

Perhaps the most significant development since the late 19th century has been the growth of political parties, which, according to Norton, has led to a fundamental shift in the role of parliament. Party, he argues, has come to dominate parliamentary activity (although, as discussed in Chapter Six, this has been somewhat less so in the House of Lords than in the House of Commons), with the result that the legislative function has moved from parliament to the Cabinet. As party cohesion has become an established feature of parliamentary life, legislation that for the most part originates in the Cabinet is passed by MPs voting loyally with the party line. Although parliament retains some residual legislative power through the ability to generate private members' bills, even these, Norton observes, can only hope to make it on to the statute books if the government agrees to provide time (Norton, 2005). As parliament is no longer involved in generating legislation several observers have noted that it has developed a new and increasingly important role, that of mobilising support for government policy (Beer, 1965; Wright, 2000; Norton, 2005). Indeed, media and scholarly coverage of parliament is increasingly dominated by attempts to trace the minutiae of party cohesion in parliamentary voting, while considerable attention has been paid to tracing the level of party discipline in successive parliaments (for example, Norton, 1980; Cowley, 2002, 2005; Russell and Sciara, 2006a).

While the identification of a complex array of developments both within and beyond Westminster tends towards the creation of ever expanding lists of parliamentary functions (see, for example, Hennessy, 1995; Riddell, 2000), it is nevertheless possible to identify a number of core functions. These may be summarised by stating that parliament is the body from which governments are recruited, legitimised and scrutinised, and through which the views of the people are heard, and redress of grievances sought.

Parliament is the body from which the executive is drawn, and an alternative government is created, in the form of an opposition. This recruiting role is an important factor in sustaining the power of parliament. Ministers, including the Prime Minister, are answerable to parliament for their own conduct and that of their departments. In addition to this, Norton has stressed that a wider consequence of parliamentary recruitment is the enforced proximity of ministers and backbenchers within parliament. While this may be an important factor in the socialisation of backbenchers into party loyalty, it also provides frequent opportunities for contact between backbenchers and ministers. In addition to taking part in debates and responding to questions in the House, ministers may also be waylaid in corridors, tearooms and division lobbies, and this, Norton observes, "presents an opportunity – and a much used one – for backbenchers to talk to ministers and put over particular points" (Norton, 2005, p 55).

However, the recruitment of ministers from parliament also provides the government with a strong element of control over parliament. The convention of collective responsibility, whereby ministers do not oppose government policy, provides the government with a large block of guaranteed votes within the Commons, often referred to as the 'payroll vote'. Moreover, the size of the payroll vote has increased considerably over the past century. In 1900, there were 60 ministers in parliament; following the 2005 General Election there were 112, 89 in the Commons and 23 in the Lords. In addition to the increase in ministerial positions, there has also been a marked increase in the number of parliamentary private secretaries. In 2005, there were 51, compared to 9 in 1900 (Rush, 2005). These unpaid ministerial aides are widely regarded as being on the first rung of the ministerial ladder and are expected to vote accordingly. The expansion in their number has therefore significantly expanded the payroll vote. In the 2005 Parliament, ministers and parliamentary private secretaries accounted for 40% of the parliamentary Labour Party. Moreover, the power of patronage ensures that in addition to the payroll vote, the government can rely on the support of a large number of MPs who aspire to ministerial office (Cowley, 2005). The effects of this, however, may be mitigated the longer a government remains in office. As one Labour MP commented, the parliamentary party is comprised of three groups, those who are ministers, those who aspire to be ministers, and those who have been ministers. While the government can generally rely on the support of the first two groups, it cannot rely on the latter, and this group is likely to increase in size the longer the government remains in office.

The fact that members of the government are drawn from parliament also serves to some degree to legitimise the actions of the government. Such legitimisation is another important function of parliament, for while parliament no longer creates the law, it does, in various ways, serve to legitimise the legislative power of the executive, although this legitimisation may be more an indication of the symbolic rather than the real power of parliament. Packenham (1970) has argued that the legitimising role of parliament may be latent, that simply by meeting on a regular basis to discuss government proposals and actions, parliament engenders in the wider public a sense of the government's right to rule. Such latent legitimisation, Norton suggests, may be most powerful in the case of legislatures, like the British Parliament, which have met regularly for a long period of time (Norton, 2005). Parliament also plays a more active role in legitimising the power of the government by assenting to legislation presented to it by the government. While legislative power has undoubtedly shifted to the executive, by giving assent to the laws presented to it parliament actively confers legitimacy on the government's plans. Conversely, if parliament does not support the government's legislation it may undermine the legitimacy of the government, and ultimately, if the government is defeated on a no-confidence motion, it may force the government to resign. Although confidence votes are rare, if the government is routinely defeated in parliament (or even finds it difficult to pass its legislation), and particularly on key aspects of its legislative programme, outside observers, in the media and in the public at large, are likely to begin to question the government's legitimacy long before a confidence motion is triggered in the House.

In many respects perhaps the most important function of parliament is that of scrutiny (Bochel and Bochel, 2004). Parliament's scrutinising function takes two forms, the scrutiny of legislation, and the scrutiny of government policy and administration. As a legislature, parliament's principal function is to examine and debate government bills, each of which must go through three readings, a committee stage and normally, a report stage. The main scrutiny of legislation takes place in standing committees, where bills are subject to clause-by-clause analysis, and proposed amendments voted on. MPs can also try to force the government to amend legislation by seeking to defeat a piece of legislation in a parliamentary vote. Although government defeats are rare, the extent of opposition to bills, particularly among the government's own party, may serve to indicate to the government areas of contention that it may wish to reconsider to ensure a smoother passage of its legislation through parliament. Votes against legislation in the Commons may also serve to highlight areas of contention that may be subject to more forensic scrutiny in the House of Lords, where a government defeat is more likely (see Chapter Six). Indeed, the House of Lords plays an important role in the revision of legislation. There is often more time to debate bills in the Lords, and consequently the number of amendments made is usually much greater than in the Commons.

In addition to the scrutiny of legislation, parliament also scrutinises the actions of government. There are a number of methods by which this is achieved. The most obvious means by which MPs can call the government to account is by raising questions in the House, during debates and ministerial question time. The weekly Prime Minister's Question Time is widely criticised as too adversarial, an opportunity for partisan point scoring and consequently devoid of substantive debate. However, the daily ministerial question time at which departmental ministers answer questions about their area of responsibility provides an opportunity for a more detailed examination of government policy (see Chapter Seven).

Detailed scrutiny also takes place in parliamentary select committees. Although the composition of select committees, and the allocation of chairs, reflects the balance of the parties in the House, they are generally accepted to be less partisan in their approach, and more forensic in their analysis. Select committees control their own agenda, and may look at broad areas of government policy such as the role of the private sector in the NHS, or specific aspects of particular pieces of legislation of public concern such as the ban on smoking in public places. Select committees examine a broad range of government policy, with departmental select committees 'shadowing' the work of individual government departments and scrutiny committees considering issues such as delegated legislation and European legislation, while other committees examine the running of the House, and broad areas of administration, notably the select committees for public accounts and public administration. Unlike standing committees they have the power to take evidence, and spend much of their time interviewing witnesses. Witnesses may include ministers, MPs and civil servants and outside experts, and interested members of the public. Moreover, since 2002, the Prime Minister has appeared twice yearly to answer questions before the Liaison Select Committee, a select committee made up of select committee chairs.

Finally, parliament provides a forum in which the voices and indeed the grievances of the people may be heard – Bagehot's expressive function. According to Norton (2005), parliament serves not one but several expressive functions. MPs express the particular views and demands of their constituents. This may be done by MPs passing constituents' concerns to relevant ministers, or asking questions in the House. MPs also express the views of different groups within society. MPs are lobbied heavily by outside interests including charities, religious groups and particular industries and occupations. The extent to which MPs give voice to concerns raised by such groups may be largely dependent on the personal interests of individual MPs and crucially, the extent of constituency interest in the issue, but many MPs certainly pursue issues on which they have been effectively lobbied. The same may be said for members of the House of Lords, who while not having a geographical constituency as such, often represent outside interests that may be related to their former occupation, as for example, trade unionists, lawyers or university lecturers. Norton also observes that MPs serve to express the views of parliament and the government to constituents and organised groups. MPs may explain policy to individual constituents and groups and select committees may in effect explain policy and administration in published reports that are widely read by interested parties and may attract media attention.

Decline of parliament?

While there is little question about the various functions of parliament, there is considerable debate about the extent to which parliament effectively fulfils these functions. In a recent study of parliament under the Blair premiership, Peter Riddell argued that there is an imbalance in the manner in which parliament carries out its various functions. "Parliament", he asserted, "is focused entirely on its role in forming, supporting or opposing the executive, and not on its long-standing other roles, especially those of scrutiny and holding the executive to account" (Riddell, 2000, pp 6-7). Such criticism, of which Riddell is by no means the most vociferous advocate, that parliament has been marginalised in the development of policy by an overly powerful executive, has been present for much of the postwar period, but has perhaps gained additional ground since the election of Tony Blair in 1997.

The most consistent and sustained explanation for the marginalisation of parliament relates to the growth in the power of political parties. It has long been argued that the growth in political parties since the mid-19th century has led to a decline in the power of parliament. Almost all MPs are now elected as representatives of highly organised political parties, on the basis of increasingly detailed manifestos that set out a programme of legislation to which they are all effectively committed. Most legislation originates in the Cabinet, and even private members' bills are unlikely to make it onto the statute books without the support of the government. As MPs have become dependent on parties for election, party cohesion has become a consistent feature of parliamentary business. Signs of independent action on the part of individual MPs are quickly headed off by party whips, whose role it is to remind MPs that they owe their privileged position to the party, and that future advancement is dependent on their continued loyalty.

Moreover, the domination of party and the power of the whips extends beyond the control of debate in the House of Commons. Standing committees, which provide detailed scrutiny of bills, are balanced to reflect the balance of the parties in the House and now almost invariably include at least one government whip. Similarly, the membership of select committees also reflects the government's majority, and membership and more importantly the allocation of chairs is largely the gift of the Whip's Office. While the domination of party is a long-term trend it has been argued that it has increased in recent years, as parties, and particularly The Labour Party, have extended control over the selection of candidates for by-elections and general elections (for example, Commission to Strengthen Parliament, 2000). The Labour Party has also become synonymous with highly organised party management, with the use of new technologies such as pagers to allow instant communication with MPs. This has led to widespread criticism, not least from some backbench Labour MPs, that the majority of Labour MPs are automatons, blindly submitting to the will of the whips, with the result that parliament under Blair has become supine and ineffective (Tyrie, 2000; Cowley, 2001).

Concerns about the lack of effective parliamentary scrutiny were further fuelled by the government's reforms of the House of Lords, dealt with in greater detail in Chapter Six. The removal of over 600 hereditary peers in 1999 transformed the Lords from a House dominated by the Conservatives to one in which no party enjoyed an overall majority. The addition of new life peers in May 2005 meant that Labour for the first time became the largest party in the House of Lords, although it remained far short of a majority. However, some observers, and particularly Conservative MPs, asserted that with an overwhelming majority in the Commons, reform of the Lords was merely designed to remove the only possible source of parliamentary resistance to the government's legislative programme. Even among those who supported the removal of hereditary peers there was concern that their replacement with appointed peers merely created another form of political patronage, which led to an influx of life peers whose principal qualification appeared to be their party loyalty. Blair's predecessor, John Major, has observed that the removal of the hereditary peers was an undoubtedly popular policy that "robbed Parliament of a revising chamber of talent and experience and independent thought ... but if they had to go they should have been replaced by others with similar virtues" (Major, 2003, p 7).

Alongside concerns about changes within Westminster, it has also been argued that parliament has failed to cope with the growth of alternative centres of power. This is the principal criticism of Riddell's (2000) *Parliament under Blair* in which he contends that parliament has been marginalised as power has been transferred to other institutions, notably the European Union, the Scottish Parliament and the National Assembly for Wales, and through the creation of elected mayors and an assembly in London. At the same time, successive governments have shifted responsibility for large areas of policy to quasi-independent bodies such as utility regulators and the Bank of England. Finally, he expresses concern about a growth in judicial activism that has been prompted in part by the failure of governments in drafting laws and the failure of parliament to scrutinise them. In addition, Riddell has argued that the incorporation of the European Convention on Human Rights into UK law has, in effect, invited a broad measure of judicial review of all legislation generated within the UK. While some of these changes have occurred under successive governments, notably the growth in quangos, Riddell argues that the drain of power from Westminster has been particularly marked since 1997 due to the unprecedented number of constitutional changes introduced by the Labour government.

Perhaps the most sustained argument for the decline of parliament since 1997 focuses on the Prime Minister himself. It is often argued that the Blair government, and the Prime Minister in particular, has neglected parliament, that the Prime Minister rarely participates in parliamentary business, and that major policy announcements are made outside the House. It is certainly true that Tony Blair has had the poorest voting record of any peacetime Prime Minister, with the exception of the ailing Churchill, and rarely participates in debates;

his appearances in the Commons seldom extend beyond the weekly Prime Minister's Question Time and statements to the House (Riddell, 2000; Tyrie, 2000). The Prime Minister participated in 8.6% of votes during the 1997-2001 Parliament, and only 7.5% in the 2001-05 Parliament. An analysis of voting records since 1969 indicates that Blair is the only Prime Minister with a voting record in single figures. His lowest voting record in a parliamentary session, at 5% in 1997-98, is considerably lower than the previous lowest record, set by Margaret Thatcher at 15% in the 1988-89 session. It is also markedly lower than his Labour predecessors, Wilson and Callaghan, who never attended less than 35% of votes in each parliamentary session as Prime Minister (Tyrie, 2000; *The Times*, 24 December 2004), although the Labour governments of 1974 to 1979 were frequently in danger of defeat in the House of Commons and the requirement to vote was therefore significantly stronger.

Critics see Tony Blair's lack of participation in parliament as significant for several reasons. It suggests that the Prime Minister has had little interest in parliament, with little appreciation that parliament has a role in scrutinising the executive; in short that parliament does not matter. The Prime Minister's absence also, in a very real sense, prevents the Prime Minister from being influenced by parliament. As Riddell argues, "it is not just the act of voting. It is much more that a Prime Minister's physical presence to vote allows MPs the chance to talk to him or her, not least as they crowd together in the division lobby" (Riddell, 2004, p 826). By avoiding this, Riddell argues, Blair is more remote, more presidential, and crucially, much more likely to brush aside the concerns of his own backbenchers. Moreover, it is argued, the Prime Minister's lack of interest has set an example for other ministers who have been similarly dismissive of parliament.

Some of the arguments for the decline of parliament are certainly politically motivated. In 2003, Blair's predecessor John Major, whose term in office was marred by the abuse of parliamentary privilege by Conservative MPs, claimed in a treatise on the decline of parliamentary democracy, that "New Labour offenders have been far closer to the centre of power than their much-maligned predecessors" (Major, 2003, p 3). Moreover, he argued, parliament was being undermined by the Prime Minister's debating style. Prime Minister's Question Time, he suggested, had been undermined by "the extent to which the Prime Minister's responses and emotions are pre-scripted by others" and questions to ministers were "becoming equally pointless" (Major, 2003, p 7). Major went on to argue that the power of parliament had been diminished by reform of the House of Lords, the transfer of powers to

Scotland, Wales and the EU, and also suggested, provocatively, that the devolution of monetary policy to the Bank of England, could be shifted at a later date to the European Central Bank.

Many of the arguments rehearsed by Major had already been made by, perhaps the most consistent Conservative critic of parliament under Blair, the Conservative MP Andrew Tyrie, who has characterised the House of Commons as 'Blair's poodle'(Tyrie, 2000). Tyrie's case for the decline of parliament centred on the Prime Minister's apparent 'disdain' for parliament, illustrated by his relative attendance and voting record, in comparison to previous 20th-century prime ministers, and the shift of political debate from the floor of the Commons to the mass media, something which he, naturally, claims has been aided and abetted by the Blair government. Tyrie's criticisms formed part of a submission to a Commission to Strengthen Parliament, established by the then Leader of the Opposition, William Hague, in 1999. The Commission was asked to examine "the cause of the decline in the effectiveness of Parliament in holding the executive to account", although did not consider whether parliament was in fact in decline. The Commission was chaired by the Conservative peer, and political scientist, Philip Norton, and produced a detailed report that included a series of recommendations for strengthening parliament, many of which had long been advocated by supporters of parliamentary reform, including strengthening the power of select committees; improved scrutiny of legislation, including more pre-legislative scrutiny; and limiting the payroll vote by reducing the number of ministers and parliamentary private secretaries (Commission to Strengthen Parliament, 2000). Norton later criticised the Prime Minister's apparent dismissal of the Commission's findings, as indicative of his "remarkable degree of detachment both from Parliament and from his own government" (Norton, 2005, p 243.).

These criticisms of the decline of parliament under Blair have not been limited to the Opposition benches. There has also been notable criticism from the Prime Minister's own benches. Cowley's conversations with Labour rebels not surprisingly uncovered some barely concealed contempt among rebellious MPs for their more loyal colleagues, one MP referring to them as a "model army of programmed zombies" (Cowley, 2001, p 818). Backbench Labour MPs interviewed in the course of the research for this book frequently referred to the limit on the power of parliament generated by the size of Labour's majorities in 1997 and 2001, often stating that this was "bad for parliament" or "bad for democracy". However, it is notable that few advocated reforms such as the introduction of proportional representation, or suggested that they were happy to lose their seats in the interests of improved parliamentary democracy. One who favours the former, if not the latter, is the Labour MP Austin Mitchell, who has attributed the decline in parliament to the rise of party. In a spectacularly mixed metaphor, he argued that backbench MPs, in theory the power elite of the British constitution, are the "workhorses of the system ... harnessed to the chariot of party", and at the same time "infantry, obeying their leaders and tramping through the lobbies to support or oppose the executive" (Mitchell, 2005, p 60).

However, while arguments for the decline of parliament have become commonplace since the 1997 General Election, there are also powerful arguments against such an interpretation. Many, including those who have criticised the decline of parliament under Blair, have observed that, whatever the current situation, there never was a 'golden age' of parliamentary sovereignty with which to compare the Blair era. As Cowley has observed, claims for the decline of parliament are not new (Cowley, 2005). The shelves of British parliamentary literature are punctuated by works lamenting the declining power of parliament, often penned by disillusioned parliamentarians (for example, Hollis, 1949; Hill and Whichelow, 1964; Hailsham, 1976; Garrett, 1992). These works suggest that current concerns about the relationship between parliament and the executive are far from exceptional.

Furthermore, while government defeats in parliament have certainly been rare since 1997, as Cowley asserts, they have always been rare. Governments usually get their way. Similarly, many other prime ministers have neglected parliament. Indeed, Tyrie's examination of prime ministerial participation is not so much an illustration of the marginalisation of parliament under Blair as confirmation of a long-term decline in prime ministerial participation throughout the 20th century, with significant drops under Blair's two immediate predecessors, Major and Thatcher (Tyrie, 2000). Moreover, as Cowley notes, the Blair government is not the first to make major policy statements outside the House of Commons. Margaret Thatcher was frequently pressed by the Speaker to come to the House to make important policy announcements (Cowley, 2001). Furthermore, Cowley argues that far from being supine:

> ... the 2001 Parliament was remarkable not for the servility of government MPs but for both the frequency and size of the backbench rebellions that took place. Between 2001 and 2005 the PLP set a number of records which the whips

> would much rather they had left well alone.... (Cowley,
> 2005, p 240)

In addition, the assertion that reform of the House of Lords has undermined parliamentary scrutiny is also questionable, and as discussed in Chapter Six, the reality has arguably been that the House of Lords has become more assertive and more willing to challenge the government, including on welfare legislation.

Ironically, perhaps the most convincing case for the continued power of parliament is made by Philip Norton, wearing the hat of a professor of politics, rather than that of Conservative peer and Chair of the party's Commission to Strengthen Parliament. He argues that the thesis for the decline of parliament is based on a narrow pluralist perspective in which power is manifested in observable decision making. Consequently, "because legislatures do not regularly say 'no' to the executive, and substitute policy of their own, they are deemed to be in decline" (Norton, 2005, p 7). This emphasis on the coercive capacity of parliament, Norton asserts, is wrong:

> It derives historically from the view that Parliament is a 'law-making' body and it is not using its coercive capacity to constrain government or to ensure the outcomes that it wants. What this neglects is the persuasive capacity of Parliament. It can be contended that this is the most vital aspect of Parliament's capacity to affect outcomes. (Norton 2005, p 245)

Both MPs and peers have a range of opportunities to influence policy beyond seeking to coerce the government by voting in the House of Commons and the House of Lords (see also Chapter Six). In this respect, Norton argues, what is happening away from the Commons chamber is as important, if not more so, than what is happening within it. MPs may press their views on ministers in a range of formal and informal settings from tearooms, and private meetings to all-party groups, backbench committees and meetings of the parliamentary parties. Furthermore, Norton adds, parliament currently offers MPs a range of other means of persuasion, rather than the threat to embarrass the government publicly by voting against it in the House:

> Pre-legislative scrutiny has added a new dimension to parliamentary influence at a formative stage. Select committees have become a central part of the parliamentary

landscape, in effect engaging in a dialogue with ministers and other political actors. Members also have at their disposal other formal as well as informal means of putting a particular point to ministers in order to induce action. The correspondence that flows between members and those of their number who are ministers is now a voluminous one, requiring ministers to respond to a wide range of concerns affecting individuals and groups in society. (Norton, 2005, pp 245-6)

This alternative view of the power of parliament is based partly on an elitist or agenda-setting perspective. While emphasising the various means by which MPs may influence decision making, it also stresses how MPs may induce non-decision making on the part of the government. By focusing on anticipated reactions rather than a narrow pluralist focus on observable decision making, Norton emphasises what parliament *can* do, rather than what it *does* do. Parliament, he suggests, may serve to keep certain matters off the agenda through the government anticipating adverse parliamentary reaction. "Ministers cannot ignore Parliament", he argues, "they can and do anticipate Parliamentary reaction. Some proposals that Ministers may instinctively wish to pursue may never reach the stage of being articulated within Government because of the negative response expected from MPs and peers" (Norton, 2005, p 246). The government may therefore be deterred from pursuing a particular policy if they believe it will attract an adverse reaction in the House, or if they fear it may be subject to forensic analysis by a parliamentary committee.

The problem with this kind of analysis, as Norton concedes, is that it is not easily observed or measured. One may be able to observe the power of parliament if the government changes a particular policy, following a vote, a critical select committee report or public criticism from a large group of MPs, in the media, or in the form of an early day motion (EDM). However, it is clearly not always possible to observe anticipated reaction and non-decision making. If proposals that ministers wish to pursue never reach the stage of being articulated because of an anticipated adverse reaction, how is it possible to observe a shift in government policy or determine the factors that influenced it? The Prime Minister's statement to the 2005 Labour Party conference, that every time he had introduced a reform in government, he wished "in retrospect" he had "gone further", suggests that anticipated reaction does have a profound effect on government policy. However, while one might presume that the Prime Minister was at least partly restrained by anticipated adverse reactions in parliament, not least on his own benches, without an intimate insight into the mind of the Prime Minister, it is not possible to weigh this against other possible agenda-setting influences such as public and media reaction. Nevertheless, in this respect it may be enough to state that ministers do anticipate reaction, and parliament does have the power to affect decision making at the executive level beyond the level of observable decision making. Interviews with MPs and peers allow us to go somewhat further in this analysis, as is done in Chapters Four, Six and Seven.

Finally, there is one further argument that suggests that to some extent irrespective of what happens in parliament, significant changes in the composition of both chambers, particularly since 1997, are symbolic of the continued importance of parliament (Cowley 2001). The 1997 General Election saw the largest turnover in the composition of the House of Commons since 1945 and this was combined with a significant increase in the number of women MPs, up from 60 in 1997 to 120, and an increase in the number of MPs from minority ethnic groups, up from 6 to 9, particularly on the Labour benches. On becoming leader of the Conservative Party in December 2005, David Cameron made clear that he saw an increase in the number of Conservative MPs from a variety of social groups as beneficial. In particular, therefore, there appears to have been a general acceptance by the political parties of the need to make parliament, and the House of Commons in particular, more characteristically representative of the population as a whole, reflecting a continued centrality, at least in some respects, of parliament in the UK's political life.

New Labour and the 'modernisation' of parliament

While the reforms of the House of Lords are covered in Chapter Six, with regard to the House of Commons, 'modernisation' since 1997 has been another contentious area, not least because it has never been particularly clear what precisely 'modernisation' has been about (for example, House of Commons Library, 2005). As Cowley (2006) has noted:

> For some, it was about making the Commons appear more modern, stripping away some of the more antiquated procedures and practices. Others wanted to make the Commons more efficient, changing the hours and making the passage of legislation more predictable. Others wanted to make the Commons more accessible, more open to the

public. Yet others wanted to make it stronger, 'shifting the balance' – a much used phrase – between the Commons and the executive. (p 46)

Since the establishment of the Select Committee on Modernisation of the House of Commons in 1997, with a remit to "consider how the practices and procedures of the House should be modernised, and to make recommendations thereon", there have been a series of reports and recommendations by the Committee (for example, Modernisation Committee, 1997, 1998 and 2004), although relatively few have sought to strengthen the powers of the House in relation to the executive, and a number of reforms to the working of the House.

However, it seems unlikely that any government would willingly surrender power to the House of Commons or make it easier for MPs to challenge its legislation and other actions, so it was not surprising that some of the proposals faced opposition, including from the government Whip's Office (for example, Cook, 2003). Despite this, the Committee's recommendations, particularly under the leadership of Robin Cook, who chaired the Committee as Leader of the House from 2001 until his resignation from the government over the Iraq war in 2003, have resulted in a number of significant changes. These have included: additional payments to chairs of select committees, in an attempt to develop an alternative career track within parliament to the ministerial path; a change to the previous sessional cut-off, allowing bills to be carried over from one session to the next, although relatively little use has been made of this and there is still the familiar end of session pattern of legislation moving back and forth between the Commons and the Lords; amendments to the parliamentary day and to the timetable with parliament starting earlier in the day and finishing in the early evening as well as returning earlier from the summer recess (but in 2005 further changes were made that involved some movement back to the previous position); the use of the grand committee room off Westminster Hall as an alternative chamber for short debates that do not involve votes on issues raised by private members as well as select committee reports; greater opportunity for pre-legislative scrutiny, with many more bills being published in draft format, allowing MPs, peers and other interested parties greater possibility for influencing legislation at an earlier stage, although as Cowley (2006) points out, pre-legislative scrutiny of bills remains the exception rather than the norm; the electronic tabling of parliamentary questions and a reduction in the period of notice required for these; and attempts to improve the connection of parliament with the public through providing better access to the Commons and the Lords, including on Saturdays.

Although separate from the package of 'modernisation' reforms, it is worth noting that there were other changes that also had the potential to impact on the relationship between the executive and the House of Commons. Following the 1997 General Election Tony Blair made changes to Prime Minister's Question Time, moving away from two 15-minute sessions each week to one 30-minute session on Wednesdays. Critics have argued that this is a reflection of his lack of attention to the House of Commons, while an alternative argument has been that it is possible to have more substantial debate in a 30-minute period than in two 15-minute sessions. Given that Prime Minister's Question Time is arguably more about scoring political points in an adversarial setting it would not seem unreasonable to suggest that neither pattern of questions allows for anything other than a media spectacle. Perhaps more significantly, in 2002 Tony Blair decided that he would appear twice yearly before the Liaison Committee (a committee consisting of the chairs of the other select committees) for two-and-a-half hours each time. Each of these sessions covers a particular theme or set of themes, with the Prime Minister knowing these in advance, but not what the particular questions will be. In many respects this was a dramatic change as no Prime Minister had appeared before a House of Commons scrutiny committee in the postwar period.

Given the lack of clarity over the purpose of 'modernisation' and the unlikelihood of any government voluntarily making it easier for parliament to amend or otherwise impede legislation or to scrutinise their work, it may be unsurprising that the reforms have done little to shed further light on the arguments discussed earlier in this chapter on the relative power of the legislature and the executive, nor on the 'decline of parliament' thesis, with critics continuing to be able to claim that "... these reforms are all on the executive's terms. None really inconvenience ministers. The basic questions of scrutiny and accountability – of power – have not been addressed" (Riddell, 2000, p 248). On the other hand, if it were the case that the reforms were intended to enable MPs to undertake their roles, including as constituency caseworkers, and to make a parliamentary career more attractive by allowing MPs to spend more time with their families, then the success of the reforms might be judged differently.

Parliament and welfare legislation under Blair

Whatever the views on the 'decline' of parliament since 1997, the Blair government's reform of parliament appears to have done little to help secure parliamentary support for its legislative programme. Not only may Labour's reform of the Lords have resulted in the emergence of a more assertive upper House (see Chapter Six), the government also had to contend with increasingly assertive backbenchers in the Commons. As Cowley has shown, a widespread assumption that Labour's substantial majorities somehow ensured a supine or compliant parliament did not stand up to scrutiny. In exhaustive analysis of parliamentary divisions throughout the Blair governments, Cowley has shown that frequent accusations that Labour MPs were unthinking automatons or sheep prepared to follow the whips into the government lobbies were somewhat wide of the mark. While there were relatively few backbench revolts in Blair's first term, 96 compared to 174 in the previous parliament, the scale of revolt was nevertheless substantial. As Cowley observes, if Labour MPs were rebelling infrequently after 1997, "when they did break ranks they did so in sizeable numbers" (Cowley, 2002, p 231). In the 1997 Parliament 133 Labour MPs voted against the party whip. Half of Labour backbenchers rebelled at least once in the course of the parliament. Moreover, the propensity to rebel increased as the parliament progressed. In the third session, 1999-2000, there were more Labour rebellions than in the first two sessions put together (Cowley, 2002). It is perhaps not surprising then that backbench rebellion increased considerably in Labour's second term. Labour backbenchers rebelled 259 times during the 2001 Parliament, more than in any other parliament since 1945. The extent of disquiet among Labour backbenchers was also remarkable, more than 200 Labour MPs rebelled, over half of the parliamentary Labour Party (Cowley, 2005).

Although Labour MPs rebelled on a range of issues, social policy legislation tended to suffer a particularly rough passage. The first major rebellion of the Blair government, in December 1997, was prompted by proposed cuts in Lone Parent Benefit. The planned cuts, included in the Social Security Bill, were inherited from the previous Conservative government and a consequence of Labour's commitment to abide by Conservative spending plans for the first two years of office. The Social Security Minister, Harriet Harman, had publicly opposed the cuts in opposition and continued to argue against the proposals within government, but the Treasury, and more particularly the Chancellor, Gordon Brown, prevailed (Pym and Kochan, 1998; Bower, 2004). Despite obvious disquiet on the backbenches, the government made little effort to explain the issue to concerned MPs, and Harman, perhaps not surprisingly, was less than convincing when seeking to justify the cuts in the Commons. As a result, 47 Labour MPs voted for a Liberal Democrat amendment that would remove the right of the government to reduce Child Benefits for lone parents. The rebellion included four members of the government who were forced to resign, while at least 20 others abstained. It was, according to one observer, "a terrible blooding for Labour's new MPs as they were dragooned through the lobbies to vote, some of them in tears" (Toynbee and Walker, 2001, p 18).

The rebellion over Lone Parent Benefit was a key lesson for the government. Even among those who voted with the government it was widely accepted that the issue was poorly handled. As a result, while the government got its way, there was, according to Cowley (2002), a change in attitudes among the executive, and ministers began to make themselves more readily available to listen and discuss the concerns of MPs. There was also a positive effort to ameliorate the effects of the cuts. In the March 1998 Budget, the Chancellor, who had been uncompromising in pushing through the cut in Lone Parent Benefit, announced a series of measures designed to support families with children. Most notably there was an increase in Child Benefit of £2.50 a week, the largest ever single increase, and the introduction of Working Families Tax Credit, and a Childcare Tax Credit. However, according to Cowley, the most significant development was a subtle shift in relations between the government and Labour backbenchers:

> The executive was forced to realise it could not rely on coercion or self-discipline alone to achieve cohesion. Labour backbenchers realised both that the sky would not fall in if they voted against the Government and that they could achieve policy change if they pressed for it. (Cowley, 2002, pp 28-9)

The combination of vocal opposition on the Labour benches and a more consultative approach by the government, extending as far as offering concessions on policy, was characteristic of the navigation of welfare reform through the Commons in Labour's first term. When backbench Labour MPs expressed concerns about proposals to cut cash benefits to asylum seekers in February 1999, the government, or rather the Home Secretary, Jack Straw, actively pursued a strategy of consultation and negotiation in tearooms and meeting rooms across Whitehall (Cowley, 2002). This process led to a series of concessions that served to head off a widely predicted sizeable Labour rebellion. These included an increase in the proportion of cash payments to vouchers, and a statutory duty on the Home Secretary to provide accommodation and living needs for children of asylum seekers. Similarly, in early 2000, Labour backbenchers combined with opposition MPs, trades unions and pensioners, charities to protest against the government's announcement that the basic state pension would rise by the rate of inflation, amounting to an increase of just 75 pence a week. In April 2000, 40 Labour MPs backed an amendment to the Child Support, Pensions and Social Security Bill that sought to increase the basic retirement pension in line with earnings or the retail price index, whichever was greater. As with the cut to Lone Parent Benefit the government ultimately got its way, but the issue was widely considered to have been badly handled, and as a result, the Chancellor responded by announcing a package of concessions targeted at those most affected. In a pre-budget statement in November 2000, he announced an increase in the basic state pension by £5 for single pensioners and £8 for couples, a dramatic rise in the winter fuel allowance from £50 to £200, and an increase in the level of the Minimum Income Guarantee.

As the revolt over pensions suggests, the government, however, was not always successful in heading off backbench revolts on welfare reform. Indeed, the largest Labour rebellion of the 1997 Parliament occurred over proposed changes to Incapacity Benefit included in the Welfare Reform and Pensions Bill in 1999. While MPs supported most of the Bill, there was considerable concern over proposals to means test new claimants of Incapacity Benefit who had not paid National Insurance Contributions for the previous two years, and to reduce payments for new claimants with private pensions or health insurance. Unlike the changes to Lone Parent Benefit the government actively sought to consult with concerned backbenchers prior to the vote. MPs who wished to express concerns were seen individually by ministers, and as Cowley reveals, even those who did not request a meeting, "often found themselves having meetings with senior Ministers" (Cowley, 2002, p 47). However, such meetings were more about promoting cohesion than offering substantive concessions. The government remained committed to the principle of moving away from universalism towards a more targeted approach to welfare benefits. A substantial proportion of the parliamentary Labour Party were not convinced, and 67 Labour MPs voted in favour of an amendment tabled by Roger Berry that proposed the removal of means testing for Incapacity Benefit, and the restoration of benefit entitlements for those without National Insurance Contributions. Not only was this the largest Labour rebellion of the parliament, but as Cowley observes, the Bill also prompted the most sustained bout of dissent by government MPs in the entire parliament, as MPs voted on a series of amendments as the Bill shuttled between the Commons and the Lords. In total there were 10 revolts on the Welfare Reform and Pensions Bill, each revolt involved an average of 39 Labour MPs, and a total of 74 Labour MPs rebelled over the Bill.

While the bulk of dissent in the House of Commons during Labour's second term centred on the war in Iraq and related anti-terrorist legislation, Labour MPs continued to rebel in substantial numbers over welfare issues. The main focus for backbench disquiet was health and education policy. In 2001 a number of Labour MPs voted against the government's proposals to expand the number of faith schools in England and Wales. Then in January 2002, a number of Labour MPs rebelled, seeking, unsuccessfully, to prevent the abolition of community health councils and their replacement with patient forums, but the following year the government faced much greater problems in relation to its healthcare agenda. In the spring of 2003, the government's proposals to create foundation hospitals, included in the Health and Social Care Bill, prompted the largest ever Labour rebellion on a health issue, when 65 Labour MPs supported an amendment designed to prevent a second reading of the Bill. Subsequent amendments calling for the removal of the clauses concerned with foundation hospitals from the Bill attracted rebellions of 62, at one point cutting the government's majority to 17, the lowest parliamentary majority since 1997. As with other contentious legislation, the government made a series of concessions that helped to massage the Bill through parliament, including capping the income the new hospitals could generate from private patients; binding the new hospitals to NHS pay arrangements to prevent poaching of staff; the creation of a regulator to ensure that the hospitals did not operate to the detriment of the NHS; and a pledge to review the first wave of trusts after 12 months (Cowley, 2005).

The opposition of Labour MPs to foundation hospitals centred on concerns about the introduction of competition, and the fear that this amounted to the return of the internal market in the NHS, and creeping privatisation of health provision. MPs also objected to the manner in which the policy was developed. Proposals for foundation hospitals had not been included in the 2001 manifesto, and as such had not emerged from the party's own policy forum. As a result they were seen by some as the ill-considered product of Downing Street advisors who were happy to sideline opinion in the parliamentary Labour Party. These concerns about the government's commitment to market reforms and the sidelining of the parliamentary Labour Party in policy formulation re-emerged when the government sought to reform the funding of higher education in 2003-04. Given that the Labour manifesto for the 2001 General Election had categorically ruled out the introduction of variable funding – so-called 'top-up fees' – for higher education, it is perhaps not surprising that many Labour MPs were exercised by proposals to allow universities to charge up to £3,000 a year, less than two years into the parliament. Arguments that the new fees would replace the existing fee structure and were not therefore top-up fees did little to persuade Labour MPs who were already angry about the lack of consultation over foundation hospitals. According to Cowley, the policy was "seen by most backbenchers as yet another example of Downing Street advisors imposing market-driven policy on the parliamentary party, without any prior discussion or debate" (Cowley, 2005, p 178). Labour MPs who had criticised the government for creating a two-tier health service with foundation hospitals now criticised them for seeking to usher in a two-tier education system.

The Labour rebellion on higher education exceeded that prompted by foundation hospitals. Seventy-two Labour MPs voted against the whip on the Bill's second reading in January 2004, stripping the government's majority to just 5, the lowest majority and the largest rebellion on a domestic issue since 1997. However, as Cowley (2005) points out, the situation could have been much worse, as almost 200 Labour MPs had publicly expressed their opposition to top-up fees by signing EDMs calling for the policy to be dropped. Moreover, the total number of Labour MPs voting against the Higher Education Bill at its various stages was 82. If these MPs had all voted against the Bill at any one stage the government may well have been defeated. However, once again the government sought to undermine opposition with a series of concessions even before the publication of the Bill, including the capping of fees at £3,000 for six years, and additional changes, such as an undertaking to report on the impact on middle-income families, as the Bill made its rocky passage through parliament.

Following the 2005 General Election, and with it a smaller, although still substantial, majority in the House of Commons, the government continued to face difficulties with its social policy proposals. The controversial Green Paper on Welfare Reform, expected in the autumn of 2005, was delayed until January 2006 following the resignation of the Secretary of State for Work and Pensions, David Blunkett. In the kind of coincidence of events that often prompt the media label, 'Blair's worst day', Blunkett's resignation coincided with a vote on the Terrorism Bill that the government won by only one vote. The label was recycled the following week when the government suffered its first ever defeat on a whipped vote over proposals to allow the detention of terrorist suspects for up to 90 days. Blunkett's resignation was undoubtedly a blow for Blair's welfare reform agenda, in particular the tricky reform of Incapacity Benefit, and coupled with the government's defeat over terrorism legislation, served to shake the government's confidence in its ability to secure parliamentary support for forthcoming legislation on education, health and welfare, which were widely predicted to prove even more controversial among the parliamentary Labour Party.

Even greater opposition was to emerge within the parliamentary Labour Party in respect of the Education and Inspection Bill in 2006. One indication of the scale of opposition within the parliamentary Labour Party came when 91 MPs signed up to an 'alternative white paper' (one of the authors of which was the former Secretary of State for Education and Skills, Estelle Morris), which called for a number of changes from the government, including making the code of practice on school admissions statutory, ensuring that trust schools were not financially advantaged compared with other schools, and that local education authorities should continue to have a significant role in ensuring that schools work together and provide good access to education for all. In turn the concerns within the parliamentary Labour Party were clearly expressed when 52 Labour MPs, in the largest rebellion of the 2005 Parliament that far, voted against the Bill's second reading. For the first time the Blair government found itself reliant on the Conservatives (or at least the Conservatives not voting against the government) to get its legislation through, although the government was successful in defeating an attempted Conservative ambush on the timetable for the remainder of the Bill's passage through parliament. Reflecting the pattern of much previous social policy legislation since 1997, the government again made a series of concessions following the Bill's introduction in attempts to try to reduce opposition within the parliamentary Labour Party, including promising a ban on schools using interviews to select pupils, strengthening the admissions code and allowing local authorities to enter competitions to provide new schools. However, the size of the revolt, particularly given Labour's smaller majority in the Commons, made it likely that there would be further similar rebellions during the remainder of the Blair premiership.

It is clear that welfare legislation has been the source of considerable internal disagreements within the parliamentary Labour Party, and that education, healthcare and social security have been particular foci for these divisions. In addition, over the years there have been substantial revolts on other aspects of social policy and Labour MPs have continued to express concerns about the treatment of immigrants and asylum seekers. A pattern has tended to emerge of the government producing legislation that then faces opposition from groups of its own backbenchers. During the legislative process the government then concedes a number of points in order to mollify opponents within the parliamentary Labour Party and thus to successfully pass its bills. What frequently remains unclear is whether such concessions are forced on the government by backbench opinion, or whether they are part of a deliberate strategy of pushing proposals further in order to later make changes that then secure support of the party in parliament.

However, while voting, and perhaps, in particular, overt rebellion, may be one measure of disagreement over policies, MPs are able to express their opinions and seek to influence government using a variety of different, and frequently less obvious mechanisms, and some, including many Labour backbenchers, will argue that these approaches are at least as effective as opposing the government in the division lobbies. Indeed, given that in over 8% of divisions there is no dissent by Labour MPs, it is important to consider the extent and effectiveness of alternative methods of influencing government legislation and policy (see Chapter Seven).

Conclusions

It is clear that there remains considerable debate about the role and functions of parliament, including both the House of Commons and the House of Lords and their relations with the public (see also Chapters Six and Seven). Among the areas often seen as key are the ability, or otherwise, of parliament to scrutinise and influence legislation and to scrutinise the work of the executive and to hold it to account. There is undoubtedly a fairly widespread view, as there has been for much of the past century, and perhaps particularly from the 1970s, that parliament's ability to fulfil these functions has been in decline, and that for some commentators at least, this has increased during the Blair governments. Among the 'evidence' frequently cited for this has been Blair's poor voting record and his lack of attendance in parliament, as well as the perceived failure of the 'modernisation' of the House of Commons to strengthen the powers of the House in relation to those of the executive. Some critics similarly suggest that the removal of the majority of the hereditary peers from the House of Lords was intended to reduce further potential opposition to the government's legislation.

However, in reality it is possible to argue that in many respects the criticisms of developments since 1997 may be overstated. In particular, as Cowley (2002, 2005) has pointed out, the level of rebellions by backbench Labour MPs was significant, and increased through the first two Labour terms. Furthermore, as will be shown in Chapter Six, the reforms to the House of Lords arguably resulted in a more assertive upper chamber, more willing to challenge and even defeat the government, rather than the disempowered and enfeebled chamber that some had predicted. Add to this the argument that much of the influence of parliament is unseen and indeed difficult to see (for example, Bochel, 1992, and Norton, 2005) and it is possible to argue that the situation during the Blair governments may not be very different, at least from their immediate predecessors.

What is certainly true is that the Labour governments since 1997 have faced considerable opposition among Labour MPs, including on its social policy agenda. Indeed, the extent of rebellion on welfare legislation suggests that many Labour MPs, at least, are not only interested in welfare, but have also been sufficiently exercised to set aside party loyalty to express their disquiet at the government's welfare reform agenda. Perhaps more significantly still, in an effort to ensure party cohesion, the government has on several occasions responded to rebellion or the threat of rebellion by offering a number of important concessions, suggesting that the attitudes of individual, or rather groups of individual MPs do matter and can have a profound influence on policy. However, while it is true that Labour, as the governing party, has been most affected by internal divisions over policy and revolts by their MPs, it is important to note that it is not the only party that has differences, and that, as will be discussed in Chapter Four, there is the potential for significant disagreement not only between but within other parties.

FOUR

Towards a new consensus? MPs' attitudes to welfare

The rocky passage of much of Labour's welfare legislation through parliament raises important questions about the extent of parliamentary support for the government's reform agenda, particularly related to welfare. It is far from clear that Labour's welfare reforms enjoy widespread parliamentary support, even on the government's own benches. Some indication of the extent of discontent among Labour MPs may be gauged by the scale and frequency of rebellions by Labour MPs on welfare issues, most notably over cuts to Lone Parent Benefit, pensions reform, the creation of foundation hospitals and successive attempts to reform Incapacity Benefit. However, while it is clear that a significant proportion of Labour MPs have been sufficiently exercised by various aspects of welfare policy to set aside party loyalty and vote against the government, what is not clear is the extent to which such backbench rebellions are indicative of a wider disquiet on Labour benches.

Conversely, while analysis of backbench rebellions highlights opposition to Labour policies, it is less helpful in explaining the extent of parliamentary support for the government's reform agenda. Despite substantial rebellions on certain aspects of welfare legislation, party cohesion remains a defining feature of parliamentary life. Cowley suggests that the broad agreement of many Labour MPs with the reform agenda of the leadership may be explained, at least in part, by a shift in political attitudes in The Labour Party (Cowley, 2002). However, the evidence for such a shift in Labour MPs' attitudes is not clear, and certainly can not be deduced from voting behaviour alone, which may be affected by other factors such as the threats and rewards offered by the Whip's Office. In order to determine whether there has been a genuine shift in the political attitudes of Labour MPs one must make a more forensic analysis of MPs' attitudes and the extent to which they correspond with party policy, and moreover, whether these views are noticeably different from those expressed by Labour MPs in the past.

Looking beyond the voting behaviour of MPs may be even more important in establishing the opinions and attitudes of MPs in opposition parties. Given that most legislation presented to parliament is government legislation, one would generally expect the voting of opposition MPs to reflect opposition to that legislation. However, voting against the government tells us little about opinion within the other parties (although voting with the government may tell us a great deal). Evidence from other sources suggests considerable intra-party debate within the opposition parties, particularly on issues related to welfare. Leadership contests in both the Conservative and Liberal Democrat Parties have served to highlight ongoing debates within both parties about the role of the state in welfare. Conservative policies since 1997, particularly under Iain Duncan Smith and David Cameron, have reflected a new interest in social policy, and a desire to distance the party from Thatcherite policies and approaches to welfare. Cameron in particular has stressed a new approach to welfare, with a firm commitment to support the NHS, and the adoption of targets for combating poverty. However, as with The Labour Party, it is not clear whether the attitudes and policies adopted by the leadership are widely held within the parliamentary party. Similarly, it is not clear whether debate within the Liberal Democrat Party, in particular about the role of the state in the management of public services, as exemplified in *The orange book*, is indicative of a broader shift to the Right in opinion within the parliamentary party, and whether this shift is a response to New Labour or Conservative policies, or a genuine attempt to reform liberalism.

Finally, it is also unclear whether these intra-party debates are part of what some have identified as a movement towards a new political consensus in approaches to welfare. As discussed in Chapter Two, the debate about a new consensus, which was largely prompted by New Labour's acceptance of the market, and the adoption of Conservative spending plans in 1997, has received new impetus since the election of a Conservative leader who has openly embraced consensus politics, and pledged to continue some Labour policies if elected, not least targets for the abolition of child poverty. However, while some have identified a broad degree of policy convergence (Williams, 2000; Taylor-Gooby, 2001), it is not clear that this reflects a convergence in thinking among MPs from both sides of the House. Lowe, for example, has highlighted sustained debates within the Conservative and Labour Parties over the extent to which the welfare state should be dismantled, or the role of the market enhanced in a range of welfare policy areas. Such tensions, Lowe suggests, are not necessarily sufficient to invalidate the concept of consensus, but are nevertheless significant and suggest that the movement towards consensus is as much a source of debate within the main parties as between them (Lowe, 2005). The extent to which the attitudes of MPs have shifted since the 1980s will reveal the depth of any new consensus on approaches to welfare and will be crucial to the direction and success of welfare policies of future governments of either political hue.

Data from a survey of MPs' attitudes to welfare undertaken between October 2004 and January 2006 was used to determine the degree of parliamentary consensus on the role of the state in welfare, and the level and nature of intra-party debate on welfare policies. MPs were asked a series of questions designed to reveal their general attitudes towards the role of the state in welfare, what might loosely be called their 'philosophy of welfare', and more detailed questions on specific aspects of welfare policy since 1997. Their replies were compared with data from Taylor-Gooby and Bochel's survey of 1986-87 (1988) in an effort to determine whether any shift in parliamentary political opinion had occurred over the past two decades, and whether that shift represented a movement towards a new consensus on welfare.

From 'safety net' to 'springboard': MPs' attitudes towards the role of the state

Taylor-Gooby and Bochel's survey of MPs' attitudes to welfare undertaken in 1986-87 (1988) supported the widely held view that there was a fundamental breakdown in the political consensus on approaches to welfare in the 1980s. On the broad philosophical question regarding the role of the state in welfare, they found an absence of consensus, and identified a strong division on party lines (see Table 4.1). Conservatives tended to favour a minimalist state that would concentrate its activities on meeting basic needs targeted at a small proportion of the population frequently described as the 'deserving' poor. The most popular description of the role of the state, used unprompted by three quarters of Conservative MPs interviewed by Taylor-Gooby and Bochel, was that of a 'safety net'. In contrast, Labour MPs were much more inclined to see the ideal role of the state as providing universal services of a high standard, and a substantial minority took the argument beyond universal provision and argued that the state should pursue policies designed to provide equality through redistribution. The SDP/Liberal group comprised only a small part of Taylor-Gooby and Bochel's sample; they tended to favour a high national minimum level of provision, but this was tempered by a concern for the preservation of community and was not necessarily seen as being universal in nature (Bochel, 1992).

Table 4.1: MPs' views on the role of the state in welfare (1986-87, % of responses by party)

	Lab	Con	Lib/SDP
Safety net/to meet genuine need only	0	70	0
To support the extension of private welfare	0	14	0
To ensure a high national minimum in an agreed range of services	56	9	75
To meet need	12	0	0
To redistribute/advance equality	29	0	0
It depends what the country can afford	3	2	25
Number	43	34	4

Note: For tables throughout Chapter Four, the following abbreviations are used: Lab: Labour, Con: Conservative, Lib Dem: Liberal Democrat, Ind: Independent, SNP: Scottish National Party, Plaid: Plaid Cymru.

Source: Bochel (1992)

When asked the same question in the current survey, although MPs continue to be divided broadly on party lines, there has been a marked movement towards the Centre on the part of the three main parties (see Table 4.2). In broad terms, Conservative MPs continue to support a more minimalist perception of the role of the state, with considerable support for private provision. Similarly, Labour and Liberal Democrat MPs continue to favour a more collectivist approach to welfare. However, almost half of Labour MPs (49%) now suggested a new role for the state in welfare; these MPs supported the idea of a broad state safety net, but augmented this with the idea that once individuals

Table 4.2: MPs' views on the role of the state in welfare (2004-06, % of responses by party)

	Labour	Conservative	Lib Dem	SNP/Plaid/Ind	Total
Safety net only for those in the most need	0	36	0	0	11
To support the extension of private provision	0	18	0	0	5
Beyond a safety net to work with individuals and the private sector to improve lives in a range of sectors	0	45	0	20	14
Beyond a safety net to provide a mechanism to enable others to lift themselves out of poverty/into work	49	0	43	0	30
Provide a national floor above the minimum level, for a range of services	31	0	50	60	28
Redistribution of wealth – advance equality	20	0	7	20	12
Number	35	22	14	5	76

were caught in the safety net it was the state's responsibility to propel them quickly back into work. They described the role of the state as 'more proactive', as 'an enabler', a 'spring-board' or 'a mechanism to lift people out of poverty'. While this view was based partly on a belief that for a host of reasons the well-being of individuals is improved through employment, it was also a question of cost. As one Labour MP observed, "the notion of the passive recipient of benefit is no longer valid, apart from anything else large numbers of people on benefit place too much pressure on the economy".

This idea of the welfare state as an enabling mechanism, which featured so prominently in the current survey, did not feature at all in MPs' responses to Taylor-Gooby and Bochel's survey. Support for this more active and selective approach to welfare has, not surprisingly, grown at the expense of support for a high level of universal provision, although support among Labour MPs for redistribution remains relatively high. A similar shift in attitudes may be discerned among Liberal Democrat MPs. Although Taylor-Gooby and Bochel did not speak to many Liberal/SDP MPs in 1986-87, their results indicated strong support for a high national minimum level of welfare provision. In the present survey Liberal Democrat support for universal provision remains high, but a significant proportion of Liberal Democrat MPs have now embraced the idea of the welfare state as an enabling mechanism. Significantly, Liberal Democrat MPs often used the same kind of language as Labour MPs to describe the role of the state in welfare, referring to the state's responsibility to provide a safety net (a metaphor used by MPs from all parties), but also to provide 'a ladder', 'a helping hand' or an 'enabling mechanism'.

It is not only those on the Left who have changed their views; Conservative MPs have also moved towards the Centre. A significantly smaller proportion of Conservative MPs (36%) now believe the government should provide only a safety net for those in the most need, compared with the position in the 1980s (70%). Thus, while there is still strong support for a minimalist approach to state provision, a significant minority of Conservative MPs now support a more active role for the state in improving people's lives. This group of MPs, which includes former ministers from both the Thatcher and Major governments and Conservative frontbenchers under Howard and Cameron, spoke about the role of government in building communities and improving life chances, in some respects coming close to Labour MPs' views of the state's enabling role. Several went out of their way to dissociate themselves from Thatcherite philosophies, explicitly declaring that "there *is* such a thing as society" and that "people are social animals, not atomised individuals". A number stressed the importance of combating poverty, particularly among children and pensioners, and one Conservative MP interviewed some time before David Cameron's election as party leader spoke forcefully about the importance of targets for combating child poverty. Conservative MPs were nevertheless keen to stress that the welfare state should not merely hand out money but should encourage people to help themselves. While Conservative MPs did not talk about an enabling role for the state, this emphasis on a positive but more selective approach to welfare, what more than one Conservative MP termed 'tough love', in which welfare provision is necessary but "handing out pounds is not enough", has brought the views of Conservative and Labour MPs increasingly into alignment.

This apparent convergence among MPs on the role of the state in welfare appears even more pronounced in the analysis of their attitudes towards the nature and extent of state involvement, and in particular the role of the state and the private sector in the delivery of services. In Taylor-Gooby and Bochel's survey there was a marked division between Conservative MPs, who believed that the state should support the extension of the private sector in welfare provision, and Labour MPs who overwhelmingly supported a high level of state provision. Indeed, Bochel reported that no Labour MPs referred to supporting the private sector as part of the state's role (Bochel, 1992). The current survey indicates a highly significant shift in Labour MPs' attitudes towards the role of the private sector in welfare provision. When discussing who should be responsible for provision (see Table 4.3), an equal proportion of Labour MPs (45%) believed that services should

Table 4.3: Who should be responsible for providing welfare services? (% of responses by party)

	Labour	Conservative	Lib Dem	SNP/Plaid/Ind	Total
Mainly the state	45	0	46	80	23
A range of providers including state, private and charitable sectors	10	33	38	0	15
The public and private sector in partnership	45	33	15	20	23
Mainly the private sector	0	33	0	0	7
Number	29	21	13	5	68

be provided mainly by the state, or by the state in partnership with the private sector. While Labour MPs continue to believe that the state should be the principal financer of welfare services, there is much less concern about who delivers those services. As one Labour MP stated, "the state will take less of a role in providing but maintain its role as the funder and a guarantor of quality". This represents a marked shift in Labour MPs' attitudes since the 1980s, and suggests a potentially substantial measure of support for the Labour leadership in seeking to expand the role of the private sector in welfare provision.

The shift in Labour MPs' attitudes towards the private sector contributes to a considerable degree of overlap between all the main parties in attitudes towards the provision of services. While there was no cross-party support for welfare services being mainly provided by the state, a view that no Conservatives supported, or for the view that provision should be mainly the responsibility of the private sector, a view only supported by Conservative MPs, the idea that there should be a range of providers, including the state, private and charitable sectors, received substantial support from all the main parties. However, interestingly, a larger proportion of Labour than Conservative MPs referred to the public and private sector working in partnership, and only three Labour MPs referred to a broader range of providers including the state, private and charitable sector, less than any of the other main parties. This commitment to diversity in the range of provision, with the emphasis on 'what matters is what works', rather than who provides services and benefits, has been central to Labour policy on welfare since 1997, and arguably lies at the heart of any new consensus on welfare.

Consensus ... what consensus? MPs' views

MPs themselves have a highly ambivalent attitude towards the question of an emerging consensus on welfare (see Table 4.4). Only 14% of MPs were unequivocal in affirming the emergence of a political consensus, while a further 41% believed there was some degree of consensus. However, a large proportion (45%) believed there to be no consensus at all. A closer examination of MPs' responses reveals an even greater degree of ambivalence. While the majority (55%) believed there to be at least some degree of consensus, their responses were generally more varied and ambiguous than those who rejected the idea of consensus. MPs who disputed the emergence of a consensus were particularly forthright, reverting to entrenched party positions and often expressing indignation at the suggestion. This was particularly

Table 4.4: Do you believe there is a political consensus around general approaches to welfare? (% of responses by party)

	Labour	Conservative	Lib Dem	SNP/Plaid/Ind	Total
Yes	13	11	0	40	14
Some consensus on objectives/language but not on methods	35	56	60	20	41
No	52	33	40	40	45
Number	31	18	10	5	64

the case with Labour and Conservative MPs. Liberal Democrat MPs as a whole were more sceptical about the idea of consensus, with none positively asserting the existence of consensus, and a common response among Liberal Democrats was, "if there is a consensus we are not part of it".

There was also a certain amount of scepticism as to whether the appearance of agreement on some aspects of welfare marked a genuine movement towards consensus. Several MPs pointed to similarities in the language used about welfare, but doubted whether this represented a genuine shift in attitudes. There was a certain degree of scepticism about Labour's commitment to welfare reform. Several Conservative MPs referred to the government's reluctance to allow Frank Field to 'think the unthinkable' on welfare reform. The use of the language of reform was, according to one Conservative MP, a smokescreen behind which Gordon Brown was expanding the 'welfare basket', or as one Liberal Democrat put it, "madly redistributing". Indeed, several MPs from all parties expressed the belief that there would be a return to more universal provision, and consequently less consensus, should Gordon Brown become Prime Minister. Similarly, Labour MPs expressed doubts that Conservative commitments to combat poverty and unemployment would be sustained in office, and pointed to Conservative plans to dismantle the New Deal as evidence of this.

It was also striking that few MPs readily viewed consensus as something to aspire to. Only five MPs, three Labour and two Conservatives, expressed the belief that the parties should be actively seeking a new consensus on welfare, and only one of these, a Conservative, expressed confidence that this could be achieved, stating rather optimistically, "we're all completely at one with Frank Field now", a view certainly not shared on the Labour benches. Many Labour

MPs were decidedly critical of the movement towards consensus, reluctantly conceding that Labour's use of the private sector in welfare provision marked the emergence of a new consensus but not one with which they were happy, or indeed wished to be part of. One Labour MP, who left parliament at the 2005 General Election, was harshly critical of competition for the 'soggy centre', which he claimed had stultified debate and undermined the welfare state. Indeed, few MPs from any party appeared to conceive of consensus as being arrived at by debate and compromise leading to movement on the part of all the parties towards some centre ground. Where MPs did recognise some consensus it was widely felt that this had been achieved by one party moving towards the position of the other. This was particularly evident among those Labour MPs who opposed the private sector, and selective provision, and also among Conservative MPs who were more inclined to believe that the balance of opinion was moving in their direction.

Nevertheless, some MPs did believe there had been a positive movement on the part of the main parties towards a new consensus on welfare and their responses suggest that this movement had been broad based and not confined to the party leadership. MPs referred to "realignment", "movement towards an imaginary middle from both sides", "a coming together of Tory and New Labour thinking", and "a realisation that we need to do things differently".

However, where MPs did identify a consensus it was largely related to objectives, and there remained fundamental differences of opinion over how to achieve these objectives. There was, for example, notable consensus on the need to combat poverty particularly among children and pensioners, but disagreements over the means of achieving this, particularly over pensions means testing and the operation of tax credits. In addition, reflecting similarities of position as outlined earlier, MPs identified a consensus on the importance of propelling people into work, based on the idea, as one Labour MP put it, "that work is normal, being on benefit is not". However, there remained areas of disagreement over the extent to which Labour's policies would achieve this. Many Conservative MPs, and a significant number of Liberal Democrat MPs, still felt the benefits system was a serious disincentive to work. Even where there was consensus over means, such as the increased use of mixed provision, there remained fundamental differences of opinion over how this provision should be managed. Thus, for example, while Conservative MPs supported the government's attempts to involve the charitable sector in welfare provision, they were critical of the fact that from their perspective, charities were not being allowed to drive need but were instead being co-opted to the government's agenda.

Paying for welfare: MPs' attitudes towards 'tax and spend'

The cost of the state provision of welfare has constituted a major theme in debates about the role of the state from the 1980s to the present day. There has, however, been a marked shift in emphasis in the debate regarding the relative merits of public spending and tax cuts. At the time of Bochel and Taylor-Gooby's survey the Conservative government openly pursued policies designed to provide tax cuts by reining in public spending, not least spending on welfare. As Bochel observed, "both the philosophical and economic theory bases of the Thatcher governments' policies called for a lower level of state expenditure than that required for a 'welfare state'" (Bochel, 1992, p 59). At the same time the Labour opposition generally advocated policies that would require increases in public expenditure – most notably increased spending on the NHS.

Interestingly, however, Taylor-Gooby and Bochel found the attitudes of individual MPs were frequently somewhat more cautious and reflexive than their respective party's positions. Despite their party's insistence on the need to reduce public expenditure, Conservative MPs evinced a lower rate of immediate concern about the cost of welfare than MPs from other parties. This position, Bochel suggested, could reflect a general feeling on the part of Conservative MPs that the government was already tackling the problem. However, it was also noted that in interviews Conservative MPs showed a clear awareness that their party's policies of spending restraint were unpopular. As one frontbencher observed, the Conservatives were "unable to present themselves as doing anything but cut". Opposition Labour MPs displayed a similar awareness that their party's policies left them open to attack, although in this case on the grounds of profligacy. A considerable minority of Labour MPs interviewed by Taylor-Gooby and Bochel emphasised the problems of costing the party's welfare policies, with several repeating the phrase often used by Conservative spokespeople that "you can't solve a problem by throwing money at it" (Bochel, 1992, p 59).

The views expressed by these small groups of MPs have become more pronounced in the intervening years, to the point at which they have today effectively become party positions. The view expressed by some Labour MPs in the 1980s, that Labour's spending plans might prove electorally damaging, has now become the established political wisdom to the extent that no party now advocates substantial increases in public spending funded by increases in direct taxation. Labour's plans for tax-funded increases in public spending are widely believed to have cost the party the 1992 General Election, and resulted in the leadership's determination that Labour should never again be presented as the party of high personal taxation (Taylor-Gooby, 2001). Such was The Labour Party's desire to shake off its image as the party of tax and spend that they promised to adopt Conservative spending plans for two years after the 1997 General Election, and in office have developed a complex system of indirect taxation. In recent years the Liberal Democrats have been the only party to advocate an increase in direct taxation in order to fund improvements in public services, with proposals in 1997 and 2001 for a hypothecated rise in Income Tax to fund education spending, and a 50 pence higher rate of Income Tax. However, by the time of the 2005 General Election, the Liberal Democrats had also dropped any commitment to an increase in general taxation, promising tax increases only for those whose annual earnings exceeded £100,000, and under Menzies Campbell have shifted further to the right with a broad commitment to cut direct taxation.

At the same time, however, it is also apparent that there is little political appetite for cuts in public services. Recent Conservative leaderships have refused to advocate cuts in services as a means of achieving tax cuts, claiming that sufficient savings could be achieved by efficiency savings through streamlining government departments and operational practices. Conservative sensitivity to accusations of being the party of cuts in services were clearly illustrated in the run-up to the 2005 General Election when the MP Howard Flight was deselected for suggesting that Conservative plans for reducing public spending went beyond efficiency savings. In the 2005 Conservative leadership contest, David Cameron consistently asserted that tax cuts had to be balanced against the need to fund decent public services, arguing that "the Conservative Party will never convince people that we can be trusted to run the economy if all we talk about is cutting taxes and cutting spending" (*The Daily Telegraph*, 28 October 2005).

The widespread acceptance of spending restraint driven by the belief that the public will not tolerate increases in taxation is a key feature of what some have identified as a new consensus on welfare, and is strongly represented in MPs' responses to the current survey (see Table 4.5). Only a third of MPs questioned favoured an increase in taxation to pay for increased services, while two thirds stated clearly that they would not be in favour of such an increase. The bulk of those opposed

Table 4.5: Would you be in favour of an increase in general taxation to pay for increased welfare provision? (% of valid responses by party)

	Labour	Conservative	Lib Dem	SNP/Plaid/Ind	Total
Yes	46	0	50	75	33
No	54	100	50	25	66
Number	24	20	12	4	60

to tax-funded increases in provision were Conservative MPs, none of whom supported this. Labour and Liberal Democrat MPs were evenly divided on the issue, with 54% and 50% respectively opposed to tax rises. Labour MPs were particularly reticent about the need for tax rises, often expressing strong support for state-funded provision, but baulking at any suggestion of improving provision by increasing tax revenue. Perhaps predictably, in explaining their opposition to tax-funded increases in provision, Labour MPs frequently pointed to the scars of 18 years of opposition, and in particular the memory of the 1992 General Election. Several Labour and Liberal Democrat MPs also pointed to the impact of Gordon Brown's 2002 Budget in which National Insurance Contributions were increased, the redistributive effects of which were widely publicised shortly before the 2005 General Election (Brewer et al, 2005; 'Tax assault on middle class cuts incomes as poll looms,' *The Times*, 31 March 2005). While generally applauded by Labour and Liberal Democrat MPs, it was felt by many that any further demands on the pay packets of the public would be unpopular, and electorally damaging. This case was made in particular by Liberal Democrat MPs in explaining their support for the party's decision to drop its previous commitment to increasing Income Tax.

Nevertheless, both Labour and the Liberal Democrats are deeply divided over the issue of tax and spend, and while many were confirmed in the belief that a commitment to raising taxes was tantamount to electoral suicide, a similar number were equally committed to improving services by increasing general taxation, and National Insurance. Several Labour MPs were highly critical of the leadership for not being bold about increasing tax revenue, arguing for more progressive taxation or more bluntly that the government should "squeeze the rich!". Among this group of Labour MPs Gordon Brown's increase in National Insurance was seen less as a one-off and more of an indicator of things to come. As one Labour MP asserted, "Gordon is more in favour of raising taxes than Tony", a view expressed in hope rather than expectation by several Labour MPs. Despite being the only party in recent years to have advocated increasing taxes to pay for public services, Liberal Democrat MPs were only slightly more supportive of this than Labour MPs. The views of Labour MPs in favour of increasing taxes corresponded closely with those expressed by half of the Liberal Democrat MPs, who also continued to advocate tax policies at some variance with party policy. Liberal Democrat MPs, however, were also highly critical of the other parties, and Labour in particular, for refusing to engage in an honest debate about taxation, observing that while there was considerable discussion about the cost of public services, the debate centred on questions of expanding private provision, rather than generating revenue through taxation. However, MPs in favour of tax-funded improvements in services from all parties conceded that the public would only accept tax rises if the money was directed at the right services, the health service and possibly education, but certainly not social security benefits.

While united in their opposition to tax rises, interviews with Conservative MPs revealed that the party is divided over the similarly sensitive question of cutting taxes and public spending. Conservative MPs, not surprisingly, frequently talked about expanding the private sector and individuals taking greater responsibility for themselves and their families. However, specific calls for cuts in taxes and services were rare. Nevertheless some Conservative MPs, including frontbenchers, had forthright opinions on the need to rein in spending. One Conservative minister interviewed shortly before the 2005 General Election not only argued for cuts in public services, but also suggested that this was what the Conservative leadership was planning to do, should they win the election. Later a very prominent Conservative backbencher and former minister spoke about open warfare within the party over Cameron's commitment not to cut taxes, asking "how can a Conservative Party not advocate tax cuts?". Several referred to the need to rein in spending on benefits, and two Conservative MPs, a shadow minister and a newly elected MP, advocated the abolition of the NHS, something which was not advocated by any of the MPs interviewed by Taylor-Gooby and Bochel in the 1980s.

Increasing polarisation? MPs' attitudes to welfare by cohort

Further evidence for shift in MPs' attitudes to welfare may be found by making cohort or generational comparisons of MPs attitudes. Taylor-Gooby and Bochel's survey offered some preliminary analysis of cohort differences in MPs' attitudes in the 1980s by comparing the attitudes of MPs elected before or at the time of Thatcher's first election victory in 1979, and those elected in or after 1983 when she had consolidated her position. This provided some evidence of increasing polarisation between Conservative and Labour MPs, with, for example, the later Conservative cohort being more in favour of expanding private provision of health, and the corresponding cohort of Labour MPs being more in favour of cutting back the private sector, than the cohorts elected earlier (Bochel, 1992). In the current survey the sample was divided into cohorts comprising those MPs elected before Labour's general election victory in 1997, and those elected in 1997 or after. Such cohort analysis can only provide tentative or preliminary conclusions as each division of the original sample of interviews involves a reduction in the numbers involved. Nevertheless, the balance of the sample in the current survey is closely representative of the situation in parliament as a whole, with 54% of MPs interviewed having been elected to parliament at the time or since Labour's election victory of 1997. The proportion for the House of Commons as a whole is 61%.

In the current survey, cohort analysis provides some further evidence of a movement towards a centre ground in MPs' attitudes to the role of the state (see Table 4.6). This was particularly so in the case of Labour and Liberal Democrat MPs, in which the later cohorts were more likely to offer a selective conception of welfare provision, and refer to the role of the state as an enabling mechanism. The shift was most marked among Liberal Democrat MPs, among whom the more selective approach was not mentioned by any of the cohort elected prior to 1997, while none of the later cohort referred to a role for the state in redistributing wealth.

However, while there is some evidence of convergence in MPs' attitudes across parties, there is also evidence of increasing intra-party differences, particularly within the two main parties. Within The Labour Party the increase in support among the later cohort for a more enabling role for the state occurs at the expense of support for a more universal concept of provision but does not result in a drop in the proportion of Labour MPs who believe the state should seek to redistribute wealth, a view which was supported by 20% of Labour MPs in both cohorts. The evidence for growing intra-party division was even more evident in the Conservative Party. While there was no difference in the proportion of Conservative MPs who believed the state should work with a range of welfare providers, the proportion of Conservative MPs who favoured a minimal safety net was much larger in the later cohort, suggesting more fundamental divisions within the Conservative

Table 4.6: Commitment to welfare provision, by cohort (% of valid responses by party)

	MPs first elected prior to 1997 General Election					MPs first elected at the 1997 General Election or later				
	Labour	Conservative	Lib Dem	SNP/Plaid/Ind	Total	Labour	Conservative	Lib Dem	SNP/Plaid/Ind	Total
Safety net only for those in the most need	0	27	0	0	9	0	45	0	0	12
To support the extension of private provision	0	27	0	0	9	0	9	0	0	2
Beyond a safety net to work with individuals and the private sector to improve lives in a range of sectors	0	45	0	0	14	0	45	0	33	15
Beyond a safety net to provide a mechanism to enable others to lift themselves out of poverty/into work	45	0	0	0	26	53	0	50	0	34
Provide a national floor above the minimum level, for a range of services	35	0	50	50	26	27	0	50	66	29
Redistribution of wealth – advance equality	20	0	50	50	17	20	0	0	0	7
Number	20	11	2	2	35	15	11	12	3	41

Party and possibly a shift to the Right in Conservative MPs' attitudes to welfare, which may be indicative of the potential for increasing polarisation between the parties in the future.

Analysis of MPs elected before and after 1997 also provides interesting information about the attitudes of Labour MPs towards the issue of 'tax and spend'. While there was no apparent difference in the attitudes of Conservative and Liberal Democrat MPs to the question of raising taxes to fund increased provision, all Conservatives being opposed, and Liberal Democrats being equally divided in both cohorts, there was a marked difference in the responses of the Labour MPs. Of those Labour MPs who favoured raising taxes, 69% were elected to parliament prior to Labour's 1997 election victory. Only three Labour MPs elected since 1997, including one elected in 2005, advocated increasing taxes to pay for improved services. Conversely, almost three quarters of those who did not think tax rises were necessary were elected in 1997 or later.

The potential for increasing polarisation both within and possibly between the parties is reinforced when one considers the views of MPs most recently elected to parliament. The survey included 15 MPs from the 2005 intake, 7 Labour, 5 Conservative, and 3 Liberal Democrat, representing 18%, 9% and 15% respectively of each party's new intake. Once again the relatively small numbers involved militate against drawing broad conclusions about attitudes within the parties as a whole. Moreover, the newly elected MPs were interviewed very early in their first term, within a few months of their election to parliament. It is therefore possible, indeed likely, that their attitudes will change as they become socialised into life as an MP, and more familiar with party policy. Nevertheless, the sample represents the attitudes of a significant proportion of the new intake, and is a useful indicator of the direction in which MPs attitudes are moving.

In response to the question about the role of the state in welfare, the views of new MPs reflected the responses from the parties as a whole, and provided further evidence of a growing consensus on approaches to welfare. Five of the seven newly elected Labour MPs described a role for the state as an enabling mechanism to lift people into work, a significantly larger proportion than those Labour MPs who adopted this position in the sample as a whole. There was also some support among new Labour MPs for the use of mixed provision in the delivery of welfare, with a belief that, as one observed, "people are now more willing to pay for what they value, for schools, hospitals, the environment". Moreover, a small but significant proportion of newly elected Conservative MPs, two out of five, described an expansive role for the state in minimising relative need and improving people's lives. While stressing that the state should not try to do everything, these MPs talked about "lifting people up" rather than maintaining them in poverty, and described welfare as "a state you pass through, not one you reside in". One of these MPs, who was a prominent supporter of David Cameron in the Conservative leadership contest, made a clear distinction between his views on the state's role in welfare, and what he identified as the Thatcherite views to be found elsewhere within the party. This distinction, he suggested, was between those who believed that poverty was an absolute and it was the role of the state to maintain a basic level of subsistence, and those, including himself who believed that "in a civilised society it was not about maintaining a subsistence level but ameliorating relative disadvantage and allowing people to live a dignified life". There was even praise from both of these Conservative MPs for Labour policies designed to encourage people into work, and target benefits at those in the most need, such as tax credits.

However, there was more support among new MPs from both the main parties than in the sample as a whole for positions that reflected the opposing poles represented by the minimal safety net and a redistributive role for the state. This was particularly evident among new Conservative MPs. Three out of five new Conservative MPs interviewed described the role of the state as no more than a minimal safety net, a proportion almost twice the size of that which expressed this view in the sample as a whole. Moreover, these MPs were particularly forthright in expressing their belief that the state should offer only minimal support for those in need, "to ensure that no-one ends up in abject poverty", or "to make sure that people are not starving". Each of them also identified growing dependence on the state as the main challenge facing the welfare state today, to the exclusion of all other challenges. They were particularly critical of the present welfare system for allowing people to be "too comfortable" on benefits, and for expanding the number of those entitled to claim, and they stressed the need to refocus state support onto those most deserving, notably pensioners and people with disabilities. The views expressed by these newly elected Conservative MPs may suggest a resurgence of the Right of the Conservative Party. Their views are certainly closer to those recorded by Taylor-Gooby and Bochel in the 1980s, when 70% of Conservatives interviewed supported a minimal safety net, and distinctions between the 'deserving' and 'undeserving' poor were particularly prominent. Indeed, several of these new Conservative MPs described being heavily influenced by Margaret Thatcher and the

Conservative governments of the 1980s, and one was particularly critical of the Conservative 2005 election campaign for not openly advocating the kind of substantive cuts in public services suggested by the deselected MP Howard Flight.

There was also a significant amount of dissent from party policy among newly elected Labour MPs. Two Labour MPs stated that it should be the role of the state to redistribute wealth. These MPs, who described themselves as "old Labour", called for a stronger role for the state in combating inequalities, although only one advocated increasing taxes for the well-off. There was also a broader concern among newly elected Labour MPs about the role of the private sector in welfare provision. This concern was expressed by four of the seven newly elected Labour MPs. There was particular concern about the use of the PFI in health and education, areas that it was felt should not be driven by profit, and were saddling future generations with excessive and possibly unforeseen costs. While only one new Labour MP expressed outright opposition to any involvement of the state with the private sector, there was a broad feeling that the government should put a brake on future partnerships. Two newly elected Labour MPs admitted that in 1997 they had accepted the use of the private sector to clear the backlog in the delivery of health services, but now had serious reservations about the long-term consequences of this policy, and felt very strongly that the government should not be looking to expand the role of the private sector in the delivery of public services.

Specific policy issues: social security, health and pensions

MPs were asked specific questions about three distinct policy areas: social security; the NHS; and pensions. Consistency between MPs' general philosophy and their attitudes on specific issues should not necessarily be expected, as attitudes may be moderated by less ideological factors such as awareness of public opinion, party policy and aspirations for office. In particular it was anticipated that questions about specific policy areas would elicit more partisan responses from MPs, with Labour MPs more inclined to express satisfaction with existing policy, while opposition MPs would naturally be expected to highlight deficiencies in current government policy. However, while partisanship was certainly evident in responses to broad questions about, for example, the effectiveness of the NHS, or whether Britain was facing a pensions crisis, there was nevertheless, evidence of consensus in MPs' priorities and proposals for changes to various aspects of welfare policy. Moreover, there was also an acceptance by some opposition MPs, albeit grudging, of the success of some policies introduced by the Labour governments since 1997, including the National Minimum Wage, increased provision in the NHS, and the use of tax credits to target those in most need.

Social security

The question of whether the benefits system is effective in getting money to those who need it, not surprisingly, revealed marked differences of opinion between Labour and opposition MPs. Only 21% of Labour MPs replied that the benefits system was not effective, compared to 73% of Conservatives and 50% of Liberal Democrats. There was, however, some consensus among those MPs who did think the benefits system was effective, with a significant proportion of MPs from all the main parties replying that the benefits system was "fairly", "reasonably" or "generally" effective, but qualifying their responses by stating that there were significant problems with some benefits, most notably the Pension Credit and Incapacity Benefit.

There was a broad cross-party consensus on the need to simplify the benefits system to improve access to benefits. This was the most frequently mentioned proposal for social security reform, identified by 45% of Labour MPs, 43% of Conservatives, 43% of Liberal Democrats, and all those MPs from the SNP and Plaid Cymru. The extent to which MPs identified problems with complexity of the benefits system is depressingly consistent with MPs' responses to Taylor-Gooby and Bochel's survey almost 20 years ago, when there was also a strong cross-party consensus on the need to simplify the rules and

Table 4.7: Do you think the benefits system is effective in getting money to people who need it? (% of valid responses by party)

	Labour	Conservative	Lib Dem	SNP/Plaid/Ind	Total
Yes	44	9	0	0	23
Reasonably effective but significant problems with some benefits	35	18	50	25	32
No	21	73	50	75	45
Number	34	22	14	4	74

improve access to benefits (Bochel, 1992). However, the proportion of MPs identifying this as a problem has almost doubled since the previous survey. Several opposition MPs argued that complexity was a product of Labour's welfare reforms, which had expanded the number of people eligible for state support, while seeking to target support at specific groups, particularly through the introduction of tax credits. As one Conservative MP argued, "there are too many benefits, too many rules". There had, he claimed, been a "massive simplification" of the benefits system in the 1980s, but this has "all been thrown away since 1997". MPs from all parties were critical of complexity and lack of flexibility in the benefits system. As a result it was argued there were "huge variations" in the take-up of benefits, with some MPs from all parties pointing to the success of universal benefits such as Child Benefit, and the problems of ensuring take-up of means-tested assistance, most notably Housing Benefit and Pension Credit.

The question of complexity in the benefits system was often mentioned in the context of benefits for old age pensioners, including Pension Credit. More support for pensioners enjoyed strong cross-party support, identified by 40% of MPs as a priority: 36% of Labour MPs, 43% of Conservatives, 29% of Liberal Democrats, and all MPs from SNP and Plaid Cymru. MPs from all parties expressed concern about the relatively low take-up of Pension Credit, although some Labour MPs highlighted improvements in take-up in recent years. The emphasis on the need for more support for pensioners reflected a more general emphasis in MPs' responses that suggested the need to improve benefits for certain groups. In part this reflected ideas about 'deserving' and 'undeserving' groups, which had been a strong theme in MPs' responses to Taylor-Gooby and Bochel's survey in the 1980s (Bochel, 1992). Consequently, there was cross-party consensus on the need to support older people and families with children, while there was little support for improved benefits for unemployed people and refugees and asylum seekers. However, rather than simply reflecting a moral judgement about those who deserved state support, in the current survey MPs' emphasis on targeting support at specific groups also reflected a desire to use a benefits system to propel people into work. Consequently, Labour and Liberal Democrat MPs who called for increased support for families with children were motivated not solely by the desire to ensure that children were not living in poverty, but also the belief that, for example, providing support for childcare would enable mothers with young children to go out to work and therefore reduce the burden this group placed on the welfare state.

This emphasis on the need to propel individuals into work for their own good, but also to reduce the financial burden of state provision, was particularly evident in MPs' attitudes towards people claiming Incapacity Benefit. At the time of Taylor-Gooby and Bochel's survey, individuals unable to work due to disability were viewed as a deserving group, and enjoyed strong support among MPs from all parties. While reform of Incapacity Benefit has been a sensitive subject for the Labour governments, as evidenced by the backbench revolts over proposed reforms in 1999 (see Chapter Three), MPs' responses to the current survey suggest a marked shift in MPs' attitudes towards those incapable of working due to ill health. Reform of Incapacity Benefit, or increased efforts to get people with disabilities into work attracted strong cross-party support from MPs, mentioned by almost half of Labour and Liberal Democrat MPs, and 29% of Conservative MPs. While one veteran of the 1999 backbench revolt warned the government "hands-off Incapacity Benefit", this was a rare dissenting voice among Labour MPs who largely supported reform of Incapacity Benefit. There was some cross-party support for existing efforts to get people with disabilities into work, most notably the pilot Pathways to Work programme of work-focused interviews and training. This was praised by MPs from all parties who called for the programme to be rolled out nationally.

However, there was some difference of opinion between MPs about the motivation for pursuing Incapacity Benefit claimants. There was a strong feeling among many MPs that many individuals claiming Incapacity Benefit were capable of some kind of work and should be made to do so. There was also a concern that supporting such a large number of individuals on benefit in perpetuity was simply not sustainable, and it was therefore fiscally prudent to get them into work. One Labour MP reported that it was unacceptable that 39% of his constituents were economically inactive, and there was clearly a feeling among some MPs that many 'economically inactive' individuals were capable of work and did not deserve state support. There were references to 'lead swingers' and support for using coercive measures, including benefit threats, to propel these individuals back into work. At the same time MPs from all parties referred to the importance of work for individual well-being, what one Conservative MP referred to as "an emerging consensus that work is good for you, inactivity is not". A small group of MPs, including most of the Liberal Democrat MPs, were critical of the government's approach to reforming Incapacity Benefit for emphasising 'benefit scroungers', and stressed the importance of creating opportunities for individuals who had not previously been considered to be part of the workforce.

Not unrelated to the question of Incapacity Benefit, there was also some consensus on the need to tackle benefit fraud. A large proportion of MPs from each party, 46% of Labour, 68% of Conservatives and 29% of Liberal Democrats, thought that benefit fraud was a significant problem. Although several qualified this by stating that it was only a problem with certain benefits, most notably Housing Benefit, MPs from all parties also made a distinction between large-scale organised fraud, which they felt was a significant problem, and individuals who may be claiming more than they were entitled to, possibly unintentionally. This they felt was more likely to be a problem created or invited by the complexity of the benefits and the tax credit systems. As one Labour member of the Work and Pensions Select Committee observed, "the boundaries are quite flexible and changeable, because the rules change, this means that something which was not allowed last week, is now allowed, and is no longer fraud". In addition, several Labour MPs observed that while benefit fraud was a problem, it was not as widespread as it had been in the past, for example during the 1980s, when large numbers of people were unemployed and the level of benefits was low. As one long-serving Labour MP observed, "there was a time in the 1980s when there was almost public approval of fraud", but he claimed, as the level of benefits, particularly Child Benefit and Income Support have risen, the amount of fraud has fallen, and the public perception has shifted, becoming less tolerant of those fraudulently claiming. Several Labour MPs also observed that while benefit fraud was wrong, it was not as significant as tax evasion, but one added, "You don't get *The Daily Mail* jumping up and down about that!".

Several of the interviews took place while the Identity Cards Bill was making its way through parliament, and although MPs were not asked specifically whether they felt ID cards would be effective in countering benefit fraud, a number offered unprompted opinions on this issue. However, of those MPs who felt that benefit fraud was a significant problem, only 29% suggested that ID cards offered a possible solution. Support was not surprisingly higher among Labour MPs, while only two Conservatives and one Liberal Democrat MP expressed confidence that ID cards would be effective in combating benefit fraud.

Despite notable areas of consensus, there remained some broad areas of disagreement between MPs on social security policy. Some of these disagreements reflected traditional Left-Right debates over entitlements to benefits and the resultant cost of welfare. A significant proportion of Labour and Liberal Democrat MPs (27% and 36%), but no

Conservatives, advocated increased spending on social security and the introduction of more universal benefits. In contrast 62% of Conservative MPs argued that there should be more restrictions on the number of people eligible to claim benefits, a proposal supported by only one Labour MP, and no Liberal Democrats. These responses are somewhat at variance with MPs' responses to the more general question of the role of the state in welfare, and indeed Labour and Conservative Party policy. In particular, those Labour MPs who called for the reintroduction of universal benefits were highly critical of the government's commitment to targeted benefits. However, it may be significant that with one exception the Labour MPs calling for a return to universalism were all elected prior to 1997 (although the same cannot be said for those Liberal Democrats taking this position).

Further evidence of Labour MPs' support for the expansion of state provision is indicated by a significant group of Labour MPs who called for more social housing. Unlike those MPs calling for more universal benefits, this group comprised MPs elected both before and after 1997, and included three elected in 2005. Their concern for more social housing, however, was less related to ideological concerns than their experience of the lack of good quality social housing in their constituencies. It may also be significant that all those MPs calling for more social housing represented constituencies with large urban centres.

However, one should not overestimate the support among Labour MPs for a return to universalism. The majority of Labour MPs advocated a more selective approach to welfare benefits and the opposition of some Labour MPs to means-tested benefits is not representative of the attitudes of the majority of Labour MPs interviewed. Indeed, Labour MPs appear to have undergone a remarkable conversion to the value of means testing in recent years. In Taylor-Gooby and Bochel's survey few issues excited as much partisan feeling as means testing. As Bochel observed:

> Use of the terms 'targeting' and 'means-testing' probably touched the ideological and emotional susceptibilities of Conservatives and certainly had this effect amongst Labour Members.... Means-testing has had long standing, largely negative, connotations for the Labour Party ('means-testing is vicious ... it can twist people's lives'); and targeting of resources on those in 'real' or 'genuine' need was a key concept in the Thatcher governments' approaches to social policy and particularly the distribution of welfare. Given these considerations it is not surprising that strong

differences were found between the two groups of MPs.
(Bochel, 1992, p 57)

Means testing continued to elicit strong differences of opinion from MPs in the current survey. However, Labour MPs are now largely supportive of means testing, while Conservative MPs expressed strong opposition. Many Labour MPs now talked about the value of targeting support at those in 'real' or 'genuine' need and argued for the need to change the public perception of means testing. Several observed that people, particularly pensioners, "need to be encouraged not to think of means-testing as demeaning". One long-standing Labour MP, who had served throughout the Thatcher years, argued:

> We shouldn't go on about means-testing as demeaning, it is this which puts people off applying for means-tested help, it is telling people that it's demeaning which puts them off, not the means-testing itself. Nobody thinks that income tax is demeaning but this is means-tested. Means-tested benefits are an entitlement, a right as a citizen and should be presented as such. These complaints about means-testing are mostly argued by those on the left. Right wing complaints are just mouthing off, jumping on the bandwagon.

However, in this survey few on the Left did complain about means testing, although there was strong opposition to means testing from Conservative MPs. Conservative MPs responded to means testing with the same kind of language used by their Labour counterparts in the 1980s, describing it as "degrading", "demeaning" and "unfair", while one went so far as to declare a "Conservative shift to universality". Conservatives objected in particular to the "perverse disincentives" created by means testing, which discouraged saving and encouraged fraud. However, it is also evident that Conservative opposition to means testing is at least in part related to its impact on their traditional support base. Conservative opposition to means testing was almost exclusively mentioned in relation to its application to pensioners through Pension Credit. This, it was argued, discriminated against pensioners who had saved all of their lives, created disincentives for people to save for the future, was degrading and highly unpopular with pensioners. However, Conservative MPs expressed little concern for the impact of means testing on other groups, and there was criticism of those "who know all the benefits to which they are entitled" and were able to effectively negotiate the necessary paperwork.

In addition to the question of benefits, MPs were also asked how they thought the government should provide support for people on low incomes. As this involved consideration of state support for people who are able to support themselves to some degree, this question, perhaps not surprisingly, elicited a more partisan response from MPs. There was very little cross-party consensus on this issue, although there were significant points on which Labour and Liberal Democrats, and Conservatives and Liberal Democrats agreed. In general Labour and Liberal Democrat MPs favoured more direct state support through the use of tax credits, the National Minimum Wage, and increased childcare provision. In contrast Conservative MPs generally favoured fiscal instruments for promoting wealth, such as stimulating job creation through supporting businesses, and using the tax system to support those in work by raising tax thresholds (something that also attracted strong support from Liberal Democrat MPs). In addition, several Liberal Democrat MPs expressed support for the introduction of a 'Citizens Income', something mentioned by only one MP from Labour and the Conservatives. There was, however, strong support from all parties for the Minimum Wage. This was mentioned by 53% of Labour MPs, 19% of Conservatives and 18% of Liberal Democrats. It was the second most frequently mentioned means of support identified by Labour MPs, and the third most popular choice among Liberal Democrats after tax credits and raising the tax thresholds. While Conservative MPs were more likely to refer to other factors such as removing disincentives, raising tax thresholds and simplifying the tax system, several Conservative MPs conceded that the Minimum Wage had been a positive and popular development that was here to stay, observing that "there will always be a need for some sort of in-work help", and "some of the predicted problems were overstated".

There was also some cross-party support for tax credits. This was the most frequently mentioned means of supporting people on low incomes identified by Labour and Liberal Democrat MPs. Tax credits were praised by MPs from all parties for targeting support at individuals in most need. They had, as one Labour MP observed, "put huge amounts of money in people's pockets". By offering support through the tax system they were also praised by Labour and Liberal Democrat MPs for removing the stigma from receiving state assistance. Several Conservative MPs also expressed support for the principal of tax credits, while expressing doubts about the effective administration of the policy under Labour. As one Conservative MP observed, "I know what Brown has tried to do, to mix tax and benefits, this is not undesirable, but it is too complicated". Similarly, another Conservative MP, a member of David Cameron's campaign team admitted, "I see the merit of tax credits, it is not an ignoble policy, the problem is it has created unforeseen problems in the administration".

However, these views were in a minority among Conservative MPs and there were some significant concerns on opposition benches about the effect of tax credits. Several Conservative MPs objected to tax credits for being "too generous" and expanding the number of people eligible for state support. In contrast to Labour MPs who asserted that tax credits targeted those in most need, some opposition MPs criticised them for extending state support to individuals who did not need it. The government, it was argued, had created a new group of people who had not previously received state support but who were now becoming dependent on that support. This view was also expressed by some Liberal Democrat MPs, one of whom criticised the government, for "building a curious middle class dependence on tax credits". Tax credits were also criticised by Conservative MPs for creating disincentives to work and save. Several Conservatives argued that they discouraged individuals from supplementing their income through their own efforts, either by finding a second job or working longer hours. Interestingly, a similar argument was made by a small minority of Labour MPs who were critical of tax credits for encouraging employers to behave badly by supplementing poor wages. A more appropriate policy, these MPs argued, would be to force employers to pay a decent wage by increasing the Minimum Wage.

However, by far the most sustained criticism of tax credits, made by many MPs from all parties, related to the complexity of the system that had led to a large number of overpayments and hardship when these were clawed back. Mistakes in the tax credit system have been widely publicised, and subject to intense parliamentary scrutiny. In September 2005 the Commons Public Accounts Committee estimated that in 2004-05, for the second year running, claimants had received £2.2 billion in overpaid tax credits. Attempts by the Inland Revenue to recover these overpayments by requesting repayment or suspending future payments have reportedly caused considerable distress and hardship and the Commons Public Accounts Committee observed that MPs "have been inundated with distressing complaints from constituents" (Public Accounts Committee, 2005a, p 4).

This was confirmed by MPs' comments. MPs from all parties reported spending a large amount of time dealing with constituents' problems related to tax credits. MPs spoke of being overwhelmed by a massive constituency caseload related to tax credits. They spoke at length about the experiences of constituents who had been overpaid and had subsequently had the payments stopped, leaving them in "real distress", "real misery" and "destitution". Both Labour and Conservative MPs questioned whether the Inland Revenue was an appropriate agency to handle social security payments. As one Conservative MP argued, "it was a great mistake to transfer the payment of benefits from social security people to the Treasury. The DHSS despite its problems got money to people who needed it". These views were echoed by a Labour MP in the Department for Work and Pensions, who observed that "benefits need to take account of human fallibility", something which, he observed, "the Treasury is reluctant to do". However, few MPs recommended abolishing the tax credit system. It was widely accepted that the problems associated with tax credits were administrative, and many MPs, including some Conservatives, were at pains to stress that there was nothing fundamentally wrong with the principle of tax credits. Despite monumental problems, one Conservative MP concluded, "I am not prepared to condemn the policy as a failure yet".

National Health Service

There was strong cross-party consensus that improvements had been made in the delivery of healthcare. Only 29% of MPs felt that the NHS was not effective in meeting healthcare in Britain today, although a similar minority (24%) were unequivocal in stating that the NHS is effective, a view adopted by no Conservative MPs. A significant group of MPs felt that despite some problems in specific areas, healthcare provision was generally good, or had improved since 1997. This position was adopted by 62% of Liberal Democrat MPs, and 38% of Conservatives. Liberal Democrat MPs were particularly critical of the Conservative management of the NHS and several stressed that standards had improved considerably since 1997. One former Liberal Democrat health spokesperson asserted that there had been "significant improvements over eight years"; others observed that the health service was "visibly improving" and was "more effective than it has ever been before". These views were echoed by some Conservative MPs, one former health minister admitted that "the health service is better than it was", that every year "the NHS treats more people, and treats more illness". Several Conservative MPs stressed that the health service was good value for money, providing a better service for less money than those of Britain's neighbours in Europe and the US, although one

Conservative MP added it was only able to do so by paying its staff poorly. There was also, not surprisingly, Conservative support for the government's efforts to expand private health provision. One Conservative MP asserted that one of the government's most significant achievements was changing attitudes towards private sector involvement in the NHS, to the extent that "nobody was now saying hands-off our NHS".

There was a general acceptance by MPs from all parties that the government had invested substantial sums of money in the NHS and this had led to improvements in some areas of provision, although several opposition MPs questioned whether improvements should have been more widespread given the sums invested. Broad acceptance of the level of investment is indicated by the relatively small number of MPs who called for increased spending on the NHS (see Table 4.8). This was identified as a priority by only six MPs: two Labour, two Liberal Democrats and one each from the Conservatives and Plaid Cymru. This is in marked contrast to the position in the 1980s, when half of Labour and Liberal/SDP MPs interviewed called for increased spending (Bochel, 1992). It may also be significant that few MPs referred to the problem of waiting lists, a particular target for Labour

Table 4.8: Changes desired in policy on the NHS (% of valid responses by party)

	Labour	Conservative	Lib Dem	SNP/Plaid/Ind	Total
Ensure consistency of output across UK	24	18	23	80	26
Extend private provision	7	50	8	0	20
Improve management/cut bureaucratic waste	10	36	15	40	22
Give more power to patients/more choice	10	27	23	0	17
Greater local control/more power for doctors	7	41	0	0	16
Greater emphasis on preventive care	24	0	46	0	19
Combat waiting lists	7	18	15	40	14
Reduce role of private sector	17	0	0	20	9
Combine healthcare and social care	10	0	8	20	7
Improve cleanliness	3	14	0	20	7
Increase spending	7	5	15	20	6
Recruit more doctors, nurses	3	9	0	20	6
Reform consultants' contracts	14	0	0	0	6
Number	27	21	9	5	62

spending on the NHS. Waiting lists were identified as a problem by 10 MPs: four Conservatives, and two each from Labour, the Liberal Democrats and the SNP. Although few MPs referred specifically to the government's success in combating waiting lists, several did refer to a drop in the amount of mail in their postbags from constituents waiting for treatment.

There was cross-party consensus on improved effectiveness in the delivery of specific services that reflected the government's spending priorities, most notably acute services such as coronary and cancer care. Almost 60% of MPs identified NHS treatment of acute conditions as particularly effective: 58% of Labour MPs, 43% of Conservatives and 71% of Liberal Democrats. As one Conservative MP observed, "if critically ill, the NHS is the best in the world". There was also some consensus that the level of primary care was good, particularly GP (general practitioner) services, which were identified as effective by 44% of MPs: 42% of Labour MPs, 43% of Conservatives and 57% of Liberal Democrats.

However, a significant minority of Labour and Conservative MPs questioned the effectiveness of primary care with particular concerns about the decline in GP out-of-hours services. There were broader concerns that while acute illnesses were benefiting from increased investment, other areas of provision have been neglected, with examples being treatment of long-term chronic conditions such as arthritis, asthma, diabetes and mental health. MPs from all parties also identified deficiencies in the provision of NHS dental care. There was also a strong feeling among Labour and Liberal Democrat MPs that there was not enough emphasis on preventative care. Several MPs commented that "the NHS is a sickness service not a health service", and called for a greater emphasis on health education, dealing with what some MPs referred to as "lifestyle" issues, such as obesity, smoking and sexual health, particularly among the young. Combating such problems, it was argued, was not only in the interests of public health, but would also be cost-effective compared to more expensive treatment later. The issue of smoking was raised in particular by several MPs interviewed late in the survey, as proposals for a smoking ban were being debated in parliament. MPs from all parties declared support for a ban, with Labour MPs in particular stressing that this was a class issue as a more limited ban focusing, for example, only on pubs serving food, would disproportionately affect the less well-off.

One of the most pressing problems in healthcare, identified by 26% of MPs, related to the lack of consistency in health provision across the UK. Several MPs identified discrepancies in provision between different geographical areas, particularly between urban and rural areas, and also between adjacent geographical areas, a point that was raised in constituency surgeries. This was particularly emphasised by MPs from Scotland and Wales, who identified a "provision gap" between healthcare in England, and that in Scotland and Wales. Scottish and Welsh Labour MPs in particular, were highly critical of the decisions about health policy made by the Scottish Parliament and the Welsh Assembly. It was claimed that the decision to spend money on personal care and reducing prescription charges rather than investing in frontline services and cutting waiting lists was "a disaster". The refusal to introduce tuition fees in Scotland was presented by one Labour MP as taking money from the health service. Another Scottish Labour MP observed that the problem in Scotland was exacerbated by the regressive policies of the SNP, suggesting that a Conservative opposition would be more desirable as it would offer less opposition to Labour policies aimed at charging and the expansion of private provision.

However, despite some broad areas of agreement on the challenges facing the health service and the effectiveness of provision in some areas, MPs' attitudes continued to reflect some fundamental differences between the parties. The proportion of Conservative MPs advocating the extension of private provision has not changed since the 1980s, remaining at 50%, although unlike the 1980s, a small number of Labour and Liberal Democrat MPs now also adopted this position. However, a larger group of Labour MPs called for a reduction in the role of the private sector in the NHS. These MPs objected strongly to the use of the PFI to build new hospitals and described foundation hospitals variously as "nonsense", "a sham" and "a load of crap".

Aside from extending private provision the main preoccupation of Conservative MPs was criticism of the centralisation of control of the health service. Almost half of Conservative MPs called for greater local control over health policy, with the devolution of more power to clinical staff. There was much criticism of the government's attempts to "micromanage" the NHS, with frequent references to the government's "Leninist", "Stalinist" and "Moscow model" of control. In response Conservative MPs advocated "more localism", even if allowing local hospitals to decide their priorities resulted in inconsistency in the delivery of services. The public, one Conservative MP asserted, "need to get away from the idea of equality of outcomes" in health.

There was, however, an acceptance on the part of MPs from all parties that some of the problems facing the NHS were intractable. Opposition MPs observed that the NHS is "as effective as it can be", that it "will always be a problem", or "never will be effective". One Conservative MP frankly admitted "the shambolic organisation is not due to political parties, we are just as bad at it". Along with a broad acceptance that the Labour governments had invested heavily in the NHS there was a broad understanding that funding could never keep pace with demand. MPs from all parties pointed to the escalating cost of new technologies and treatments, and the increase in demand generated by an ageing population, and conceded that some form of rationing was "inevitable". At the same time there was an appreciation that the public seemed largely unaware of the escalating cost of health provision and that there was a need to make them aware that increased provision across a wide range of services was only possible if people were prepared to pay either through some charging or increased taxation.

Pensions

MPs' comments frequently suggested that pensions are the most pressing welfare concern on the current political agenda. When asked to identify the main challenges facing the welfare state today, an ageing population was the most frequently mentioned challenge, identified by 43% of MPs. This was not, however, solely related to the challenge of pensions provision but also included concerns regarding strains on healthcare provision and long-term care for older people. But when asked to identify priorities for extra government spending on welfare, pensions was the most popular choice, mentioned by 51% of MPs, considerably higher than the next most frequently mentioned priority – spending on families with children/combating child poverty – which was mentioned by 39% of MPs (see Table 5.4, Chapter Five). Pensions was mentioned by almost twice as many MPs as identified the NHS as a priority for extra spending, and three times the number who called for increased spending on education. Moreover, there was widespread consensus on this issue, with pensions as the most frequently mentioned priority for extra spending among Labour and Conservative MPs and in the case of the Liberal Democrats, second only to support families with children/combating child poverty. However, there was also widespread consensus that simply increasing state spending was not sufficient to meet the challenges created by an ageing population. When asked if there were any important policy changes they would like to see in the welfare arena, pensions reform was identified by 40% of MPs, second only to calls for simplification of the benefits system.

Asking about a perceived pensions 'crisis' invited partisan divisions between MPs. All but two Conservative MPs and 68% of Liberal Democrats unequivocally supported the view that the UK was facing a pensions crisis. Labour MPs were more circumspect, were reluctant to use the word 'crisis' and were more inclined to suggest that there was a potential for crisis, in perhaps 20 or 30 years' time, if measures were not taken soon. Of course, the extent to which MPs were prepared to identify a crisis as current or potential has a direct relation to the degree to which they considered that pensions reform to be a pressing issue, although several MPs who identified a current pensions crisis were somewhat more optimistic about the long-term prospects, observing that the demographic pressures of an ageing population may not be inexorable. Today's pensioners, it was suggested, had a healthier lifestyle and better diet than the generations following. With rising obesity and increasingly sedentary lifestyles, it was suggested, life expectancy in the future may level off or indeed begin to fall. Nevertheless, of the whole sample only a quarter of MPs (35% of Labour MPs, 5% of Conservatives and 31% of Liberal Democrats), believed that Britain was not facing some kind of crisis – current or potential – in pensions provision.

There was, again not surprisingly, a certain degree of partisanship in explaining the current pensions difficulties. There was broad consensus on the overall strain created by an ageing population, and also on the inadequacy of individuals' personal arrangements for pension provision, particularly among the young. However, these problems, it was variously suggested, had been exacerbated by the policies of successive governments. Thus, Conservative MPs were particularly vocal in apportioning blame to "Gordon Brown's £5 billion tax raid on company pensions schemes". This, it was also claimed, was exacerbated by the introduction of means testing that had acted as a disincentive to personal saving. In contrast several Labour MPs blamed the present difficulties on the Thatcher government for removing the link between pensions and earnings. They were also more likely to point to the failure of the market and problems with the regulation of company pension schemes.

In seeking to provide solutions to the predicted shortfall in pensions, MPs identified a range of possible options that attracted varying degrees of cross-party support (see Table 4.9). It was clear, however, that this is a question MPs approached with some trepidation. Several Labour MPs were reluctant to offer suggestions, asserting that this was the job of the Pensions Commission. Indeed, the interim report of the Commission was published at an early stage in this research and clearly informed MPs' responses. It was certainly apparent that MPs from all

Table 4.9: MPs' proposals for pensions reform (% of valid responses by party)

	Labour	Conservative	Lib Dem	SNP/Plaid/Ind	Total
Encourage/create incentives for individuals to save	44	91	50	0	57
People work for longer/flexible arrangements to allow longer working	59	50	43	25	51
Improve basic state pension/provide stable state provision	29	14	21	25	23
Some form of compulsory saving	18	5	36	75	20
Improve/reform occupational pensions	24	5	14	25	16
Some kind of non-contributory/citizen's pension	15	0	50	25	18
Increase taxes/National Insurance	18	0	7	0	9
Increase regulation/support for those affected by failing company pensions	9	0	14	25	8
Create stability in the housing market/enable equity release	6	14	0	0	7
Deregulate/remove tax burden on pension funds	0	23	0	0	7
Increase immigration	3	5	7	25	5
Use tax credits	9	0	0	0	4
Restore link between pensions and earnings	0	9	0	0	3
Number	34	22	14	4	74

parties were acutely aware that placing pensions provision on a more stable footing was likely to involve some unpalatable options for whatever government is in power: extending the working life and increased personal provision, as well as increased state spending. Consequently, while MPs were often happy to set out a range of possible solutions, they were rather less prepared to say in detail which options they preferred. Interestingly, two Labour members of the Department for Work and Pensions team, interviewed before the publication of the final report of the Pensions Commission, were at pains to stress that the government might well choose not to adopt some of the Commission's proposals.

Nevertheless, there were some broad areas of consensus among MPs when seeking to offer solutions to the pensions problem. This consensus lies in three key areas: the need to encourage individual saving; the need for people to work longer; and the need for the government to be active in seeking to restore confidence or trust in pensions. The need to encourage individuals to save was the most frequently identified solution, mentioned by 57% of MPs, although there were some marked divisions in the proportion of support between the parties, with 91% of Conservatives, 50% of Liberal Democrat MPs and 44% of Labour MPs advocating this solution. There were also some differences in approaches to providing incentives, with Conservatives stressing the deregulation of the financial services industry, something that attracted no support among the other parties, and some form of co-payment through lifetime savings accounts. The introduction of some form of compulsory saving enjoyed strong support among Labour, Liberal Democrat, SNP and Plaid MPs, but was only supported by one Conservative MP.

Longer working lives also attracted strong support among MPs from all parties, 51% of the total sample. Several MPs accepted that this may be an unpalatable option to some, and were unhappy at the idea that people may be forced to work for longer. Others, however, pointed to the iniquity of forcing people to retire at 65. These MPs preferred to talk about the extent to which many individuals were not only willing to continue working beyond the statutory retirement age, but also had much left to contribute. Several, particularly older, MPs used themselves as examples of this. However, there was also a strong emphasis on the need for a more flexible working environment to encourage this. It was suggested, for example, that older workers should, if they wished, be more able to step back into less responsible roles in their final years of work without adversely affecting their pension.

Finally, there was some consensus on a role for the government in restoring trust in pensions, although support for this was not as great or as broad as that for increased individual saving or longer working lives. While Liberal Democrat MPs spoke about the problems created by a lack of confidence in pensions, none specifically mentioned an active role for the government in building confidence. Once again, however, there was considerable difference in emphasis in approaches to restoring trust, with some Labour MPs stressing the importance of increased regulation of occupational pensions schemes, something that attracted no support among Conservatives. There was also some support among Labour and Plaid Cymru MPs for the government to "step-in" and provide help for those affected by failing company pension schemes. There was more consensus between Labour and Conservative MPs regarding the importance of placing state provision on a long-term stable footing, in order that individuals are able to make provision to meet any shortfall.

Interestingly, however, there was little cross-party support for increased state provision. Conservative MPs expressed strong opposition to pensions means testing; their opposition, however, was largely based on the disincentive effect on personal savings, and was not matched by support for a high level of universal provision. In contrast a significant proportion of Labour MPs (29%) supported improvements in basic state pension provision. Support for an increase in state provision among Labour MPs was not translated into support for the introduction of a 'citizen's pension', based on entitlement rather than contributions, which received fairly strong support among Liberal Democrat MPs (50%), but was only supported by 15% of Labour MPs, and no Conservatives.

Conclusions

There has been some significant movement towards a middle ground in MPs' attitudes to welfare, suggesting the emergence of a new consensus on welfare. This is particularly evident when MPs' attitudes today are compared with MPs' attitudes to welfare in the 1980s, in a period when there was little or no discernible consensus on approaches to welfare. If there is a consensus on welfare, it is, however, a new consensus. There has not been a return to the postwar consensus that defined attitudes towards the welfare state up to the 1970s. This postwar consensus involved considerable cross-party agreement on means: commitment to a mixed economy; the maintenance of full employment through Keynesian economic management; and a high level of state welfare provision. There were, however, fundamental differences of opinion over objectives with The Labour Party committed to the redistribution of wealth, while the Conservatives sought a degree of intervention only compatible with market efficiency and personal initiative. The current survey reveals a significantly different situation within parliament. Labour MPs, aware of the escalating costs of welfare provision, have moved away from ideas centred on universal provision towards a more selective targeted approach to welfare. At the same time some Conservative MPs, aware of the damaging social costs of poverty, have shifted away from a strictly minimal approach to welfare towards a more collectivist position. There is therefore some convergence of attitudes on a middle ground defined by financial restraint and the mixed provision of welfare services, designed to help those in most need, while enabling others to help themselves. There is now arguably a broad consensus on ends, the elimination of poverty particularly among pensioners and children, the movement of people off welfare and into work, and the creation of a competitive economy by restraining spending and the burden of taxation. There are some areas of consensus on the means of achieving this, most notably through a commitment to mixed provision. However, the fundamental differences now relate to the delivery of these objectives with areas of disagreement over issues such as means testing and tax credits.

However, while there has clearly been some movement of MPs towards a centre ground on approaches to welfare, it is not clear how firm this ground is. There is considerable intra-party debate about the role of the state in welfare. This was not evident in the 1980s, when Bochel (1992) found that MPs' attitudes generally reflected those of the party leadership. In contrast, in the current survey there was considerable dissent from party policy among backbench MPs from each of the three main parties. A significant proportion of Labour MPs (20%) continued to believe that the role of the state should be to redistribute wealth. Many Labour MPs who took part in this survey expressed grave misgivings about aspects of Labour's programme of welfare reform, most notably the involvement of the private sector, and expressed strong opposition to the movement towards a new consensus based on selective and mixed provision. This is reflected in marked divisions within The Labour Party in the data related to the financing and provision of welfare. Perhaps more significantly these MPs were not primarily well-known Labour rebels, but MPs whose voting records generally suggest agreement with party policy. Moreover, although these views were particularly strong among Labour MPs elected prior to Labour's victory in 1997, the post-1997 cohort is also divided on the level of state provision and attitudes towards issues such as tax and spend, as is the cohort elected in 2005. There were similar divisions among Liberal Democrat MPs between those MPs who favour a high level of universal state provision, and continued to support the policy of tax-funded improvements in provision, and those Liberal Democrat MPs who favour spending restraint and a more selective approach to provision, although Liberal Democrat MPs were much less critical of the leadership when expressing dissent from party policy.

This research also suggests that there are significant divisions within the Conservative Party. Interviews with Conservative MPs revealed the existence of a group of MPs keen to distance themselves from Thatcherite approaches to welfare, and to develop policies designed to provide considerable state support for individuals and communities in need. These views broadly coincide with the Cameron leadership, and, moreover, suggest the basis for cross-party consensus. However, it is not clear how representative these views are of the Conservative Party as a whole. Conservative MPs interviewed before Cameron's election as party leader were unable to estimate the depth of support for this position within the parliamentary party, but certainly did not give the impression that these views were widely held. In contrast there was strong support among Conservative MPs for a limited approach to welfare. A significant proportion of Conservative MPs (36%) continue to believe that the state should provide nothing more than a minimal safety net for those in the most need. There were powerful arguments about the disincentive nature of state provision and several calls for increased charging or fundamental cuts in services. These views were particularly prominent among Conservative MPs elected in 2005.

The impact of these intra-party divisions on the future of welfare policy is not clear. There is clearly scope for a broad cross-party consensus on a range of issues. The decline in ideological opposition among Labour MPs to the involvement of the private sector in welfare provision, coupled with Conservative commitments to reduce poverty, suggest the basis for consensus on a number of specific policies such as the Minimum Wage, tax credits, and the PFI. However, in each of the parties, efforts will need to be made to accommodate the divergent opinions of different groups of MPs. The extent to which the parliamentary parties are successful in achieving this may affect their success at the polls, and will certainly have an impact on the scrutiny of welfare legislation by the Commons, and perhaps the House of Lords, in the future.

FIVE

MPs' attitudes to welfare and public opinion

Labour's welfare reforms have generated considerable interest and debate both within parliament and in the public arena. However, it is far from clear that shifts in political attitudes towards welfare have been reflected in public opinion. MPs act as an important channel of communication between the public and the executive. Constituency work remains an important, and arguably growing (Healey et al, 2005), part of MPs' work, and, as noted in Chapter Three, some of the changes to the parliamentary timetable as part of the 'modernisation' process were intended to help them in fulfilling that role. This chapter examines the role of parliament in representing the interests of citizens, by comparing MPs' attitudes to welfare, as discussed in Chapter Four, with evidence of public attitudes to welfare collated from the annual *British Social Attitudes* survey and public opinion polls. The chapter will seek to identify and explain areas of disagreement and consensus between public and parliamentary attitudes to welfare, focusing in particular on questions regarding commitment to state welfare provision, priorities in welfare spending, and attitudes towards funding for welfare provision.

Studies of political representation have offered several interpretations of the representative function of MPs. These often begin with the notion of trusteeship expressed by Edmund Burke on his election to parliament in 1774, when he famously informed his new constituents that while he would put 'great weight' on their wishes and accord their opinions the highest respect, he would not be bound by them. "Your representative", he asserted, "owes you, not his industry only, but his judgement; and he betrays, instead of serving you, if he sacrifices it to your opinion" (Burke, 1808, p 19).

Modern commentators have increasingly questioned the relevance of Burkean notions of representation, or at least sought to limit the occasions when Burke should be applied. In a seminal work on representation published in 1967, Pitkin argued that, while representatives must be capable of independent action or judgement, representative government must be characterised by a "constant condition of responsiveness" (Pitkin, 1967, p 233). Conflict between representative and represented, Pitkin argued, "must not normally take place. The representative ... must not be found persistently at odds with the wishes of the represented without good reason..." (Pitkin, 1967, p 209). Scholars working on the British political process have argued that developments such as the emergence of a mass electorate, an educated public, improved communications and modern political parties, have served to undermine altogether Burkean notions of representation which, it is claimed, are based on an elitist conception of aristocratic paternalism that is no longer relevant (Judge, 1999; Rush, 2001; Beetham, 2003). It has been suggested that in practice MPs may draw on a range of ideas to defend or justify their actions, including party loyalty, the representation of interests, constituents or individual conscience. Crucially, however, the degree to which MPs are prepared to exercise independent judgement is contingent on the interests and indeed the issue involved (Judge, 1999).

It is clear that MPs are aware of a complex web of relationships that define their representative function, referring to their role in representing a range of interests including constituents, their party, and a range of organised interest groups both within their constituency and beyond. In recent years both Houses of Parliament have seen an increase in lobbying by pressure groups and professional lobbyists. Much of this involves contact by letter, or increasingly, by email. Such contacts can be useful to MPs and peers, by providing background information on a complicated issue making its way through parliament, but may also have a substantive impact on debate in parliament. Norton (2005), for example, highlights references made during the second reading debate of the Children Bill in September 2004 to briefings by a variety of interested pressure groups. Moreover, Labour MPs interviewed for this research suggested that the influence of various charitable groups had increased since 1997, because in many instances they were seeking policy changes in roughly the same direction as the government was moving.

Nevertheless, it is possible to argue that one issue on which MPs' attitudes may most closely reflect those of their constituents is welfare. It is certainly the case that MPs can have little excuse for not knowing the views of the public on welfare issues. What MPs in this survey referred to as their 'social work' or 'ombudsman' function is a particularly strong feature of the British constituency system and provides MPs with a useful, if not always welcome, barometer of public experience of the public services. As one former Conservative social security minister observed:

"You get some members of the public who are experts in foreign affairs, but you probably get a better picture of foreign affairs from here at Westminster. But in the welfare field, the punter is the expert. There is no doubt that the debates on the Child Support Agency, and Tax Credits have been driven by constituents. That is one of the strengths of the constituency system, you go back to your constituencies on a Friday and people tell you what's really going on."

The relationship between the MP and his or her constituent is, of course, a complicated one. MPs are clearly aware that constituents are far more likely to approach them with complaints than compliments, and several MPs admitted that they were more inclined to take on board those complaints that supported their own political views. Most noted, however, that it was their own observations of the experiences of constituents, rather than constituents' particular complaints that were influential. Whatever the case, it is clear that in the case of welfare most MPs are not only aware of their constituents' experiences, but also that these have been influential in informing their own views on welfare. When MPs were asked what sort of influences had been important in determining their position on welfare issues, the experience of constituents or constituency casework was the most frequent response, with 61% of MPs identifying this as an important influence. The next most frequently mentioned influence was personal experience or upbringing, cited by 57% of MPs. Burkean notions of the importance of parliamentary debate were significantly less important with only 7% of MPs identifying debate in the House as an important influence on their thinking, while only three MPs stated that lobbying had been influential in determining their thinking rather than simply providing background information.

Public attitudes to welfare: an enduring commitment to state welfare provision

Surveys of public opinion such as *British Social Attitudes* consistently reveal a widely held view that support for individuals in a range of social policy areas is primarily the responsibility of the government. Apparent shifts in the political consensus regarding welfare provision have not, it seems, served to dampen public enthusiasm for a high level of state involvement in welfare provision. In the past 25 years, despite the election of radically reforming governments of both Left and Right, both of which have been committed to a fundamental reform of the welfare state, and to changing public attitudes towards the relationship between individuals and the state, there is only limited evidence to suggest that there has been any movement in public attitudes away from a conception of cradle-to-grave state welfare provision grounded in the late 1940s.

In particular, while the Blair governments have sought to introduce a more selective approach to welfare, public support for a broad range of state provision has, if anything, increased since 1997. When asked whether provision in a range of areas was mainly the responsibility of the government, the person's employer, or individuals and their families, a consistently high proportion feel that it is mainly the government's responsibility to pay for healthcare for the sick, to ensure that long-term sick and disabled people have enough to live on, and to provide for unemployed people. Only in the case of providing enough support for individuals to live on in retirement does public support fall below 80%, although a growing majority still favour state support in this area (see Table 5.1).

Even taking into account a relative lack of support for state retirement provision, and declining support for government spending on social benefits, it is apparent that a large proportion of the public continue to feel that welfare provision is mainly the responsibility of the government. Evidence for a broad public consensus in support of state provision is reinforced when people are asked to choose their priorities for extra government spending from a long list of policy areas. The mass public services, health and education, consistently head the list by a very large margin. Support for spending on housing and social security benefits, once consistently listed in third and fourth place, has slipped in recent years with public transport and police and

Table 5.1: Public attitudes to state versus personal responsibility (1998 and 2003)

% saying that the responsibility should be:	1998				2003			
	Health	Retirement	Sickness	Unemployment	Health	Retirement	Sickness	Unemployment
Mainly the government	82	56	80	85	83	58	83	81
Mainly the person's employer	9	9	9	3	7	11	8	3
Mainly the person and their family	6	33	10	10	7	29	7	14

Sources: Jowell et al (1999); Park et al (2004)

prisons now garnering more support. In contrast, areas such as roads, defence, help for industry and overseas aid, receive little priority for extra expenditure (Sefton, 2003; Park et al, 2005).

However, recent *British Social Attitudes* surveys have led some to question whether these broad indicators of public support for the welfare state mask a subtler shift in public attitudes towards welfare provision. In particular, it has been argued that New Labour's attempts to change the way the British people think about the welfare state and the nature of the duties a state has towards its citizens are beginning to bear fruit. In 1999 Hills and Lelkes (1999) observed that despite a persistent public appetite for increased welfare spending, the spending people want is selective, focused on health, education and benefits for carers, people with disabilities and pensioners. There is, in contrast, little public support for blanket benefit increases, not least because of widespread public concern about unemployment benefits undermining independence and incentives, and fraud. This public support for selective increases in welfare spending, they suggest, is closely in line with Labour government policy (Hills and Lelkes, 1999).

Similarly, in 2003, Curtice and Fisher (2003) argued that Blair's tenure as Prime Minister has been marked by a significant shift to the Right in public attitudes. They illustrate their argument with reference to shifts in opinion on redistribution and attitudes towards benefits levels, which began to display significant movement to the Right after Blair's election in 1997 (see Table 5.2). Ironically, they observe, Blair has achieved something which Thatcher failed to do, that is to bring public thinking closer to the views espoused by the Prime Minister, which because of Labour's movement towards the Centre, has at the same time brought the public much closer to the views expressed by Thatcher in the 1980s. This shift has been achieved, Curtice and Fisher suggest (2003), primarily by changing the attitudes of Labour supporters, while the views of Conservative supporters have changed little. The result, they conclude, is a significant narrowing of some of the differences between Labour and Conservative supporters, and the emergence of an important electoral battleground in the centre of British politics.

Claims for a narrowing of differences between Labour and Conservative supporters are further reinforced in evidence presented by Taylor-Gooby on shifts in opinion by members of the public across the political spectrum (see Table 5.3). Looking at attitudes to welfare by groups of individuals positioned on the Left–Right scale in 1987 and 2003 Taylor-Gooby found that, while the proportion in favour of welfare recipients has declined among all groups, the gap between

Table 5.2: How Britain moved to the Right (1983-2002)

	% saying unemployment benefits are too low	% saying government should redistribute from rich to poor	% Left of Centre
1983	46	n/a	n/a
1984	49	n/a	n/a
1985	44	n/a	53
1986	44	43	52
1987	51	45	55
1989	53	51	58
1990	52	51	59
1991	54	50	54
1993	58	48	59
1994	53	51	64
1995	51	47	61
1996	48	44	58
1997	46	n/a	51
1998	29	39	52
1999	33	36	50
2000	40	39	52
2001	37	38	49
2002	29	39	53

Note: n/a = not asked.

Source: Curtice and Fisher (2003, p 236)

Table 5.3: Public attitudes towards welfare by position on the Left–Right scale (1987 and 2003)

	1987			2003		
% saying that:	Left	Centre	Right	Left	Centre	Right
Government should spend more money on welfare benefits for the poor, even if it leads to higher taxes	76	57	35	63	44	29
Many people who get social security don't really deserve help	32	28	33	47	38	33
If welfare benefits weren't so generous people would learn to stand on their own two feet	28	27	42	48	43	37

Source: Taylor-Gooby (2004)

those on the Left and Right was smaller in 2003 than in 1987. Moreover, the number of those agreeing with the statement that "Many people who get social security do not really deserve help" has increased on the Left, while the proportion of those on the Right who agree remains the same, with the result that those on the Left are now more likely to support the statement. At the same time there has been a fall in the number of those on the Right who agreed with the proposition that generous welfare benefits discouraged people from standing on their own two feet.

Growing convergence? MPs' attitudes and public attitudes

Comparisons of public attitudes with MPs' attitudes to welfare suggest some broad similarities between the opinions of MPs and those of party supporters. As indicated in Chapter Four, there has been a clear move towards the Centre in MPs' attitudes to welfare, particularly when compared with MPs' attitudes in the 1980s. This is in part the result of a shift to the Right in the attitudes of a large proportion of Labour and Liberal Democrat MPs, many of whom now express a more selective approach to welfare. This may reflect the shift in opinion of those on the Left of the political spectrum identified by Taylor-Gooby. Similarly, there has been a movement, albeit less marked, towards the Centre on the part of some Conservative MPs who now advocate policies designed to combat poverty and relative inequality. This is also reflected in the table above, by those on the Right of the political spectrum whose views on recipients of social security have changed less markedly than those on the Left, but which nevertheless reflect a more positive attitude to benefits recipients than in the past.

However, the convergence of MPs' attitudes around a more selective approach to welfare is somewhat more marked than that of the general public. As the first line of Table 5.3 indicates, and as Taylor-Gooby reminds us, while there has been a significant hardening of public attitudes since the 1980s, support for generous and costly welfare provision remains relatively high, particularly on the Left of the political spectrum. While MPs from all the major parties have sought to grapple with the global technological and demographic pressures placed on welfare states at the end of the 20th century, public attitudes towards the responsibilities of the state have remained more static. While Taylor-Gooby and others have found little evidence of widespread public support for rolling back state responsibility, it is quite clear that the broad public support for a high level of state welfare provision across a range of services is not reflected in MPs' attitudes. Looking at opinion across the House of Commons, only 40% of MPs interviewed advocated a role for the state to provide at least a high national minimum level of welfare provision in a range of services. This compares to figures for public commitment to state provision that, with the exception of pensions, routinely exceed 80%. "Britain," Taylor-Gooby concludes, "is still very much wedded to the idea of government responsibility for a broad range of policy areas", including support in areas which are not current policy in England, such as care needs of older people in nursing homes (Taylor-Gooby, 2004, p 19).

This commitment to state provision is also reflected in public ambivalence towards the role of the private sector in the delivery of welfare services. As indicated in Chapter Four (Table 4.3), MPs are divided about whether the state should be the main provider of welfare services, with 45% of Labour MPs, 46% of Liberal Democrats and no Conservatives expressing the view that welfare services should be provided mainly by the state, the remainder advocating mixed provision or in the case of some Conservative MPs, a predominant role for the private sector.

The public's strong commitment to state provision (Table 5.1) suggests a marked difference of opinion with MPs about the role of the private sector. However, the question in *British Social Attitudes* implies opting out of the state sector to pay for private provision; consequently the public's responses do not necessarily indicate opposition to a role for the private sector in the delivery of state-funded services, as advocated by many, particularly Labour, MPs. A clearer indication of public attitudes to private provision was revealed in 2004, when the survey asked whether important services such as health and education would be better run by the government or private companies. In response to this question the public were much more equivocal in their support of state provision. Significantly there was still strong support for state provision – 73% of respondents believed that the government would be better at making sure the services went to those in the most need. However, 51% believed the private sector would provide a better quality service, and 55% believed the private sector would be more cost-effective (Park et al, 2005). This suggests a much broader measure of public support for mixed provision, particularly if services remain free at the point of need.

Deserving and undeserving poor: conflicting priorities in welfare provision

The *British Social Attitudes* surveys not only reveal a strong public attachment to state welfare provision, they also provide a clear indication of public priorities in welfare spending. As has already been observed, the mass public services, health and education, consistently head the public's list of overall spending priorities. When asked more specifically to prioritise spending on social benefits, the public has consistently distinguished between services for the 'deserving' and the 'undeserving' poor. When asked to choose priorities from a list of social benefits, the old and infirm top the list, while there is little support for benefits for unemployed people and single parents, and, as shown in Tables 5.2 and 5.3, there has been a significant hardening of public attitudes towards benefits for unemployed people since Labour's election in 1997. There is more support for helping families with children than those without. In 2004, 15% thought the government should spend more on benefits for unemployed people compared to 35% who advocated increased spending on benefits for single parents. However, there is considerably more support for state assistance for parents who work on low incomes than those who do not, with 63% advocating increased spending on working parents on low incomes (Park et al, 2005); yet there is little evidence of support either for single adults or couples without children, whether unemployed or working on a low income (Taylor-Gooby, 2005).

While public priorities for welfare spending reflect a consistent measure of support for mass services and the 'deserving' poor, MPs' responses were more varied and arguably more closely reflect currently perceived needs in particular sectors rather than a consistent endorsement of state provision (see Table 5.4). Thus, while most MPs spoke of the importance of state provision in health and education, these services were not prioritised as in need of additional spending. Health and education have benefited from large increases in funding since Labour's election in 1997 and MPs, including Conservatives, conceded that real improvements (often reflected in MPs' postbags) had been made in provision in these areas – most notably in the reduction of hospital waiting lists. In contrast, the widely predicted

Table 5.4: MPs' priorities for extra welfare spending (% of valid responses by party)

% giving as highest priority for extra spending:	Labour	Conservative	Lib Dem	SNP/Plaid/Ind	Total
Pensions/old people	50	68	36	40	51
Families/children/child poverty/childcare	41	32	50	20	39
NHS	26	26	29	60	29
Housing	26	5	21	0	18
Education	21	11	14	0	15
More support for disabled people and carers	9	21	29	0	15
Mental health	3	0	7	20	4
Benefits for unemployed (not housing)	0	0	0	20	2
Number	34	19	14	5	72

Note: Lib Dem: Liberal Democrat, SNP: Scottish National Party, Plaid: Plaid Cymru, Ind: Independent.

shortfall in pension provision meant that support for increased provision for old age was the most pressing priority, mentioned by 51% of MPs. Similarly, support for increased spending on social housing often reflected specific constituency concerns, and publicity surrounding a shortage of childcare for working parents, and pre-election statements from Labour politicians pledging extra support in this area ensured that family policies were clearly to the forefront in MPs' views of the welfare landscape (Brown, 2005). While MPs were more concerned than the public to identify need, there was nevertheless some adherence to ideas about deserving and undeserving recipients of state support. MPs' support for old people and families with children generally mirrored public perceptions of 'deserving' groups. In contrast social benefits were mentioned by relatively few MPs, only one MP mentioned benefits for unemployed people, and there was no voicing of support for single adults, or for families without children.

However, once again MPs' attitudes towards drawing back state support go somewhat further than those of the general public. This is particularly the case with respect to attitudes towards benefits for people with disabilities. Relatively few MPs advocated extra support for people with disabilities and carers, an area that attracts strong public support, and was marked by a particularly high level of cross-party consensus among MPs in the 1980s (Bochel, 1992). While support for improved benefits for people with disabilities is still characterised by a measure of cross-party consensus, there has been a marked decline in support particularly among Labour MPs. This results from concerns among MPs from all parties about the large number of individuals claiming Incapacity Benefit, and successive attempts by the Labour government to cut the on-flow of individuals claiming it. In contrast to the public, MPs have now developed a more nuanced appreciation of those unable to work due to disability. In interviews many MPs distinguished between the 'deserving' disabled, those with severe physical and mental illnesses who could not reasonably be expected to work, and those with long-term chronic conditions such as backache and depression who, many felt, could be economically active to some degree, and are therefore less deserving of state support. There is little evidence to suggest that the public make such distinctions.

Paying for welfare: attitudes towards 'tax and spend'

Surveys of British public opinion indicate considerable and consistent support for increasing taxes to pay for spending on health, education and social benefits (Sefton, 2003; Page, 2005; Taylor-Gooby, 2005).

Every year since 1987, a majority of respondents to the *British Social Attitudes* survey have supported an increase in state spending, even if that meant an increase in taxes. The proportion of people supporting an increase began to rise steeply in the 1980s, from around one third to more than a half, and has remained above that level ever since (see Table 5.5). Similarly, there is strong public support for a role for the government in redistributing wealth. In 2003, 42% agreed that "the government should redistribute income to the less well off" while only 26% disagreed. Taylor-Gooby observes that while support for redistribution is lower now than in the late 1980s and 1990s, when around 50% supported it, opinions against redistribution have not hardened under Labour, and there has been a slight rise in support since 1999 (Taylor-Gooby, 2005, pp 112-13).

This apparent enthusiasm for tax-funded improvements in services, and a role for the government in redistributing wealth is in marked contrast to the prevailing attitudes of MPs. While most MPs readily accepted that the government should finance welfare, they were much more reticent about the suggestion that increased provision could be financed by an increase in general taxation. One third of MPs favoured an increase in taxation to pay for increased services, while the remainder clearly stated that they would not be in favour of such a change. Although Labour and Liberal Democrat MPs were fairly evenly divided, and much closer to public opinion, with tax increases supported by 46% and 50% of their MPs respectively, support for a role for the state in advancing equality through redistribution was supported by only 20% of Labour MPs and 7% of Liberal Democrats.

Even among those MPs who supported it there was widespread scepticism at evidence from surveys such as the *British Social Attitudes* surveys that the public would support tax increases to pay for improved services. "People say they would pay more tax when asked", observed one Labour MP, "but this is not reflected in the ballot box". Several MPs argued that when people advocate tax increases they mean other people's taxes and not their own. There is some evidence to support this. When asked about personal levels of Income Tax the public generally respond that they are too high (Lipsey, 1994). Moreover, *British Social Attitudes* has also shown that over 60% of respondents consistently believe that those on higher incomes should pay a 'larger' or 'much larger' proportion of their incomes in tax. This is supported by qualitative research carried out to accompany the 2004 survey, which used focus groups to explore public attitudes to tax, and found little support for tax increases for any groups earning less than £100,000 (Hedges, 2005; Taylor-Gooby, 2005, p 119).

Table 5.5: Public attitudes to taxation and expenditure (1983-2004)

% saying that if the government had to choose, it should ...	1983	1986	1990	1993	1996	1999	2000	2001	2003	2004
... reduce taxes and spend less	9	5	3	4	4	4	5	3	6	6
... keep taxes and spending at same level	54	44	37	29	34	35	40	34	38	42
... increase taxes and spend more	32	46	54	63	59	58	50	59	51	49

Note: The spending areas asked about were 'health, education and social benefits'.

Perhaps even more significant is the shift in public attitudes towards tax and spend since Labour came to power. Public support for tax-funded increases in provision fell in 2000, and again in the two most recent editions of the survey in 2003 and 2004. In 2004, support fell below 50% for the first time since the late 1980s. While there has been no corresponding increase in the number of people advocating cuts in taxes and spending, the gap between those who support tax increases, and those who advocate the status quo has narrowed considerably (see Table 5.5). Several observers have attributed this to a growing appreciation on the part of the public that Labour has in fact increased the tax burden not least through the increase in National Insurance in 2003, but also through less direct means such as stamp duty and Council Tax (Page, 2005; Taylor-Gooby, 2005, p 120; Toynbee and Walker, 2005, pp 154-5). This view was echoed by several MPs, who suggested in particular that the rise in National Insurance represented the limits to which the public would tolerate demands on their income.

Conclusions

Analysis of MPs' attitudes to welfare reveals a complex relationship between the public and their representatives in parliament. A broad comparison of attitudes suggests marked divisions between the public and MPs on the role of the state in welfare, with each believing the other should play a greater role in provision. *British Social Attitudes* reveals a strong and consistent public commitment to a high level of state provision, while interviews with MPs suggest a shift in parliamentary opinion away from support for a high level of national provision towards a more limited safety net, coupled with a more active approach to getting people off benefits and into work. This shift towards the idea of state provision as an enabling mechanism rather than a passive provider of services is not limited to The Labour Party, but has also attracted strong support from Liberal Democrat MPs. There has undoubtedly been some movement in the opposite direction by Conservative MPs, a significantly large proportion of whom advocate greater state intervention to improve the lives of individuals and communities. However, Conservative attitudes towards a state-funded safety net remain somewhat more limited than that advocated by the other parties and at some distance from the kind of system supported by the majority of the public.

However, the convergence of MPs' attitudes towards a more selective approach to welfare does find some reflection in public attitudes. Analysis of recent *British Social Attitudes* surveys indicates a comparable hardening of public attitudes towards welfare recipients, particularly on the part of those members of the public identified as being politically Left of Centre (see Tables 5.2 and 5.3). Similarly, public support for tax-funded increases in provision has certainly wavered in recent years, suggesting that this is a widely but perhaps not deeply held opinion (see Table 5.5).

Nevertheless, one should be cautious about overestimating any shift to the Right on the part of the public or MPs. Evidence for a movement to the Right in public attitudes is tentative and in recent *British Social Attitudes* reports, Peter Taylor-Gooby, in particular, is reluctant to attribute this apparent shift to the emergence of a new culture of welfare (Taylor-Gooby, 2004). Public support for state provision, and indeed increased taxes and spending, remains relatively high when compared with the status quo, or support for cuts in taxes and spending, which receives very little public support. This also reflects the attitudes expressed by some MPs. While a significant proportion of Labour MPs wish to see a more selective role for the state in welfare provision, a larger proportion continue to embrace traditional ideas about universal provision and the role of the state in the redistribution of wealth. Similarly, while the question of tax and spend has been marginalised by party leaders reluctant to engage in a debate about tax rises, or cuts in public services, as discussed in Chapter Four, a more forensic examination of MPs' attitudes indicates marked differences between the parties on this issue, with a great deal more support among Labour and Liberal Democrat MPs for tax-raising improvements in services, and among Conservative MPs for rolling back state provision, than might be inferred from party positions. However, while the evidence would suggest that the attitudes of those MPs in favour of tax and spend lie closest to public opinion, MPs as a whole remain sceptical about the degree of public support for tax-funded improvements in services. MPs' views on this issue tend to be limited by their beliefs that the public is not willing to support either increases in taxation to pay for welfare, and at the same time a belief that the public at present has no appetite for major reductions in expenditure that would allow cuts in levels of taxation. While the evidence from recent *British Social Attitudes* surveys suggests that they may be right about the fragility, if not the extent, of public support for tax and spend, MPs' resultant caution means that the parties in parliament are pushed towards common ground around the status quo, with the result that the public's apparent support for extensive and costly state welfare provision is unlikely to be tested.

SIX

A more assertive chamber: the House of Lords and the scrutiny of welfare

Not only have social policy and welfare been key elements of the Labour governments' modernisation and reform programmes since 1997, but reform of the structures and practices of policy making and the constitution have also been central to the modernisation agenda. This has included reform of parliamentary procedure in attempts to 'modernise' the House of Commons, particularly during Robin Cook's period as Leader of the House (see Chapter Two), and substantive reform of the House of Lords, in an effort to make the upper chamber more representative and legitimate. This was widely recognised with the removal of the bulk of hereditary peers from the House in 1999, but following this there was no consensus on the direction of the future composition of the chamber, and after a free vote in the House of Commons all seven options, ranging from a fully appointed to a fully elected chamber, were rejected. As a result the 'interim' House of Lords has continued to develop in its own way. However, reform of the House of Lords was again included in The Labour Party's 2005 General Election manifesto, with a commitment to introducing further reforms but without allowing the upper chamber to challenge the primacy of the House of Commons. Also in May 2005, with the creation of 27 new life peers, of whom 12 were Labour, The Labour Party became, for the first time, the largest Party in the Lords.

The House of Lords has generally been ignored in considerations of social policy (indeed in relation to many policy areas, the term 'parliament' has frequently been used synonymously with 'House of Commons'); this chapter therefore considers the role of the House of Lords in relation to welfare issues, arguing that a combination of factors, including the policies put forward by the government, the government's reforms of the chamber, and a growth in external inputs, mean that the House is now playing a more significant part in influencing and scrutinising social policies than it has done for many years.

Experience and expertise: the role and functions of the House of Lords

It is widely recognised that the House of Lords is less powerful than the House of Commons, but nevertheless it remains an important component of the legislative and scrutiny processes of British government. All government legislation is required to pass through the Lords and it has been an important revising chamber, with amendments being introduced by both governments and opposition. On average between 1995 and 2004 60% of the time of the House was spent on the revision of legislation (55% on Bills and 5% on Statutory Instruments) and 40% on scrutiny, including debates (22%), questions (14%) and statements (4%) (House of Lords, 2004). The House of Lords has also played a major role in judicial affairs as the highest court of appeal, but as that is essentially separate from its legislative and scrutinising work that aspect of its activities is not dealt with here.

The powers of the House of Lords are limited by the Parliament Acts of 1911 and 1949, so that the upper chamber has no power to amend or delay a 'money bill' (any financial measure), although it does have the power to delay other legislation for up to a year, which can give it increased power towards the end of a parliament when governments may be under significant pressure to get their legislation through both Houses. The House has also limited its own powers through abiding by the 'Salisbury convention', which has normally been interpreted as stating that the House of Lords should not defeat legislation that had been foreshadowed in the governing party's election manifesto, although the future of this convention has recently been questioned by prominent Conservative and Liberal Democrat peers (Hazell, 2006; House of Commons Library, 2006).

Composition of the House of Lords

As Norton (2003) has noted, the House of Lords shares a number of characteristics with other second chambers, but until the reforms of 1999 it was unique among western legislatures in having a majority of its members being there on a hereditary basis. There is no limit on the total number of members and this reached 1,330 in October 1999 (including a large number of hereditary peers) before falling to 666 in November 1999 following the removal of the hereditaries (Norton, 2003) and rising again to 720 in December 2005. Since the introduction of reforms in 1999 the number of hereditary peers has been limited to 92, but there remains no overall limit on the size of the House.

Even following the reforms, the House of Lords remains largely male, with fewer than 20% of peers being female in June 2006, although this is comparable to the proportion of women in the Commons. The Conservatives have a smaller proportion of women peers (16%) than Labour (26%) and the Liberal Democrats (25%). The upper House is also overwhelmingly white, having only a small number of non-white members (around 3% in December 2005). The Lords is also, inevitably given the existence of appointments for life, a more elderly chamber than the House of Commons, and relatively few peers are aged under 50 (7% in 2000), with the average age of members being 68 in 2005. Similarly, the Lords is generally viewed as a middle and upper class chamber (Lord Chancellor's Department, 2001), with, for example, the Sutton Trust (2005) finding that 62% of peers had attended private schools.

In May 2000 a change was made to the way in which non-party-political members of the House of Lords are appointed. The Appointments Commission was given the role of determining the names of individuals who should be appointed on merit (it also vets, but does not choose, party nominees). Of the first 15 peers appointed in 2001 a number had backgrounds in social welfare or related areas, including Victor Adebowale, Chief Executive of the charity Turning Point, Richard Best, Director of the Joseph Rowntree Foundation, Valerie Howarth, Chief Executive of the charity Childline and Sir Herman Ouseley, formerly Executive Chairman and Chief Executive of the Commission for Racial Equality; others included Professor Illona Finlay, a palliative medicine expert from the University of Wales College of Medicine, Sir Paul Condon, formerly Commissioner of the Metropolitan Police and Professor Michael Chan, a paediatrician and Chair of the Chinese in Britain Forum. This pattern appears to be continuing with a number of appointees having welfare interests in the years since 2001.

While there is clearly no form of electoral representation in the upper chamber, the House of Lords can, to some degree, be depicted as performing a different representative function. In interviews peers frequently referred to their role in representing the interests of particular groups. In some cases peers like MPs consider themselves to be representing particular geographic areas. This may be based on the area in which they live or from where their title is derived, and is particularly the case with peers who previously served as MPs. As of June 2006, 189 members of the House of Lords had previously served in the Commons. Many of these peers maintain links with their former constituencies, and as one peer put it, "carry the shadow of that mandate up here". However, representation in the Lords is more diverse than in the Commons, and as one peer observed, "is more likely to be sectoral than geographic.... Thus the doctors and consultants represent a medical constituency, the professors represent the education constituency...". This sectoral representation may involve peers being lobbied and representing the interests of particular groups in the Lords. For example, a number of those peers interviewed were former trades union officials and maintained links with the unions for whom they had worked. As a result they referred to being lobbied by their union and by the Trades Union Congress (TUC), when relevant legislation was making its way through the Lords, for example, the Pensions Bill. However, they were also at pains to stress that it was not their role to act as a union representative in the Lords. As one Labour peer and former trades union leader asserted, "I have a voice borne out of experience but I don't represent them, I take an interest in trades unions but I don't represent them!". The extent of any 'representative' role is therefore clearly limited.

In addition to changes in the composition of the upper House, there have also been improvements in terms of attendance that may suggest a more rigorous and professional approach to scrutiny in the Lords. The past 50 years has seen a marked increase in average levels of attendance, from fewer than 100 in the early 1950s to a high of 446 in 1998-99, although as a proportion of possible attendance the 338 in the election year of 2004-05 represents a further increase.

Limited role of parties

Like the House of Commons, the House of Lords has developed party organisations, and most peers belong to a party, although there are a significant number who do not (as at June 2006 there were 209 Labour peers, 206 Conservatives, 79 Liberal Democrats and 190 crossbenchers, along with 25 bishops and 9 'others'). However, the Lords has not been dominated by party interests in the same way as the Commons. As in the House of Commons, each party has a leader, frontbenchers and whips, and whips and votes are recorded in *Hansard*, yet peers remain relatively free of party discipline; as they face no electoral constraints, they cannot be removed, and it is difficult for parties to threaten significant sanctions. As one Labour peer observed:

> "The Lords can vote against the whip with impunity. There is very little the whips can do to enforce obedience. They can call you in for a little chat, but nothing like what goes on in the Commons. It is much more relaxed."

However, despite this, in reality peers seldom vote against the party whip. Norton (2003) notes that even given the lack of 'sticks' or 'carrots' available to the parties, cohesion in terms of voting is generally high, with 70% of votes in the three sessions between 1999 and 2002 seeing no peer voting against their party; and where there is dissent, it is relatively small, particularly when compared with dissent in the House of Commons (see also Russell and Sciara, 2006a). This was reinforced by several peers who asserted that despite the lack of sanctions for rebels, they would not often vote against the party, favouring, as one observed, "quiet diplomacy". What is less clear, because of the generally lower levels of attendance among peers and weaker whipping, is the extent to which a level of dissent may be expressed through absences from the House, rather than through voting against the party line.

In another respect, too, party discipline is much less apparent in the Lords, and that is that the chamber has been almost entirely self-regulating. There is no Speaker to enforce order and there is no procedure for guillotining business. There is generally a broader and more spontaneous questioning of ministers, often in greater depth than is possible in the House of Commons (Hansard Society, 2001).

Nevertheless, parties do remain important in the upper House. Party peers are expected to attend party meetings and to take the party whip, and the whip can be withdrawn from those who are disloyal or who do not otherwise meet the expectations of them. As with MPs, peers may find that they do not agree with everything that their party puts forward, but similarly will vote for the party, as they expect others to do when their views may not be in agreement with them. While it is harder for the whips to maintain discipline in the Lords, there may also be costs to those who deviate too frequently from the party line, as they may be taken less seriously within the party, and they may lose influence, including access to the ears of ministers or colleagues.

The existence of the crossbenchers in the House of Lords adds another dimension that does not exist in the Commons, with around one quarter of peers being crossbenchers following the reforms. Crewe (2005) argues that as party whips have become increasingly active in the House of Lords, the crossbenches, which allow for greater independence of thought, speech and voting, have become more appealing. They also appeal to those who wish to appear as neutral, including many who have formerly held positions as judges or civil servants or have served in the armed forces. Anecdotal evidence also suggests that the crossbenchers have in recent years become increasingly diverse in their views. In an interview one prominent long-serving crossbencher observed, "the attitudes of the crossbenchers have changed, there are less crypto-Conservatives now, they're more Left of Centre, and represent a greater cross-section of views".

The crossbench peers do have an organisation, including an elected convenor who receives some office support, and there is a sharing of information on the business of the chamber. However, crossbench peers receive much less support and information than do those who are party members. They also lack group power and cohesion, which limits their input into places on committees and the business and management of the House and they do not take a collective position on matters discussed, so that there are no agreed approaches towards the government's proposals. The potential influence of the crossbenchers is also limited by the generally lower levels of attendance and voting than their party counterparts, which can be explained by the lack of a salary and the fact that many have employment or other responsibilities outside the chamber, by the lack of a whip to inform or guide them on how to vote and to pressure them to attend, and by the need for them to familiarise them with issues and papers if they are to make an informed decision.

Ministers in the House of Lords

It is worth noting that the House of Lords remains a source of personnel for the government, including for ministers. Indeed, in the spring of 2006 of 93 ministers, 16 were drawn from the upper chamber. These included Lord Adonis, as Parliamentary Under-secretary of State for Schools in the Department for Education and Skills, Lord Hunt of Kings Heath as Parliamentary Under-secretary in the Department for Work and Pensions, Lord Warner, as Minister of State in the Department of Health and Baroness Scotland, as Minister of State in the Home Office with responsibility for the criminal justice system and offender management.

This also allows most government departments to be represented in the Lords and therefore allows ministers to be questioned by peers. In addition, the system of questions in the Lords places a greater emphasis on the depth of questions, rather than numbers as in the Commons (Norton, 2005), with no more than four questions being asked in a 30-minute period, thus arguably requiring ministers to be knowledgeable and well briefed, particularly if their questioner is an expert on the subject at issue.

Operating in the House of Lords

As a result of the more limited role of parties, and the nature of the composition of the upper House, it is often claimed that peers operate in a different manner to MPs in the Commons. Crewe (2005) has undertaken an in-depth anthropological study of the House of Lords. Based on her observations she has suggested that peers adopt particular strategies in their activities in the chamber, although she acknowledges that all peers employ whatever approach seems appropriate to their objectives at a particular time. As idealised types she suggests that one approach is to be seen as *specialists* – most peers have some expertise, often professional, and even if they do not, many choose to concentrate on a small number of issues in order to be taken seriously when speaking about them in the chamber. Those who are seen as leaders in their fields tend to be taken very seriously. The parties also provide briefings for members, while crossbenchers may have to do their own research but are freer to form their own opinions. All peers increasingly receive briefings from interest groups, non-governmental organisations and sometimes ministers. Crewe (2005) notes that one of the ways in which peers can influence policy is "Peers who are members of the party in government have some access to the top ministers in the Commons, and are invited to briefings at which their views are sought (and then often ignored); the rest can lobby the ministers in the Lords" (Crewe, 2005, p 4).

Another approach is taken by *networkers* – Crewe suggests that much networking tends to be confined to the House of Lords itself, although contact with ministers from the Commons can be important for exerting pressure on the government. Face-to-face contact in all-party groups, bars and corridors is important in gathering support. Those from the Conservative and Labour Parties tend to concentrate on their fellow party members, while Liberal Democrats and crossbenchers may work with those from other parties. Crewe cites the Countess of Mar's campaign on the dangers of organophosphates and the work of peers who have worked with the disability lobby as examples of the successful use of networking. She describes others as *party creatures* – some peers choose to follow the party line closely, in some cases to seek office. However, backbenchers' opportunities for influencing frontbenchers are increased by membership of the same party, while parties, and to a much lesser extent the crossbenchers, have funds to employ advisers and researchers to inform members and to keep them up to date about legislation and the timing of debates. She defines one approach as *eccentrics* – a few peers choose to present themselves as 'mavericks', 'rebels' or other forms of eccentric; a few of these command respect, even if they sometimes ignore their party whips, with Crewe (2005) giving the example of Lord Ashley of Stoke, a long-time campaigner on disability issues. Finally she describes *elders* – usually regular attenders of many years' standing; this group are likely to have held ministerial posts, including those who have held senior government posts before moving to the Lords, such as Lord Carrington and Lord Callaghan. They are taken seriously for their experience and the consideration that they are often viewed as having given their interventions.

Legislation

The assent of the House of Lords is required for Bills, although in certain circumstances its refusal to give assent can be overridden by the Commons. The powers of the House of Lords in relation to the House of Commons are limited by the Parliament Acts of 1911 and 1949. These mean that money bills, dealing with taxation and public expenditure, must start in the Commons and must receive Royal Assent no more than one month after being introduced in the Lords, even if they have not been passed by the Lords. In addition, while the Parliament Acts allow the Lords to hold up a bill for about a year, the bill can be reintroduced into the House of Commons in the following session and then passed without the agreement of the Lords. The Salisbury Convention allows governments without a majority in the Lords to pass their major bills, with the Lords not voting down at second or third reading a government bill that is mentioned in an election manifesto.

One of the features of legislative activity is that an increasing number of government bills are being introduced in the Lords. In the 2003-04 session 11 government bills were introduced in the Lords, including the Children Bill and the Domestic Violence, Crime and Victims Bill. This compares with the 22 bills that went to the Lords from the Commons. The Lords is also important in the scrutiny that it gives to legislation and the opportunities for amendments to be made, both by supporters and opponents of particular proposals. To take the earlier examples, 536 amendments were tabled in the Lords to the Children Bill, of which 83 were made and the government was defeated once, while 340 amendments were tabled to the Domestic Violence, Crime and Victims Bill, of which 108 were made, and the government was defeated on four occasions.

One consequence of the lesser role of parties in the upper House is that the 'usual channels' (the "meetings and discussions between the Leader of the House, the Chief Whip and parliamentary personnel in both the Commons and the Lords to decide how business will be arranged in each House" [Rush and Ettinghausen, 2002, p 6]) are of great importance in the Lords. With the self-regulation of the Lords, the usual channels involve considerable give and take, but there is a general recognition by the main parties that government needs to get its business through the chamber. Although backbenchers and crossbenchers can sometimes resist the usual channels, they are normally unsuccessful in their attempts. Nevertheless, recent years have seen not only the Countess of Mar's successful campaign for the banning of organophosphates, but also six private members' bills reach the statute books (Crewe, 2005), including the 1999 Protection of Children Act, sponsored by Lord Laming in the Lords and Debra Shipley MP in the Commons, which sought to prevent paedophiles working with children.

Scrutiny

There are two principal means of undertaking work in the House of Lords: the system of select committees, which provides some degree of collective scrutiny, and the more individualistic method based on both oral and written questions and answers.

Select committees

Where scrutiny is concerned, like the House of Commons, the Lords has select committees; however, whereas those in the lower chamber are departmental select committees, shadowing the work of particular departments, those in the upper chamber are more generalist and cross-cutting in their coverage. The Lords has had two long-standing committees, one focusing on Science and Technology and the other being the European Union Select Committee, which has seven sub-committees, including Social and Consumer Affairs (set up in January 2004 to improve the scrutiny of EU social policy and consumer affairs), Education and Home Affairs. In recent years these have been augmented by others, such as those on the constitution and on economic affairs. These have been wide-ranging in their work and able to take an approach to issues that cuts across traditional departmental boundaries, as well as drawing on expertise from both inside and outside the House. Some inquiries have attracted considerable attention, such as the report *Complementary and alternative medicine*, which made a number of recommendations about the need for evidence and research, and the training and regulation of practitioners, as well as the delivery of such therapies (Science and Technology Committee, 2000). The EU Select Committee seeks to complement the activity of the Commons European Scrutiny Committee, and rather than looking at all proposals, works by identifying a number of items for in-depth study and analysis, normally focusing on those that raise issues of policy or principle. For example, Sub-Committee G has reported on the Working Time Directive (EU Committee, 2004a) and Sexual Equality in Access to Goods and Services (EU Committee, 2004b).

In addition to these, the Lords also makes use of ad hoc committees that are established from time to time to examine issues that fall outside the remit of the main committees. One notable example was the committee set up to look at stem cell research in 2001-02. This committee made a number of recommendations, with its report being debated in the Lords on 5 December 2002 and receiving a response from the government in July 2002 that accepted many of the recommendations (DH, 2002).

In a new development, since 2001 there has been a Joint Committee on Human Rights, consisting of equal numbers of members from both chambers, which has a fairly wide remit to consider "matters relating to human rights in the United Kingdom (but excluding consideration of individual cases)" and to propose remedial orders under the 1998 Human Rights Act.

Generally, while the departmental select committees in the Commons may be able to undertake in-depth work shadowing government departments, the Lords offers greater flexibility and the opportunity to respond to issues and developments as they emerge. In many respects therefore the select committee systems of the two Houses arguably complement each other and provide a spread of possibilities to scrutinise the work of government.

Questions

In addition to the work of the select committees, like MPs, peers have the opportunity to question the government, using both oral and written questions. Each day oral questions are asked of ministers. These are termed 'starred questions' and take up about 15% of the time of the chamber. Starred questions can be asked on any topic for which the government is responsible and are tabled on a first-come, first-served basis, although each week two 'topical questions' are drawn by ballot. There is a time limit of 30 minutes for the four questions each day, thus allowing much longer for each question than is available in the Commons. Any peer may ask supplementary questions. Six hundred and thirty-four questions were asked in the Lords during the 2003-04 session.

The Hansard Society has argued that, "The topicality and random nature of the questions provide useful lessons for the Commons" (2001, p 71). However, while the range and depth of questioning may be greater in the Lords than in the Commons, the decline in the number of ministers drawn from the House means that there are fewer ministers available to question. While peers are able to question ministers from the Commons in committees (and vice versa), the primary role of questioning ministers remains with the House of Commons.

Peers may also table questions for written answer, in which case the minister responsible will reply in writing to the peer and the answer is published in *Hansard*. A response is given within a fortnight. In addition to providing information, the government also sometimes uses written answers to questions to make an announcement or to publish information. The number of written questions in the Lords has increased dramatically from 72 in 1961-62, to more than 1,000 per session in the late 1980s, and to between 4,000 and 5,000 since 1997 (reaching 5,798 in the admittedly long session of 2001-02).

The Lords also has 'unstarred questions', which are questions for debate, proceedings for which are time limited to one-and-a-half hours. At the end of the debate a minister answers the question and there is no right to reply. There were 46 such 'mini debates' during 2003-04, including on the protection of children, abortion and adolescent health, as well as on select committee reports on illegal immigration and on asylum.

Debates

In addition to the opportunities for debates given by unstarred questions, discussed above, opposition parties and backbenchers are able to initiate debates. The days for debates are allocated by agreement between party whips (Rogers and Walters, 2004), with the bulk of time going to the main opposition parties. There is also some possibility for backbench-initiated debates. In recent sessions up to about 15% of sitting time has been spent debating opposition and backbench motions. During the 2003-04 session these included on aspects of the Queen's

Speech, including pensions, home and social affairs, health and education; cancer registration; development aid and world poverty; special educational needs; Alzheimer's disease and dementia; the social purposes of sentencing; housing supply; alcohol abuse; charitable giving; healthcare and public health. There were also a number of debates on select committee reports, including *The Working Time Directive: A response to the European Commission's review* (EU Committee, 2004a) and *Aspects of the economics of an ageing population* (Economic Affairs Committee, 2003).

It is frequently argued that due to the composition of the Lords, and the existence of groups of peers with particular expertise, debates in the Lords are more informed than in the Commons. When interviewed, one peer observed that in contrast to the Commons where MPs were required to know a little about a great many subjects, peers tended to bring professional expertise and experience to the upper House. Moreover, he argued, peers are more able to maintain their expertise because, unlike MPs, their time is not dominated by the needs of individual constituents. Because they are not required to act like social workers, this peer observed, peers have more time to specialise and more time to "consider and reflect" on issues. Several peers also asserted that because of their recognised expertise peers are more likely to listen to each other, regardless of party loyalty. As in the Commons, those with a specialist knowledge are more likely to be listened to in debate; however, even more so than in the Commons, members of the Lords referred to actively seeking out those with expertise when legislation was being debated in the Lords, rather than looking to the party whips for guidance. Peers referred in particular to the Labour peer Lord Ashley of Stoke, and the crossbench peer, and Secretary-general of Mencap, Lord Rix, as recognised experts in the field of welfare, and Baroness Warwick, in the field of education.

A more legitimate and more assertive House: the reformed House of Lords and the scrutiny of welfare

As outlined above, the House of Lords has played a number of roles, including legislative, deliberative, interrogative and judicial (for example, Rush, 1999). The government's initial proposals for reform (Cabinet Office, 1998) asked whether these were all necessary for the second chamber to properly complement the House of Commons, and concluded that while the first three were all important functions of the Lords there was scope for consideration over the location of judicial authority. The proposals made clear that the removal of hereditary peers would "radically alter the complexion and composition of the House" and that while the upper chamber would be in a transitional stage, "Even so, we are determined to ensure that even in transitional form, the House of Lords is a more modern and fairer chamber" (Cabinet Office, 1998, ch 6, para 1). The White Paper suggested that a reformed second chamber should be able to offer a distinctive and informed view on the issues that come before it and should have the legitimacy to ensure that its recommendations for improvements to legislation are valued; should retain its scrutiny function; and should retain direct access to ministers as part of its interrogative role.

The removal of the bulk of the hereditary peers has arguably served to increase and intensify debate over the role and functions of the upper House. The continued importance of the House of Lords can be demonstrated in a number of ways: government and the opposition parties have continued to pay close attention to the reform of the House of Lords (for example, the publication of *Constitutional reform: Next steps for the House of Lords* [DCA, 2003]); the proposals for the creation of a Supreme Court; and continued defeats for the government in votes in the House of Lords (56 in 2001-02, 88 in 2002-03, 64 in 2003-04 and 37 in 2004-05), including not only amendments to high profile issues such as foundation hospitals and tuition fees for higher education, but also over a wide range of other topics, including many social policy-related issues, such as the age of consent for gay men, the abolition of community health councils and reform of private pensions.

Given these developments, Russell (2003) has argued that the House of Lords has already made the transition to a more effective and powerful body, having what she suggests are three essential features that contribute to the effective functioning of a second chamber: adequate powers, distinct composition and perceived legitimacy. She suggests that the removal of the bulk of the hereditary peers has already enhanced the legitimacy of the Lords, as well as changing the party balance in the chamber. She notes that during the 2001-02 parliamentary session the government was defeated on 56 votes in the Lords, compared with 36 in 1997-98, suggesting that this may be because the "chamber's belief in its own legitimacy is already making it more assertive" (Russell, 2003, p 316). In addition, Russell and Sciara's (2006a) research has shown that around 40% of defeats for the government in the upper House have not been overturned, giving the chamber potentially a significant impact on legislation and thus on policy.

However, while there has been a growth in scholarship about the reform and role of the House of Lords, little of it has yet focused on specific policy areas. Welfare is clearly a major area of government activity and expenditure, involving considerable amounts of new primary and secondary legislation and scrutiny of a number of government departments. It is also an area where there is a significant degree of lobbying within parliament by pressure groups and professional lobbyists, and a field where there are a considerable number of all-party parliamentary groups in existence, consisting of both MPs and peers. Here therefore is an initial consideration of the formal and informal mechanisms and workings of the Lords in relation to welfare during its period of 'transition'.

The literature around the government's reform proposals does indicate a number of areas that suggest potentially important topics and developments relating to the work of the House of Lords, a number of which are of relevance to the chamber's roles with regard to social policy:

• the existence of specialised abilities, experience and expertise, and individuals of personal distinction (Archer, 1999; Rush, 1999; Wakeham, 2000a; Joint Committee on House of Lords Reform, 2002) such as doctors, academics, lawyers and those from the voluntary sector; Wakeham (2000b), for example, sees this as a source of authority for a reformed second chamber; Russell (2003) sees the "distinct composition" (2003, p 314) as a key feature; this aspect also raises interesting questions about the balance of interests and expertise in the House of Lords across subject specialisms, including, for example, the practical and ethical dimensions of social policy, and state provision against private or not-for-profit provision);
• perceived legitimacy (Joint Committee on House of Lords Reform, 2002; Russell, 2003) and authority to exercise its powers effectively (Wakeham, 2000b); clearly the House of Lords, lacking democratic legitimacy, is dependent on other sources of power, including, as outlined above, the expertise and experience of its members, and to some extent that of the 'communities' from which they come;
• scrutinising work, such as the questioning of ministers, and the work of the select committees, as noted above, including the Select Committee on Science and Technology, which has included investigations into areas such as ageing (Archer, 1999; Baldwin, 1999; Rush, 1999; Joint Committee on House of Lords Reform, 2002);
• amending legislation (Baldwin, 1999; Rush, 1999; Joint Committee on House of Lords Reform, 2002), including, as noted earlier, both government and opposition amendments;

- pre-legislative scrutiny (Wakeham, 2000a; Joint Committee on House of Lords Reform, 2002), with Norton (2005) observing that since 1997 the government has been publishing more bills at the draft stage, allowing for a growth in this activity, and consequently giving both chambers, and through them other interests, greater capacity and scope to influence the contents of legislation. For example, during the 2002-03 session the Draft Mental Incapacity Bill was considered by a joint committee of the two Houses and the Draft Gender Recognition Bill by the Joint Committee on Human Rights;
- the House's primary role in the examination of European and delegated legislation (Archer, 1999; Baldwin, 1999; Bogdanor, 1999; Rush, 1999; Wakeham, 2000a; Russell and Cornes, 2001) including the work of the EU Social Policy and Consumer Affairs Sub-committee);
- scrutiny over constitutional change, including the Constitution Committee (Archer, 1999; Baldwin, 1999; Russell and Cornes, 2001);
- self-regulation, and the importance of the 'usual channels' in ensuring that business proceeds (Baldwin, 1999; Wheeler-Booth, 2001).

While it is perhaps too early, and as yet little research has been done, to examine precisely how far these have an impact, they do provide useful guidance to the potential operation, roles and influence of the reformed House of Lords.

Challenging the government

While some critics argued that through its reforms of the House of Lords and the removal of the hereditary peers the New Labour government was weakening one of the few remaining checks on its power, in reality this does not appear to have been the outcome. Tables 6.1 and 6.2, which depict government legislation introduced into both chambers during 2003-04, demonstrate the scale of activity in the Lords with respect to legislation, including on social and welfare issues, with substantial numbers of amendments being tabled and made in the upper chamber, and with a number of significant government defeats, including those on the Higher Education Bill. In addition, of the 12 private members' bills introduced in the House of Lords during 2003-04, three could be seen to be in the broad area of social policy: the Assisted Dying for the Terminally Ill Bill, the Smoking in Public Places (Wales) Bill and the Tobacco Smoking (Public Places and

Table 6.1: Government bills brought from the House of Commons (2003-04)

Title	Amendments tabled	Amendments made	Government defeats
Age-related Payments	0	0	0
Armed Forces (Pensions and Compensation)	62	4	2
Asylum and Immigration (Treatment of Claimants, etc)	291	99	2
Child Trust Funds	119	13	0
Civil Contingencies	309	59	3
Consolidated Fund	0	0	0
Consolidated Fund (No 2)	0	0	0
Consolidated Fund (Appropriation)	0	0	0
Employment Relations	192	91	0
European Parliamentary and Local Elections (Pilots)	116	51	2
Finance	0	0	0
Fire and Rescue Services	281	24	0
Higher Education	220	31	4
Horserace Betting and Olympic Lottery	150	4	0
Housing	871	330	2
Human Tissue	250	77	1
Hunting	123	56	0
National Insurance Contributions and Statutory Payments	4	0	0
Pensions	1,408	684	6
Planning and Compulsory Purchase	703	159	9
Scottish Parliament (Constituencies)	32	0	0
Traffic Management	388	113	1

Source: House of Lords Information Office (2005)

Workplaces) Bill. An alternative view of the House would be that while the pre-reform Lords, perhaps in part due to a consciousness that their legitimacy was limited, frequently pulled back from conflicts with the government, the reformed House became more assertive. As Cowley (2005) notes, the number of government defeats in the Lords more than doubled, increasing from 108 during the 1999-2001 parliament to 245 in the 2001-05 parliament.

It is certainly true to say that historically Labour governments have suffered more defeats in votes in the House of Lords than have Conservative governments. House of Lords figures show that the 1974-79 Labour governments suffered an average of 60 defeats per parliamentary session (1974-75 figures not available), far higher than the Conservative governments of 1979-83 (11 defeats per session),

Table 6.2: Government bills introduced in the House of Lords (2003-04)

Title	Amendments tabled	Amendments made	Government defeats
Children	536	83	1
Civil Partnership	541	206	1
Companies (Audit, Investigations and Community Enterprise)	269	67	0
Constitutional Reform	814	523	1
Domestic Violence, Crime and Victims	340	108	4
Energy	696	252	11
Gender Recognition	262	16	0
Health Protection Agency	117	50	0
Justice (Northern Ireland)	111	42	1
Patents	44	16	0
Public Audit (Wales)	115	32	0

Source: House of Lords Information Office (2005)

1983-87 (16 defeats per session), 1987-92 (14 defeats per session) and 1992-97 (12 defeats per session). The 1997-2001 Labour government saw defeats rise to an average of 27 per session. Given the inbuilt Conservative majority in the House of Lords until 1999 it is unsurprising that Labour governments should have suffered more at the hands of the upper chamber; indeed, the fact that the Conservative governments suffered significant numbers of defeats is perhaps of interest in itself. However, of greater relevance for current purposes is that following the removal of the hereditary peers there was an increase in defeats for the Labour governments: 56 defeats in 2001-02, 88 in 2002-03 and 64 in 2003-04. Indeed, this could have been significantly higher if it had not been for a higher proportion of Conservative than Labour peers not voting in divisions (for example, Russell and Sciara, 2006a).

In 2002-03 among the significant defeats for the government in the House of Lords were those on plans to remove trial by jury and proposals to introduce foundation hospitals. With the Lords reluctant to back down, the government was forced to arrange for the Commons to sit later into the session and although the Lords did eventually give way on foundation hospitals the government did make concessions on trial by jury (Cowley and Stuart, 2004). During that session the

Lords defeated the government 22 times on the Criminal Justice Bill, 10 times on the Health and Social Care (Community Health and Standards) Bill, 7 times on the Community Care (Delayed Discharges, etc) Bill, and 3 times on the Sexual Offences Bill (Cowley and Stuart, 2004).

There are a number of potential explanations for this apparently greater willingness of the House to challenge the government. Firstly, although Labour increased its membership of the House of Lords, becoming the largest party in the chamber for the first time in 2005, the government continued to lack a majority in the Lords. Secondly, as noted above, the reformed chamber may have felt less constrained with the removal of the bulk of the hereditary peers. As Russell and Sciara (2006b) have observed, the words of Baroness Jay, the leader of the House at the time of reform, that the new chamber would be "far more legitimate" (p 5), are now frequently cited by peers as justification for their actions, and have even been dubbed the 'Jay doctrine'. It may also be the case that the nature of the legislation put forward has been more open to challenge, either because it was more controversial or because there had been less discussion before it was introduced to parliament. Finally, it has been suggested that the increased level of dissent in the House of Commons (Cowley, 2005), either on its own or in combination with the other explanations, has contributed to the willingness of the Lords to challenge the government. For example, Cowley (2002) notes that following backbench concerns in the House of Commons and a defeat in the Lords on 20 January 2000 on an amendment that effectively negated the aims of the Criminal Justice (Mode of Trial) Bill, the government strengthened the safeguards in the Bill, including the right of appeal to a High Court judge against a magistrates' decision. Despite some further concessions there still remained dissent among Labour MPs and when the revised Criminal Justice (Mode of Trial) (No 2) Bill went to the Lords for its second reading it was again defeated. Similarly, over foundation hospitals, two backbench Labour MPs circulated a memorandum to Labour and crossbench peers arguing that the convention that the House of Lords does not defy the will of the elected House of Commons did not apply in this instance, pointing out that the proposals had not been in the 2001 General Election manifesto; peers voted by 150 to 100 to defeat the government and to set up "another battle between Labour rebels and the government when the Bill returned to the House of Commons on 19 November" (Cowley, 2005, p 152).

Indeed, the government's problems with the Lords have also reinforced their problems with some of the Labour rebels in the House of Commons. Cowley (2005) suggests not only that the House of Lords has been becoming more obstructive, but also that "the tendency for controversial Bills to ping-pong between Commons and Lords provides yet more opportunities for backbenchers to stick their oar in" (Cowley, 2005, pp 12-13). The government's difficulties in each chamber were therefore reinforcing each other, as both the House of Commons and the House of Lords came to seek concessions on some pieces of legislation. Moreover, with the government lacking a majority in the Lords it was tempting for it to make concessions there, as it could generally rely on a majority in the Commons. However, Cowley suggests that this strategy has led to larger rebellions in the Commons where some backbench Labour MPs have been unhappy to vote for a Bill that they knew would be changed in the Lords, as was the case with the Mental Capacity Bill (Cowley, 2005, p 231), and the Asylum and Immigration (Treatment of Claimants) Bill, about which the Independent MP Richard Taylor observed:

> The Government refuse to consider logical or reasonable amendments before a Bill goes to the House of Lords in order to leave themselves bargaining space for Lords amendments. That is like a second-hand car salesman who sets a high asking price that he can later reduce, and Labour members clearly alluded to such conduct in that debate. (*Hansard*, 9 March 2004, col 1476)

There is also evidence to suggest that MPs have begun to take a different view about how the House of Lords is operating in its 'transitional period'. For example, while many of the MPs interviewed for this research were, in principle, unicameralists, many supported a role for the Lords and there was a view among some that in its 'transitional' state the role and operations of the Lords have changed and that in some respects its importance has increased. Consequently, MPs made statements such as:"If I want to change legislation I go to the Lords.... If I wanted to lobby on something I would lobby the Lords, that is where the power is..." (Conservative), and "Scrutiny in the Lords is more informed, leisurely, and thorough, and in a number of areas it is more effective than the Commons" (Labour).

Yet in terms of outright rebellion by Labour peers, internal dissent in the House of Lords has generally been relatively small scale, particularly compared to the Commons, with Russell and Sciara (2006a) noting that on only 13 occasions between 1999 and 2005 did more than 10 Labour peers rebel, and on six of those, although the votes were whipped, there was arguably a 'conscience' dimension, such as over the repeal of Section 28 (of the Local Government Act 1988) and the proposal to allow unmarried couples to adopt children. Although rebellions by Labour members contributed to over 100 defeats, in relatively few instances were the rebellions alone enough to make the difference, as Conservative, Liberal Democrats and crossbenchers had sufficient numbers to defeat the government. A further complicating factor is again the role of the crossbenchers, as they do not vote cohesively, with Russell and Sciara (2006a) pointing out that over the period between 1999 and 2005 around one third of crossbench votes were cast in support of the government, while at the same time low levels of turnout among the crossbenchers serves to dilute their potential influence.

Given their political position and the lack of a majority for either Conservative or Labour parties in the House of Lords, the Liberal Democrats are clearly in a position to play an important pivotal role (much more so than the crossbench peers who, although greater in number, as already noted, are both less likely to attend and who do not vote as a group). In the period following the 1997 General Election the Liberal Democrats frequently voted with the government, supporting it on divisions that were called by the Conservatives, but over time this situation changed and the Liberal Democrats have increasingly opposed the government (for example, Russell and Sciara, 2006a). While some of this change undoubtedly reflects the declining relationship between Labour and Liberal Democratic Parties from the relatively warm position in 1997 it may also be due to the changed composition of the Lords, with the Conservatives now requiring Liberal Democrat support to defeat the government.

However, although there are difficulties in defining exactly what counts as a final 'defeat' or 'victory' for the government, a preliminary analysis by Russell and Sciara (2006a) suggests that in reality a relatively high proportion (around 37%) of defeats in the House of Lords were not overturned by the government, although around 60% of defeats in divisions did see them successfully reverse the changes. They use examples such as the 2002 Adoption and Children Bill, where a Lords defeat for the government ensured that a child has legal representation during the adoption process, and the Higher Education Bill (2004), where another defeat meant that students who were offered university places for 2005 but who did not take these up until 2006 were not charged the new fees, to illustrate that such defeats can result in policy change.

Finally, while perhaps inevitably the greatest attention is generally paid to overt conflict, either between the government and the House of Lords or the House of Commons and the House of Lords (which may indeed often be the same thing), it is important to note that as with internal party opposition in the lower House, peers generally seek to influence the government without recourse to attempts to inflict defeat in the division lobbies. There are many attempts to persuade governments to reconsider proposals both during policy formulation and at early stages of legislation (including, for example, tabling amendments but not moving to a vote if the government undertakes to review its position), and where these are viewed as successful, or where ministers respond with a winning argument, there is unlikely to be a defeat for the government. The process of taking legislation through the House of Lords therefore frequently results in government concessions (Shell, 1992) without the need to proceed to a vote. In addition, because attendance and voting rates among peers is so much lower than for MPs, it is not possible to tell whether absence represents dissent or is for other reasons. It is therefore important to be aware that the influence of the Lords on policy and legislation is therefore likely to be significantly greater than it appears if simply measured in terms of defeats in the chamber.

Lobbying by outside interests

It is not just the apparently greater interaction between 'rebels' in the House of Commons and peers that appears to be increasing. While the House of Lords has always been subject to lobbying by particular groups, anecdotal evidence suggests that this has increased markedly in recent years. This is partly because of the increase in the number of groups and the availability of new means of communication (and email in particular). Norton (2005) points out that the volume of post entering the House of Lords in 2003 amounted to more than 3,500 items per peer, not including emails. Another development has been the growth of professional lobbyists, either from consultancies or in some cases from in-house organisations. Like pressure groups, these have been active in the House of Commons for many years, but anecdotal evidence suggests that there has been some increase in lobbying of the Lords in recent years, including both general lobbying and individual peers who are targeted according to their personal interests, for example by groups representing disabled people, those campaigning on pensions and medical groups. One peer reported that of the average of around 20 letters that she received per day, typically about eight or nine are lobbying in nature.

Another explanation for increased lobbying of the Lords is a growing perception that the upper House has become more assertive and influential and consequently interested groups have become more aware of the possibilities of lobbying the upper chamber. Several peers interviewed for this research suggested that this is an explanation for the increase in lobbying of the Lords, and pointed in particular to the growth in professional targeted lobbying of peers as evidence of a growing awareness that changes to legislation could more effectively be pursued in the House of Lords.

As with MPs, peers are likely to find the bulk of material provided by groups and lobbyists of little use. However, some of it is undoubtedly useful in providing information, independent of that provided by both the government and by the parties. One peer with a particular interest in welfare issues claimed that in the absence of the wealth of information provided to MPs through constituency casework, peers may "rely a lot" on material provided by outside interest groups in order to maintain their expertise. Similarly, a crossbench peer observed that in the absence of a party organisation, the crossbenchers in particular rely on material coming in from individuals and outside groups. This material can therefore assist peers in their scrutiny role, with both individual members and select committees potentially being better informed and more able to question and challenge government. As Norton (2005) notes, in terms of amending legislation the provision of good quality information can be of benefit to members of both houses, and in particular:

> The House of Lords offers particular scope to pursue amendments. Government is less in control of proceedings – and the outcome of votes – in the Lords than in the Commons, and peers with a particular knowledge of a subject can pursue it in order to elicit a response from the government. The capacity of members to have a significant impact on the legislative process remains limited, but the link with outside groups ensures that it is not quite so limited as it once was. (Norton, 2005, p 207)

Among those peers interviewed for this research the most frequent reference to lobbying was in relation to the Mental Capacity Bill. This Bill, introduced as the Mental Incapacity Bill in June 2003, had its origins in a Law Commission report on mental incapacity in 1995 and followed several years of consultation intended to clarify the position of people who were deemed to 'lack capacity'. The Bill was examined by a joint scrutiny committee of both Houses in the summer of 2003. In addition to the evidence presented to the committee, the Bill was the subject of extensive lobbying of both Houses of parliament by a wide range of organisations, one of the outcomes of which was that a renamed Mental Capacity Bill was introduced to parliament in June 2004 and finally received the Royal Assent on 7 April 2005.

However, Norton (2005) also notes, "Equally remarkable is the number of groups who fail to recognise and exploit the value of the House of Lords in influencing legislation" (p 209). This point was also made by a number of peers in interviews, several of whom took the opportunity to call for more lobbying of the upper House. One peer in particular noted that there was relatively little organised lobbying of individual peers, and in particular that lobbying groups appeared to lose interest in MPs as soon as they moved to the upper House. However, it is also apparent that one of the reasons that lobbying is more effective in the Lords is that there is less of it, with peers feeling less overwhelmed and consequently, more inclined to read it than MPs. The generally positive attitude of peers to lobbying, particularly compared to MPs, may be a direct result of the less intensive lobbying of the Lords; consequently one may be inclined to caution members of the upper House to be careful what they wish for.

Conclusions

It seems likely that the House of Lords is playing a greater role in relation to welfare policy than it has done for some time. Although the Conservative governments of the 1980s and 1990s did suffer a considerable number of defeats in the Lords, the changes to the upper House in recent years have led to a more active chamber, and peers from specialist backgrounds have been willing to contribute to debates on which they have particular knowledge. The lack of electoral pressure may also sometimes make it easier for peers to speak out on controversial issues.

Following the arguments about the impact of the reforms outlined in this chapter it is apparent that peers continue to believe that the specialised abilities and experience of individual members allows for more informed debate than they perceive exists in the House of Commons. In addition, the creation of new peers, including those emerging from the House of Lords Appointment Commission, arguably reflects and supports the arguments that peers bring specialisms to the House, including a number of newly created peers who have significant backgrounds relevant to social policy. Nevertheless, it is also the case that relatively small numbers of peers are likely to have backgrounds in this field, and that given that little is known about their beliefs and attitudes it is difficult to make a judgement about their ability to undertake the scrutiny and influencing of welfare policy. The majority of party peers are therefore, like the counterparts in the House of Commons, to take the lead from their parties on the great majority of issues. Similarly, the scrutiny activity of the House of Lords' select committees is different in nature from that undertaken in the House of Commons, and while there is perhaps greater opportunity for reports on issues that cut across the work of several government departments, conversely there is less prospect for detailed scrutiny of the work of major departments such as the Department of Health, Department for Education and Skills and the Department for Work and Pensions.

Where the reforms do appear to have had a significant impact is in the upper House's willingness to challenge the government and to ensure that both the government and the House of Commons take it seriously. The House continues to play an important role in amending legislation, both through the government's own amendments and through attempts by others to introduce amendments. Given that in the past the comparative lack of influence of the House of Lords has been self-imposed and depended "at least as much upon its lack of legitimacy as upon the statutory restrictions on its powers" (Bogdanor, 1999, p 376), it is perhaps not surprising that the reforms to its composition may have affected peers' views of their own status in relation to the House of Commons. The number of defeats for the government has increased since the reforms, although the precise reasons for this remain debatable. Similarly, the government has made a number of concessions on major pieces of legislation, although again it is difficult to apportion the reasons for this to the House of Lords (including through a greater sense of legitimacy arising from the removal of the bulk of the hereditary peers), to 'rebel' MPs in the House of Commons, or indeed to the impact of interested parties in both chambers working together to exercise influence. The extent to which the Salisbury Convention continues to be accepted will be a major consideration for future governments.

Moreover, the 'hung' nature of the upper House has implications for future governments, as they too will be unlikely to be able to be sure of getting their legislation through the Lords as combinations of other parties and crossbenchers will continue to be able to inflict defeats, while even the threat of this may be sufficient in some cases to ensure that legislation is amended.

There is some evidence that some members of the House of Commons have become more aware of the potential for influencing government through the House of Lords, and MPs and peers have worked together to influence legislation. In the same vein, the media and pressure groups also appear to have begun to view the Lords as a legitimate instrument through which to influence policy, so that the level of lobbying of the upper chamber appears to have grown significantly, by both professional lobbyists and by organised interests, with welfare issues being one of the major areas of growth. Cowley (2002) wrote that "… Labour backbenchers were often not the only people pressurising the Government. When change came about, therefore, it was not solely because of the actions of backbench MPs. This was perhaps most clear in the case of pensions up-rating but it was also true in other cases as well. The role of the House of Lords was, for example, crucial in gaining a number of the concessions achieved. And pressure on the Government over issues such as incapacity benefit was strengthened by the lobbying of outside groups, especially those normally sympathetic to Labour" (Cowley, 2002, p 231). As noted earlier in the chapter, peers interviewed for this research gave both the Mental Capacity Bill and the Pensions Bill as examples of this increased lobbying. One peer also noted that this may have arisen in part because the rules governing the House of Lords are less rigorous and more open to interpretation than those applying to the House of Commons. The power of the media may be likely to be more limited due to the lack of electoral accountability of peers. However, there may be some degree of 'sectoral representation' in the upper chamber, with some peers feeling some allegiance to the specialist 'constituency' that they come from.

It is also the case that the House of Lords in recent years has provided a forum for debate on issues that governments and parties are unwilling to address, as has been the case over issues such as euthanasia (Lord Joffe's Patient [Assisted Dying] Bill in 2003 and Assisted Dying for the Terminally Ill Bill in 2004), and stem cell research. In addition to the 'normal' relationships with outside interests, the House of Lords therefore contributes to parliament's role a channel for communication to government on what may be difficult moral issues.

The responses of peers interviewed for the research largely reflected those of their counterparts in the Commons. There was a strong view that the Lords is increasingly "where politics is happening", in part because of the large Labour majority in the House of Commons, in part because of the alteration in political balance and to some extent attitude in the Lords following the removal of the hereditary peers, and in part reflecting increased lobbying of the House. However, it is perhaps worth noting the words of one peer, that it is "influence not power that has increased over recent years".

SEVEN

'Exercising influence and setting limits': MPs' influence on welfare policy

The preceding chapters have included discussion of the wide range of views expressed by MPs on the role of government in welfare and on specific aspects of welfare policy (Chapter Four), and the extent to which MPs are influenced by public experiences of state welfare provision (Chapter Five). Some of these views, even among Labour MPs, are clearly at some variance with government policy. However, the extent to which MPs are able to communicate to the government their own concerns and those of the individuals and groups they represent is not clear. As discussed in Chapter Three, recent years have seen renewed claims that the power of parliament is in decline, particularly in relation to the executive, and that backbench MPs have little opportunity to influence policy. At the same time, a wealth of literature has focused on the one most obvious means by which MPs may seek to influence the government, by voting against legislation in the division lobbies. As discussed in Chapter Three, the Blair governments have certainly experienced some difficulties in seeking to pass parts of their welfare legislation due to rebellions by Labour MPs. However, overt rebellion in votes in the House of Commons (as discussed in Chapter Three), or the House of Lords (as discussed in Chapter Six), is only one means of seeking to influence the government, and arguably is often only resorted to when other attempts to persuade the government have failed.

It is also important to recognise that there are many other factors influencing government policy, including pressures from the party more generally (and indeed the opposition parties), public opinion, the media, pressure groups, the civil service, public expenditure limits and other policy and economic pressures. Parliament, and indeed the House of Commons, is therefore only one among many potential influences, although its place in the policy arena does provide it with certain advantages (and also limitations). When interviewed for this research MPs from all parties identified a number of means of influencing welfare policy (Table 7.1). This chapter therefore examines

Table 7.1: How can MPs influence or set limits on what government does? (% of valid responses by party)

	Labour	Conservative	Lib Dem	SNP/Plaid/Ind	Total
Through select committees	33	25	62	20	35
Voting/threatening to vote against the government	39	25	31	20	32
Informal means/personal contact with ministers	45	10	15	20	28
Through the House of Lords	6	25	31	20	17
By coalescing in interest groups to raise issues	27	5	8	0	15
Through parliamentary questions/debate	12	20	31	20	18
Persistent single issue campaigning	12	20	8	20	14
Stimulate debate beyond Westminster/in the media	3	10	15	20	8
Through party machinery eg NEC, backbench committees	9	5	0	0	6
Through APGs	9	5	0	0	6
Through devolved assemblies	0	0	8	20	3
Adjournment debates	0	5	8	0	3
Private members' bills	0	5	0	0	1
EDMs	3	0	0	0	1
Backbench MPs have little/no real influence	18	20	15	40	20
Number	33	20	13	5	71

Note: Lib Dem: Liberal Democrat, SNP: Scottish National Party, Plaid: Plaid Cymru, Ind: Independent, NEC: National Executive Committee, APGs: all-party groups, EDMs: early day motions.

the variety of methods used by MPs in their efforts to scrutinise and influence government policy, focusing on the wide range of procedures and practices within parliament that are available for and used by MPs and peers (see also Chapter Six), and the extent to which MPs consider these to be effective in enabling them to provide effective oversight of, and influence over, welfare policy, including reflecting both their views and the views of those who they represent.

Legislation

As has been discussed in greater detail in Chapter Three, involvement in the scrutiny and passage of legislation is one of the best known roles for MPs, and, like parliamentary questions, generally takes place within the Commons chamber. One of the changes since 1997 is that more bills are now published at the draft stage, thus affording MPs and others some greater opportunity to influence them. It is, however, at a bill's second reading that MPs normally get the opportunity for a full debate on the principle of the measure. For example, on the second reading of the 2006 Education and Inspection Bill, which the government won with Conservative support (see Chapter Three), the Conservative MP David Gaucke, who voted with the government on this occasion, was able to argue:

> A few weeks ago in the White Paper, the Government's position was that there should be no new community schools. Under intense pressure from their Back Benchers, they now say that there can be new community schools subject to a veto. When the pressure dissipates after the Bill is passed, what is to stop the Secretary of State, or indeed any of her successors, changing her mind, going back to the White Paper position and vetoing any new proposals for community schools? Some of us think that that would be a very good idea. Will the Government go back to where they were with the White Paper? (*Hansard*, 15 March 2006, col 1466)

while the Labour MP Helen Jones, who, together with 29 other Labour backbenchers, voted against the government, said:

> There is much in this Bill that is sensible and well thought out and builds on the Government's excellent progress in education. But I deeply regret that I cannot support the Government's proposals for trust schools because I believe them to be wrong in principle and flawed in practice. Moreover, I believe that far from improving education for the most disadvantaged children, they will in fact disadvantage them further. (*Hansard*, 15 March 2006, cols 1539-40)

However, it is rare for a government bill to suffer a defeat at this stage, although concessions and changes may be made, as, for example, happened prior to the second reading with the Education and Inspection Bill, and the Higher Education Bill in 2004 (see also Chapter Three). Following the second reading a bill proceeds to the committee stage, which is normally taken by a standing committee, although very simple and uncontroversial or very important bills with constitutional implications may be taken by a standing committee of the whole House, while it is also now possible for bills to be referred to a select committee or to a special standing committee.

It is at the committee stage that a bill is considered in detail, and amendments may be proposed either by the government, for example to improve or tidy up the measure, or by government or opposition MPs. MPs often have extensive communication and consultation with outside interests, such as pressure groups, which may seek to encourage MPs to introduce amendments. Where the government has a majority in the House of Commons it has a commensurate majority on committees, and it is therefore normal for a government's own amendments to be passed, although it may also sometimes accept amendments proposed by backbenchers or even the opposition. The committee stage is often seen as important in improving legislation, for example through leading to better implementation, or highlighting and dealing with possible problems, as well as allowing for input from outside interests.

The committee stage is followed by the report stage, with the amended bill returning to the House of Commons, and further amendments may be considered before the bill passes to its third reading. Following the third reading the bill moves to the House of Lords.

In general MPs were sceptical about the ability of parliament to make changes to legislation through scrutiny in the chamber. MPs from all parties referred to the size of the government's majority allowing them to force through legislation without the need to make concessions. There was also criticism of the government's use of timetabling, which, it was claimed, had truncated debate, allowed amendments to fall at the report stage due to lack of time, and allowed bills to be sent to the upper House without consideration of all clauses. This was echoed in interviews with peers, several of whom referred to the increasingly poor quality of the bills they were called on to revise. Although one Conservative MP observed that the government was "continually" amending legislation at the committee stage, MPs were largely sceptical about the work of standing committees, arguing that the government often retained controversial aspects of legislation to which they were not committed, to allow them room for manoeuvre later. The Labour MP Tony Wright has described his experiences as a member of the standing committee considering the 1993 Education Act, when members of the government party on that bill spent their committee time writing their Christmas cards (Wright, 1997). Interviews with MPs suggest that the situation has been little better under the present government. One MP interviewed for this research observed that:

"When the government had a majority of 160, standing committees were a laugh. There was always a huge government majority and on the ones I was on there was always a government whip there, so the chance of getting an amendment through were nil."

Faced with a lack of opportunities to influence legislation as it passes through the House, a significant proportion of Labour MPs interviewed as part of this research identified voting against the government, or threatening to vote against the government, as an important means of influencing policy. As discussed in Chapter Three, voting in divisions on government legislation is one of the key activities of MPs, and by its nature is one which is both highly visible and measurable. A frequent criticism of MPs is that they are effectively 'lobby fodder', trooping through the division lobbies at the behest of the party whips, and there is a fairly widespread assumption that MPs have become more obedient in recent years. However, as writers such as Norton (1975, 1980) and Cowley (2002, 2005) have shown, both of these views are inaccurate. In reality backbench discipline was probably at its tightest during the 1950s and early 1960s, with the level of cohesion falling from the late 1960s and through the 1970s. Indeed, arguably the highest level of rebellion, in the postwar years, was during the 2001-05 Labour government, with over 250 revolts by Labour MPs, frequently on welfare issues (such as foundation hospitals and university tuition fees). That Labour survived from 1997 to 2005 without a defeat on a whipped vote was due to the very large majority in the House of Commons, and the government making concessions on legislation to stave off potential defeat (Cowley, 2006; see also Chapter Three).

Seeking to exert influence in the division lobbies was identified by MPs from all parties as the only way of influencing a government that enjoyed the size of majorities that Labour held from 1997-2005. As one Labour MP, who is not a frequent rebel, observed, "when facing a big majority like this, getting together with other MPs to rebel may be the only option". Not surprisingly voting against the government as a means of exerting influence was identified predominantly by Labour MPs, 39% of whom mentioned it. Although large, this figure is not surprising when one considers that 54% of the parliamentary Labour Party rebelled against the government at least once in the 2001-05 parliament. Moreover, just as the ranks of Labour rebels include MPs from across the party and not just the 'usual suspects' fêted by the media, those Labour MPs who expressed their notional willingness to vote against the government during this research represented a broad cross-section of the parliamentary Labour Party including MPs interviewed shortly after their first election to parliament in 2005. However, it remains to be seen how many of the newly elected Labour MPs who, having boldly declared their willingness to vote against the government if the issue merits, will do so in practice, and some long-serving Labour MPs were predictably critical of the career-minded younger MPs.

Several Labour MPs provided positive examples of the influence exerted by rebellions. Most notably, the increase in Child Benefit, following the rebellion over cuts to Lone Parent Benefit, the reintroduction of grants following the rebellion over tuition fees, and the increase in non-means-tested benefits that followed the rebellion over reform of Incapacity Benefit. Moreover, some Labour MPs also argued that their willingness to rebel also had an impact on future policy considerations. As one Labour MP observed, the rebellion over Incapacity Benefit in 1999 ensured that the government would not raise the issue again in the run-up to the 2005 General Election.

For opposition MPs, of course, voting against the government is an everyday event but not one that many considered to be an effective means of influence when facing a government with a large majority. Several Conservative MPs, who had experienced the tiny majorities of the Major government, expressed their hope or indeed expectation that it would be "different" after the 2005 General Election, while some MPs interviewed after that election suggested that the government would now be forced to take more notice of parliament. Opposition MPs also recognised that rebellion against the leadership was only an effective tool for MPs whose party is in government. Several noted that when in opposition, voting against the frontbench was potentially much more damaging by presenting an image of a divided party. Given the size of Labour's majority, it was observed, they could afford to accommodate rebellion to an extent that among the opposition parties would fatally damage the leadership and their election prospects. However, the relatively large number of opposition MPs who identified rebellion as an effective means of influencing government policy does suggest that they have learnt from observing the extent or frequency of rebellions by Labour MPs and now see rebellion as an effective and legitimate means of influencing the government, which may in turn create problems when these parties come to form a government.

Private members' bills

Backbench MPs are also able to initiate legislation themselves through private members' bills. While there are a variety of procedures by which these can be introduced, the only method that provides any realistic chance of success is the annual ballot under which a small number of backbenchers (usually around half a dozen) can introduce bills with some hope of them completing their passage, on a number of Friday sittings that are set aside for such measures. However, private members' bills suffer a number of difficulties: they are not supposed to entail the expenditure of public money, they face major time constraints, they are unlikely to progress if the government is opposed to them, and even if the government does not oppose a measure, a bill that arouses strong negative feelings among even a minority of MPs can often be blocked. Private members' bills have also been used in relation to welfare, both to display concerns over issues and to introduce bills with a real chance of passing (see, for example, Bochel, 1992). Since 1997, successful measures have included the 1999 Protection of Children Act, introduced by the Labour MP Debra Shipley, the 2000 Health Service Commissioners Amendment Act, introduced by the Conservative MP Sir Geoffrey Johnson Smith, the 2003 Female Genital Mutilation Act, introduced by the Labour MP Ann Clwyd, and the 2004 Carers (Equal Opportunities) Act, introduced by the Labour MP Hywel Francis. Over the years, private members' legislation has been widely used on social issues and those with a strong moral dimension, such as abortion, capital punishment, divorce, homosexuality and restrictions on cigarette advertising. Such issues often cut across party lines and it therefore suits both government and opposition parties to leave such measures to private members' legislation and a free vote.

Debates

In addition to legislation and government-sponsored debates, the opposition parties are allocated 'opposition days' that are generally used to debate issues on which the opposition believes that the government might be vulnerable or embarrassed, or to highlight their own policies. These days can, if the opposition wishes, be split in two in order to allow two topics to be debated. In recent years welfare issues have regularly formed the focus for more than one third of these debates, including, for example, during the 2005-06 session 'the need for the government to appoint a turnaround team to the

Department of Health', welfare reform and Incapacity Benefit, dentistry and cancer services, and during the 2003-04 session NHS performance indicators (Conservatives), protection of vulnerable children (Conservatives), pensions policy (Conservatives), higher education (Liberal Democrats) and older women (Liberal Democrats). The smaller parties have also used this time to raise social policy topics, such as the future of education in Northern Ireland (Ulster Unionists) and policing in Northern Ireland (Democratic Unionists) during 2002-03. In addition the more general topics sometimes chosen, such as 'value for taxpayers' money' and 'Council Tax' (both chosen by the Conservatives from the 2004-05 session) frequently draw on debates relevant to social policy. The debates are normally led by the relevant frontbenchers from the parties, and following the debate there is a vote that is usually a strongly-worded attack on the government's policies on the issue, to which the government tables an amendment that instead endorses warmly their approach (Rogers and Walters, 2004).

Since 2000, backbench MPs have also been able to raise issues for short debates in Westminster Hall, by submitting their names to the Speaker and being chosen through a ballot. Following a speech by the member initiating the debate, and contributions from other MPs, a minister replies. These debates are widely used to raise issues of constituency or regional interest (Norton, 1995), and although attendance is normally small, they do allow MPs to raise topics, including social policy issues, that might be unlikely to reach the Commons chamber, as is well illustrated by the topics for the week beginning 16 May 2006, which included: 'Nottingham's city strategy on Incapacity Benefit'; 'government policy on further education and adult learning'; 'effects of the problems with the tax credit system on people in Angus'; 'second chance education in Liverpool'; and the 'Child Support Agency and the case of Diane Mellor'.

In addition to all of the above there are opportunities for backbench MPs to raise issues in the daily half-hour adjournment debate. This allows an MP to speak on a subject for 15 minutes followed by a reply from a minister for the remainder of the time. MPs' applications are put into a ballot to decide who has this opportunity, with the exception of Thursdays when the Speaker chooses the subject. These adjournment debates allow around 150 opportunities for backbenchers each year.

As Bochel (1992) found in the 1980s, so in the research undertaken for this book, MPs viewed specialisation as advantageous in efforts to influence policy. MPs who are recognised specialists are more likely to be consulted by or have access to ministers, and they may be more likely to catch the Speaker's eye in debates on which they are considered to be knowledgeable. However, given the breadth of topics that MPs are required to cover, relatively few are able to develop great depth of knowledge in any one area, although a handful, such as the Labour MP Frank Field, the Conservative MP David Willets, and the Liberal Democrat MP Steve Webb, are seen by MPs from all parties as experts and as such are more likely to be listened to.

Interestingly several MPs suggested that it was not enough to raise issues in parliament alone but that parliament offered backbenchers the opportunity to draw attention to issues, and hopefully attract the interest of the media. One Conservative MP stressed the importance of making "flamboyant speeches", which might attract media attention. Adjournment debates and 10-minute rule bills were seen by some as important only insofar as they attracted attention beyond parliament. Liberal Democrat MPs seemed particularly aware of the importance of raising issues simultaneously in parliament and in the media. Several Liberal Democrats referred to the lack of real power wielded by third party MPs, but added that by stimulating debate in parliament and the country they had exerted considerable influence. One Liberal Democrat MP cited as an example the issue of raising taxes, claiming that the government's decision to raise National Insurance in 2003 was a response to Liberal Democrat well-publicised policy of tax rises to fund the NHS.

Parliamentary questions

While Prime Minister's Question Time is one of the most high profile of the potential means of MPs seeking to hold the executive to account, it is arguably also one of the least useful. The 30 minutes each week may be a focus of attention for the media, but they do not present an accurate picture of the potential usefulness of questions in providing information. Government departments also respond to oral questions from MPs, on a set rota, with ministers and their advisers being given a minimum of three days to prepare their answer. Following the first question an MP can ask a supplementary question on the same topic, after which the Speaker may also allow other MPs to add further supplementaries, normally alternating between government and opposition members. Oral questions are often used to raise issues or to criticise (and sometimes to praise) ministers and their policies, as well as raising matters of importance to constituents.

In addition to oral questions MPs are also able to submit questions for written answer, and these often provide factual information, sometimes in a format that might not be achievable during question time. For instance, on 4 May 2006, Eric Pickles, Conservative MP for Brentwood and Ongar, asked the Deputy Prime Minister "what the Government's definition is of affordable housing" (*Hansard*, col 1802W). Questions, and particularly written questions, often have a constituency focus, reflecting MPs' emphasis on this aspect of their work. For example, also on 4 May 2006, David Amess, Conservative MP for Southend West, asked the "Secretary of State for the Home Department how many persons aged *(a)* 11 to 15, *(b)* 16, *(c)* 17 and *(d)* 18 years were (i) prosecuted for and (ii) convicted of a criminal offence in (A) Southend-on-Sea, (B) Essex, (C) the Metropolitan Police area of London and (D) England and Wales in each year since 1990" (*Hansard*, col 1830W). Such questions are indicative of the type of information sought by MPs through this means. Given that there is no limit on the number of questions each MP can ask, it is not surprising that they form an important activity and that a large number of questions for written answer are submitted, with around 46,000 being tabled in the 2002-03 session, although only 21,176 were printed in *Hansard* in the shorter 2004-05 session.

Analysis by the House of Commons Library (2003) showed that for the 2001-02 session not only did MPs from opposition parties ask more questions on average than Labour backbenchers, so too did Conservative frontbenchers and Liberal Democrat spokespeople, leading Norton (2005) to suggest that, beyond their use as a source of information for backbench MPs, "Written questions are thus employed as a significant weapon in the armoury of opposition front-benchers in questioning ministers" (Norton, 2005, p 115).

Interestingly, the role of parliamentary debate and questions was by no means the most popular method of influencing policy identified by MPs (Table 7.1), although a larger proportion of opposition MPs identified this as a means of influence than Labour MPs. Departmental questions were generally felt to be more important and effective than Prime Minister's Questions, which were dismissed by several MPs as overly stage-managed and designed for media consumption. Questions to ministers were highlighted as particularly important, as they allow backbench MPs to directly challenge the government. This was considered to be particularly valuable by MPs from smaller parties such as the Liberal Democrats, the SNP and Plaid Cymru, as one of the few opportunities they had to directly challenge the government. As one Plaid Cymru MP observed, they allow MPs from small parties to "punch above our weight". However, parliamentary questions are not just of symbolic importance; several MPs asserted that they provided genuine opportunities to scrutinise the government by raising "awkward questions" and stimulating action. Raising questions on the floor of the House, one MP observed, can often expose "weak thinking" by ministers, while another noted "you can get an instant response from ministers, and this may prod ministers into action". Despite this, one Conservative MP added that raising an issue in ministerial questions was no guarantee of action:

> "The real problem is ministers' capacity to get the bureaucracy moving. A minister may go back to his department and say 'we must do something about this' and pass it on to his civil servants where the issue will become bogged down, lost or ignored."

Early day motions

Another means for individual MPs to draw attention to issues is the use of early day motions (EDMs), an expression of a view that could be debated by the House (Rogers and Walters, 2004), that other MPs can add their name to, thus giving some indication of feelings in the House of Commons. There was a significant increase in the number of EDMs from the early 1980s and in recent years there have been around 1,900 in each parliamentary session (House of Commons Information Office, 2005).

EDMs can be used for a variety of purposes, but among the most common and relevant for current purposes is their use by a group within a party, typically government backbenchers, to express a view that is different from the official position of their party, although these may be supported by MPs from other parties. One example of this would be that sponsored by the Labour MP Paul Farrelly on the introduction of university tuition fees:

> That this House notes with concern that a number of elite universities are making contingency plans for top up fees, which would create a two tier university system; and urges the Government to adhere to its policy of ruling out such extra charges in this and successive future parliaments. (EDM 2, 2002-03 [see http://edmi.parliament.uk/edmi/])

This EDM was supported by 138 Labour backbenchers, clearly wishing to express their concern with aspects of the government's higher education policy, but also attracted 25 Liberal Democrats, 4 Plaid Cymru MPs, 3 Ulster Unionists and 1 Scottish Nationalist.

There are also EDMs that seek to express an opinion on an issue that runs across party lines, such as that sponsored by Julia Drown in 2004-05, which stated:

> That this House welcomes the United Kingdom Government's commitment to the Millennium Development Goals; notes with concern that the current debt crisis, trade injustice and shortcomings of aid further exacerbate poverty, inequality, the HIV/AIDS crisis and environmental degradation across the developing world; notes that if the international community is to make poverty history then there needs to be further co-ordinated political action by the world's governments, including the United Kingdom, aimed at trade justice, dropping the debt and providing more and better aid; and calls on the United Kingdom Government to lead the way for change and use its influence when it holds the presidency of the G8 and chairs the EU to make poverty history in 2005. (EDM 9, 2004-05 [see http://edmi.parliament.uk/edmi/])

This EDM attracted 454 supporters from across the House. Given the ease of producing an EDM and also the lack of direct parliamentary consequence of them, it is not surprising that they are a popular means (although not one that is necessarily widely used by all backbenchers) for MPs to express their feelings, nor that there are a wide range of social policy-related EDMs. For example, in the 2004-05 session these included one congratulating Hull City Council on its approach to primary school meals (signed by 25 MPs), one seeking to raise awareness of Parkinson's disease and in particular Parkinson's Awareness week (88 signatures), and one expressing dismay that the gap between rich and poor had grown since 1997 (45 signatures).

As noted in the Introduction to this book, some commentators have seen these as potentially a useful means of gauging the feelings of MPs, but not every MP who supports a position will necessarily sign a motion, while there is no indication of the extent or strength of opposition to the views put forward. They are therefore perhaps best seen as a means for MPs to express and test views. EDMs also frequently attract media attention, if not nationally, at least regionally or locally, and therefore provide a mechanism for MPs to be seen to be expressing a concern over an issue. Perhaps not surprisingly they frequently relate to local issues. In most parliamentary sessions only a few EDMs achieve more than 200 signatures, and many will only receive the support of only a handful of MPs.

All-party parliamentary groups

Several MPs pointed to the importance of all-party groups, both in raising the profile of issues and also in directly influencing the government. The number of all-party groups, which may be joined by both MPs and peers, has increased in recent years, with around 300 subject groups in existence in 2004-05 (and more than 100 country groups). One of the frequent aims of these groups is to help raise awareness of a topic or issue, and there are a large number that relate to social issues, ranging alphabetically from Adoption and Fostering, Ageing and Older People, AIDS, through Maternity and Mental Health to University, Victims of Crime and Youth Affairs. Some groups exist largely in name only, but others are very active, such as the All-party Disability Group, which has long worked closely with outside organisations such as RADAR (the Royal Association for Disability and Resettlement) (see Whiteley and Winyard, 1987; Bochel, 1992), which provides secretariat support and funding for receptions.

Such links with outside organisations can give these groups a value to both MPs and to pressure groups. For MPs they can provide a source of information and support, for example in suggesting and drafting amendments to legislation, or even in producing ideas for private members' bills. For groups, they provide a means of accessing sympathetic MPs and peers, and through them, potentially ministers. Indeed, several MPs suggested that all-party groups may have a direct influence on policy. They are considered to be particularly important because of the access they have to ministers and leading experts. One example cited by an MP was the all-party breast cancer group whose recent meetings had been attended by a health minister and the government's cancer tsar. Moreover, MPs pointed to the importance of the cross-party membership of such groups that allowed them to "work with government" and "exert influence, gently, behind the scenes".

However, while often valuable, the effectiveness of all-party groups varies enormously. One MP, whose parliamentary profile listed membership of a long list of all-party groups, confessed that she rarely attended any of them and likened them to university societies that recruit large numbers of people at the beginning of the year but are either sustained by a small number of committed individuals or lapse into inactivity. Moreover, the close relationships of some groups with outside interests can be seen as a weakness. Recent press reports have highlighted financial support provided for some groups by industry and lobbying firms, which has increased considerably since MPs were banned from working directly for political consultancies ('How business pays for a say in Parliament', *The Times*, 13 January 2006). One MP pointed in particular to the financial assistance given by the pharmaceutical industry to a number of health-related groups.

Select committees

The most effective means of influencing policy identified by MPs from all parties is through parliamentary select committees. In recent decades the select committee system has often been seen as providing a potential mechanism for helping to redress the balance of power between parliament and the executive. In 1979 a new system of departmental select committees was established by the House of Commons to run alongside the existing Public Accounts Committee and the Select Committee on the Parliamentary Commissioner for Administration. Since then departmental select committees have formed the basis of the system although there have been a number of alterations to reflect organisational changes to government departments. Prior to the changes to departments in May 2006, the main departmental select committees covering social policy issues included: the Education and Skills Committee, the Health Committee, the Home Affairs Committee, the Committee on the Office of the Deputy Prime Minister, and the Work and Pensions Committee. The scope of inquiries can be illustrated by the reports of two committees during the 2004–05 session (see Table 7.2).

Beyond the 'spending departments', the Treasury Committee has taken an increasing interest in welfare issues, reflecting the growing role of the Treasury in social policy under Gordon Brown as Chancellor of the Exchequer. The Treasury Committee has produced reports on topics such as the administration of tax credits, financial inclusion and child trust funds. In addition other committees undertake work relevant to welfare and social policy. The Public Accounts Committee, consisting of 15 members and chaired by a member of the Opposition, plays a central role in the House of Commons' scrutiny of government expenditure, and has frequently displayed a concern over achieving value for taxpayers' money. It works with the National Audit Office, an independent body headed by the Comptroller and Auditor-General, which audits the account of government departments and provides parliament with value-for-money reports on government departments

Table 7.2: Examples of select committee reports, session 2004-05

Education and Skills Committee
- Secondary education: teacher retention and recruitment
- Public expenditure on education and skills
- Education outside the classroom
- UK e-university
- Secondary education
- National skills strategy 14-19
- Education
- Prison education
- *Every child matters*
- Teaching children to read

Health Committee
- The prevention of venous thromboembolism in hospitalised patients
- New developments in sexual health and HIV/AIDS policy
- The influence of the pharmaceutical industry
- The use of new medical technologies within the NHS
- NHS continuing care

and other public bodies. The Public Accounts Committee produces reports on a wide range of topics including NHS dentistry, welfare-to-work and the Home Office and Crime and Disorder Reduction Partnerships (all in the 2004-05 session), as well as more generic reports such as that on managing risks to improve public services (Public Accounts Committee, 2005b). Similarly, the Public Administration Committee produces reports such as that on *Choice, voice and public services* (Public Administration Committee, 2005), suggesting, for example, that while choice might be important for users of public services, it may not be their highest priority, and that it is important to be aware of limitations on choice. The European Scrutiny Committee, which, as outlined in Chapter Four, works broadly in parallel with the House of Lords' EU Committee, also has an interest in social policy issues.

Arguably one of the purposes of the departmental select committee system has been to allow small groups of MPs to develop specialist knowledge of a particular area, and to focus on the work – administration, policy and expenditure – of the relevant government department, thus improving the quality of scrutiny. The committees themselves choose which topics to examine and are able to question ministers and civil servants, as well as calling other witnesses. Although prime ministers have traditionally refused to give evidence to committees, Tony Blair's announcement in April 2002 that he would appear twice a year before the Liaison Committee (consisting of the chairs of the select committees), has to some extent, responded to this criticism (see also Chapter Three). Most committees also make use of specialist advisers from outside parliament, either for particular enquiries or throughout a parliament. There has been general recognition that the committees are successful at producing often authoritative reports, that they have led to increased transparency (Judge, 1990), making the work of departments more visible to parliament, the media and the public, and that "... they also have some impact on departmental thinking. This impact does not usually extend to initiating significant new policies, but it can affect the implementation of existing policies and administrative practices" (Norton, 2005, p 121).

There was strong cross-party consensus among MPs about the effectiveness and influence of select committees. They were praised for allowing MPs to specialise, and for providing perhaps the only forum in parliament in which government policy is examined in detail. The non-partisan nature of select committees was one positive feature stressed by MPs from all parties. They were generally accepted as more consensual, authoritative and less susceptible to whipping. "The culture of committees", one Conservative MP observed, "is to oppose any pressure from the whips". The Work and Pensions Select Committee, under the chairship of the Liberal Democrat MP, Archy Kirkwood, was praised by several MPs from across the House as a 'model' committee producing detailed reports and resisting the urge to go "scalp hunting". Many MPs also stressed that select committees had a direct influence on policy, although few were forthcoming with specific examples. Select committee members suggested that committee reports were often not as influential as the process of a committee's inquiry. Several MPs suggested that the mere announcement that a select committee was about to investigate an issue often prompted the government to take action. One Labour member of the Work and Pensions Select Committee observed that in many cases the government will begin to make changes in advance of a report being published in an effort to head off potential criticism, citing as an example government statements on the future of the Child Support Agency, and the resignation of the head of the Agency in November 2004, in advance of the publication of the committee's critical report on the subject in January 2005. Another prominent example of a policy change announced in response to a select committee report, mentioned by a number of MPs, was the change in the government's position on banning smoking in public places that followed the Health Select Committee report on the subject in January 2006.

However, there are many problems that perhaps prevent the scrutiny work of the committees being as effective and non-partisan as some of their supporters would hope. Among these is a significant turnover of membership (for example, between 1997 and 1999 the Social Security Committee had a turnover of 64% [Brazier, 2000]), with many MPs choosing to move on to government or opposition posts when these become available. One of the main criticisms of the work of the select committees since the 1979 reforms has been that their reports have rarely been debated in the House. While government departments are expected to respond to reports, normally within 60 days, relatively few reach the floor of the House, although the use of Westminster Hall as a second debating chamber since 1999 has allowed some increase in the number of reports that can be debated. In addition, there have always been doubts about the extent to which select committees can achieve a genuinely consensual, non-partisan approach (for example, Johnson, 1988), particularly with the governing party having a majority on the committee that some have suggested encourages them to choose issues that may be less likely to lead to divides along party lines (Bochel, 1992). Indeed, when committees have conducted inquiries on issues that are clearly of less cross-party appeal, such as the Health Committee report on the role of the private sector in health provision in 2002, then consensus has been notably absent (Health Select Committee, 2002).

Since 1997 there have been a number of reports that have suggested ways in which the system could be made more effective (for example, Commission to Strengthen Parliament, 2000; Liaison Committee, 2000; Hansard Society, 2001; Modernisation Committee, 2002b), including recommendations such as the creation of an alternative career path to the ministerial route, provision of greater staffing and other support, improving the impact of reports, and increasing their role in the scrutiny of legislation. However, while there were some changes following the Modernisation Committee's report, such as the introduction of additional payments for select committee chairs, they remain well short of any significant shift in power away from the executive.

Overall, there appears to be broad agreement between political commentators and MPs that while the select committee system works well in some respects, such as the provision of information and making ministers and civil servants more open to public scrutiny and accountability, it could be more effective, particularly in relation to increasing the impact of their reports and their influence on policy (for example, Liaison Committee, 2000; Riddell, 2000; Hansard Society 2001; Norton, 2005). There was considerable concern among MPs from all parties that select committees were not given enough resources with which to carry out detailed scrutiny, particularly as one Labour

MP observed, they are "faced with the combined strength of government departments".Two highly experienced select committee chairs, one a Labour MP and the other a Conservative, were highly critical of the lack of resources available to select committees, and compared them unfavourably to US congressional committees.There was criticism from both Labour and Conservative MPs of the government's built-in majority, although no alternative was suggested, and there were calls from Labour MPs to remove control over the appointment of select committee chairs from the whips office.While MPs from across the House suggested that select committees provided the greatest potential for parliamentary scrutiny of the executive, there was also some concern that committees were being presented as the only effective opposition. As one Labour chair of a select committee argued, "the trouble with this government is that they see select committees as the opposition whereas they could really use select committees to inform and support policy". However, as several MPs suggested, select committees may well be victims of their own success, with governments of any party unlikely to reinforce them if they are perceived to be an effective means of limiting the power of the executive.

Informal methods of influence

One significant feature of MPs' comments was not only the variety of parliamentary practices and procedures employed by MPs in seeking to influence policy, but also the emphasis given to informal means of exerting influence. This was highlighted in particular by MPs who questioned the value of voting against the government in the division lobbies. Several Labour MPs, but also Conservative MPs who had experience of being the party of government, stressed that publicly challenging the frontbench by rebelling in parliamentary votes was unlikely to achieve results. By the time an issue comes to the vote, it was suggested, the government was unlikely to change policy in response to a direct challenge from its backbenches. "Rebellion is at the end of the process, it is less effective than doing it earlier", suggested one Labour MP, while another observed that MPs' influence was undermined by regularly voting against the government, "when you have a reputation [for rebelling] no-one listens to you". It was, several MPs suggested, better to seek to exert influence "gently", or "quietly" behind the scenes through informal contacts with ministers, in conversation, or by letter. One experienced Labour backbencher, who was highly critical of the group of well-known Labour rebels, argued that:

> "Every other week there is a rebellion here ... and serious change can and does happen, but it is done by people beavering away. Not by rebelling and appearing on the 6 o'clock news."

This MP cited as an example the government's introduction of the Pension Protection Fund (PPF) to protect members of private sector pension schemes whose companies become insolvent, introduced as part of the 2004 Pensions Act. The government's original proposal did not make provision for retrospective cases, but following backbench pressure the government set up an additional financial assistance scheme for them. Interestingly, the PPF was also cited as an example of backbench influence by one of the Labour ministers involved in the legislation. Indeed, as this example suggests, and as several MPs observed, backbench pressure is not simply used to "threaten" or coerce the government but also to highlight positive policy developments. For example, several MPs had positive things to say about the Pathways to Work pilot, and about the Sure Start scheme, and had pressed the government to roll out the schemes nationally.

Significantly the importance of informal contacts with ministers was mentioned by all but one of the newly elected Labour MPs interviewed. Informal contact with ministers and whips was part of the induction process for new Labour MPs and clearly designed to promote party cohesion. Five out of the six newly elected Labour MPs interviewed referred to contacts with government ministers. Two referred to a formalised induction process in which they met with ministers including Cabinet ministers, at receptions and seminars organised by the PLP resource centre, while others referred to small meetings with the Chancellor and the Prime Minister. One new MP who had expressed some concern about the role of the private sector in health was surprised to receive a personal 'phone call from the Health Secretary Patricia Hewitt. While some of the new MPs expressed an awareness that this process was undoubtedly designed to stimulate loyalty, they were nevertheless genuinely impressed by the level of access and pleased that the party leadership was "willing to listen" to new MPs.

While informal means of exerting influence are clearly more open to MPs on the government benches, several opposition MPs did refer to informal contacts with government ministers. On less contentious issues related to the concerns of individual constituents, opposition MPs stated that they would approach the minister concerned rather than seek to make political capital out of an issue. Good "personal relations" with government ministers were very important, according to one Liberal Democrat MP who confessed to being friends with someone on the government frontbench, although such outward expressions of fraternal feeling were rare among the MPs interviewed.

The use of informal methods of influence has been discussed in particular in relation to the way in which women MPs operate. Childs (2004) has examined whether the influx of New Labour women into the House of Commons in 1997 might have a new, 'feminised', style of politics, noting that there are some expectations that women might be more cooperative and consensual, rather than adversarial and confrontational, in their approach to the practice of politics. She found that many of the New Labour women elected in 1997 did believe that there was a difference in style between women and men, and that, according to them, this is "due to women and men's differently gendered socialization and experiences" (p 181); in addition, in a second round of interviews in 2000, she suggested that this perception had been heightened. Childs' interviewees characterised their political style as working behind the scenes, in contrast to involvement on the floor of the House or in rebellions in the division lobbies.

Childs' findings are to some extent reinforced by interviews with women from the three main parties undertaken for this research. The use of informal methods of influence was mentioned by a third of women MPs interviewed, compared to a quarter of male MPs. Moreover, some of the comments made by female MPs reinforced Childs' findings. One female Liberal Democrat MP contrasted the "quiet methods of influence" adopted by women with the "yah-boo politics" sometimes seen in the House, while several were critical of the adversarial "macho" attitudes evident in the House. There were also some suggestions that some policy developments had been lifted up the agenda or driven forwards by the presence of women MPs, most notably the government's childcare agenda, and domestic violence legislation. However, when women MPs spoke about their gender it was generally in the context of the importance of their presence in making parliament more representative, and on a more personal note on the importance of the support provided by other women MPs (albeit in the same party) in what is clearly a male-dominated, and at times, hostile environment.

Conclusions

Opportunities for MPs to transform their own, or public, concerns about the government's approach to welfare into changes in policy are limited. It is arguably the case that the increase in dissent from the 1980s means that MPs are more prepared to be critical of government policies and legislation than they once were. There may therefore appear to be a greater need for governments to consult with and take note of backbenchers' views at an earlier stage of the legislative process. Yet one of the frequent complaints from (at least some) Labour MPs has been that the government has been unwilling to do this. This may in part explain the increase in dissent during the second and third Labour terms and the consequent need for the government to make concessions during the passage of some of its welfare legislation. Alternatively it may be that, knowing that some of their backbenchers or peers will demand concessions, ministers introduce legislation with at least some expectation of making changes during its passage, and include aspects that they may be willing to concede.

Indeed, evidence from interviews with MPs reinforces the argument made in Chapter Three, that the power of parliament lies not so much in an ability to coerce the government, but rather in its power to influence the government through a range of parliamentary and informal procedures, and to exercise some control of the agenda by forcing ministers to anticipate parliamentary reaction. As one former Labour Cabinet minister observed:

> "Just because parliament isn't voting government proposals down doesn't mean it isn't exercising influence or setting limits…. Parliament does exert considerable influence, both through the mechanisms of accountability – select committee inquiries, questions, debates – and because account will be taken by ministers of likely public and parliamentary reaction in framing their proposals."

However, while the more 'collective' sources of potential influence available to MPs, such as the select committee system and all-party groups, do provide opportunities, in the case of the former it is arguably in relation to transparency and provision of information that they have been successful, as there remains little evidence that they have had any significant impact on the formulation and implementation of social policy. Where all-party groups are concerned, they can provide outside interests with a channel of influence to MPs and through them to ministers, although the extent to which this enables legislation or policy to be influenced should not be overstated. Similarly, although there has been a growth in lobbying by interest groups and professional lobbyists in both chambers of parliament, the formulation and implementation of policy and legislation remains the purview of government, rather than MPs and peers.

Overall, the nature of politics and the different mechanisms open to MPs and peers make it difficult to separate out parliamentarians' influence from that of others, such as pressure groups and the media. It is also difficult to judge the extent to which governments take pre-emptive action, for example through the whips informing ministers that particular proposals may be unacceptable to their party, or the House as a whole. Nevertheless, it is in this process of backbench pressure, agenda setting and non-decision making that the real power of parliament lies.

EIGHT

Conclusions

This book has drawn on a variety of evidence, including interviews with 76 MPs and 10 peers, to examine the beliefs, roles and activities of MPs, and to some extent peers, in relation to welfare policy since 1997. The empirical research was undertaken largely during the second Blair term, a period that saw considerable change in many areas of welfare policy. It is also a period in which many commentators suggested that there was a significant increase in the power of the executive, and perhaps in particular the Prime Minister, compared with that of the House of Commons (for example, Riddell, 2000). In addition, however, this period also saw other significant changes within parliament, including reform of the House of Lords, and to the governance of social policy outside parliament, for example the creation of the Scottish Parliament and the National Assembly for Wales, which has led to new forums for the making of social policy within the devolved administrations.

In addition, this book has been able to draw on previous research, also drawing on interviews with a significant number of MPs, undertaken at a similar stage of the second Thatcher administration (1986-87), a period during which there were also radical shifts in welfare policy. This enables comparison to be made across a variety of topics including MPs' beliefs and their approaches to influencing government policy.

The New Labour governments have made significant changes to social policy, in some areas building on changes introduced by the preceding Conservative governments, and in some areas varying considerably. Some of the debate about the nature of New Labour's policies has been focused around the idea of a 'Third Way' (for example, Giddens, 2000). At the same time, there have inevitably been changes in the social policies of the other political parties, with the Conservatives in particular attempting to respond not only to the challenge of New Labour but also the legacy of Thatcherism. However, in recent years social issues have become more of a focus for the Conservative Party, and following David Cameron's election as leader, the announcement of a number of significant policy shifts have brought the Conservatives closer to Labour's position in many areas, such as a commitment to ending child poverty and to maintaining an NHS free at the point of delivery.

There have been considerable claims for the development of a new welfare consensus (for example, Williams, 2000; Taylor-Gooby, 2001), with the political parties converging on a 'middle ground' of limited spending, privatisation of some provision, a movement towards more selective provision through the increased use of targeting of benefits, including means testing, and an emphasis on labour market activation through the development of incentives, training and welfare-to-work.

In examining the extent to which such a consensus might be developing within the House of Commons, it is certainly true that there have been significant changes in MPs' attitudes to welfare, particularly compared with those of 20 years ago, with a general move towards a middle ground. While in the 1980s there was little or no consensus on approaches to welfare between MPs of different parties, in 2005-06 there was considerable agreement on some key features of welfare provision. However, as discussed in Chapter Four, any such convergence is not a return to the postwar consensus, or an acceptance of the New Right influences of the 1980s, but is a new consensus, based on what MPs see as the realities of the early 21st century. Relatively few Labour MPs now call for higher taxation, and there is a much greater acceptance within the party of a need for greater selectivity and targeting in welfare provision. Similarly, relatively few Conservative MPs now demand significant tax cuts, and there is within the party in parliament a greater acceptance of a role for the state in helping those in need, and particularly in helping people escape from poverty.

There are, however, limits to this 'consensus', both within and across the parties. In marked contrast to the situation in the 1980s, when there was considerable agreement in all parties between backbench MPs and their party leadership, all parties are now divided, sometimes sharply so, in their attitudes towards welfare. For example, in contrast to the government's position, around one fifth of Labour MPs continue to assert that one of the roles of the state should be to redistribute wealth, while others, by no means habitual rebels, expressed grave misgivings about the involvement of the private sector in welfare and the shift towards selectivity. Similar divisions exist within the Liberal Democrats, with economic liberals, who favour spending restraint and selectivity, expressing very different views from those who favour high levels of universal provision by the state, including some desire for tax increases.

Within the Conservative Party too there are fundamental divisions, with some MPs taking a view that broadly coincides with that of their leader since late 2005, David Cameron, which supports considerable levels of state support in meeting individual and community needs. However, at the time of most of the interviews this group of MPs were clearly aware that their commitment to state provision marked a major departure from recent Conservative thinking and the views of most of their colleagues, and were unable to estimate the level of support for this position within the Conservative Party in parliament or the country. In contrast, around one third of Conservative MPs' preferred role for the state was as a minimal safety net for those in greatest needs, a position much closer to the bulk of Conservatives interviewed in the mid-1980s. Perhaps significantly for the longer term this view was more strongly supported by Conservative MPs newly elected to parliament in 2005 than among the party as a whole.

These intra-party divisions help to explain the difficult passage of Labour's welfare reform legislation through parliament, and also suggest that the leadership of the other main parties will need to accommodate dissent when seeking to develop welfare policy, and subsequently if elected to government.

The shift in the political consensus on welfare also presents the main parties with different and distinct challenges in terms of securing public support. While there has certainly been some shift in public attitudes to welfare since the 1980s, in particular a hardening of attitudes towards benefits recipients, the public remains broadly committed to a large measure of state provision. This presents the Labour government with the challenge of leading public opinion away from entrenched ideas about the role of the state, while the Conservatives under David Cameron must convince the public of their commitment to state provision. The success of the parties in achieving this may well be dependent on the extent to which the leadership of both parties is able to accommodate and assuage the dissent on their own backbenches, which, in the case of The Labour Party, appears to be somewhat closer to the public's commitment to state provision, while in the case of the Conservatives would seek to lead the party away from state provision.

The emergence of a new consensus, and the consequent increase in intra-party debate on the question of welfare, has to some extent served to reinvigorate parliamentary debate, albeit within the parties, rather than between them. Among the arguments put forward to support the 'decline of parliament' thesis has been the dominance of parties in the House of Commons (and to some extent, although less so) in the House of Lords, with the power of the whips extending not only to voting in division lobbies but to influencing the membership of select committees and standing committees. However, there is considerable evidence (for example, Cowley, 2005) that the frequency and size of backbench rebellions in the division lobbies has been high under New Labour, particularly in the second and at the start of the third term, as discussed in Chapter Three. Nevertheless, as in the 1980s, the evidence generally suggests that despite some degree of dissent among Labour backbenchers, including some large rebellions and some concessions from the government on welfare legislation, such as foundation hospitals and university tuition fees, it remains the case that MPs have relatively little influence either on the passage of government legislation or in originating private members' legislation.

It is, however, possible to identify a number of factors that may contribute to MPs being able to successfully influence the government. As was the position in the 1980s, those (few) MPs who specialise in welfare issues are seen by MPs from all parties as influential voices. However, the extent to which even the most knowledgeable are in a position to influence policy is limited. In reality, the extent to which backbench MPs are able to influence government remains largely dependent on, for example, the extent to which their views chime with those expressed by pressure groups and the media, as well as the strength with which particular views are held within government. There have been suggestions that under Labour the government has been more open to organised interests (Marsh et al, 2001; Richards and Smith, 2002), in part arising from links that had developed while the party was in opposition, but perhaps also due to attempts to develop a more inclusive approach to policy making (Cabinet Office, 1999b). However, many interest groups also lobby at the level of individual MPs, both seeking to influence MPs and through them the government, but also frequently providing them with information with which they may, if they wish, be more able to challenge the executive. MPs therefore continue to act as a channel of communication and influence, not just from their constituents, but also organised interests.

Where the scrutiny of government policy and actions is concerned, perhaps the main tools for both Houses are their committees, and in particular the select committees. The departmental select committees introduced in the House of Commons in 1979 have generally been recognised as valuable in that they have produced authoritative reports that have at times been highly critical of governments, and this has certainly been the case with regard to the committees that shadow the work of the major welfare departments. The select committees in the Lords have also produced some significant reports, although despite the opportunity for them to take a more wide-ranging approach, and one that can cut across the work of several government departments, they have not generally looked in depth at social policy, the one notable exception being the Social and Consumer Affairs Sub-committee of the EU Committee that does play an important role in looking at proposals from the EU. Where the committees have perhaps been less successful is in having any major impact on government policies and legislation, although the gradual move towards a greater degree of pre-legislative scrutiny may provide some opportunity for this to change. However, parliamentarians do have a variety of other mechanisms at their disposal and many argue that these can be at least as influential, if not more so, than higher profile statements in the media and rebellions (or threats of them) in the division lobbies.

It is, however, difficult to assess accurately the abilities of MPs and peers to influence policy. While certain aspects of their work, such as voting in the division lobbies and select committee reports, are both visible and measurable, it is important to recognise that some forms of influence may be unseen. Norton (2005) has argued that parliament can serve to keep issues off the agenda, with governments anticipating adverse reaction within parliament, or detailed scrutiny in committee, so that some proposals may never reach the stage of legislative or other action. This view has been reinforced by comments from backbenchers and from former Cabinet ministers who have attested to the informal influence of backbench MPs, the government's propensity to anticipate parliamentary reaction, and the ability of parliament to influence the agenda. While the type of influence implied by this view is difficult to observe or measure, it is supported by the comments of many MPs and peers, who report that they seek to exercise government through activities behind the scenes.

One of the changes that is developing within parliament appears to be the emergence of a greater assertiveness and potentially a greater influence of the House of Lords. While some critics accused Labour of seeking to weaken one of the last bastions of opposition with its reforms, and in particular the removal of the hereditary peers, in reality the opposite has happened. The House of Lords arguably now takes a greater interest in, and plays a greater role in relation to, welfare policy than it has for some time, although it remains limited. The reformed House also appears to have a greater belief in its own legitimacy and as a result to be more willing to challenge the government. There also appears to be some evidence of outside interests, such as interest groups and the media, taking the Lords more seriously, with a greater degree of lobbying by pressure groups and professional lobbyists than previously. This has also been reflected in the House of Commons, with MPs, including backbench Labour MPs, reflecting on the ability of the upper House to influence policy. This suggests that in contrast to those who claim that parliament is increasingly insignificant, in relation to the scrutiny of welfare policy under Labour, members of both Houses have sought by various means, and with varying degrees of success, to reassert the power of parliament.

References

Appleby, J. and Coote, A. (2002) *Five year health check: A review of health policy, 1997-2002*, London: King's Fund.

Archer, P. (1999) 'The House of Lords, past, present and future', *The Political Quarterly*, vol 70, no 4, pp 396-403.

Bache, I. and Flinders, M. (2004) 'Multi-level governance and the study of the British state', *Public Policy and Administration*, vol 19, no 1, pp 31-51.

Bagehot, W. (1867) *The English constitution*, London: Fontana.

Baker, D. (1997) 'Collaborative research and the Members of Parliament project', *Politics*, vol 17, no 1, pp 59-66.

Baker, D., Fountain, I., Gamble, A. and Ludlam, S. (1995) 'Backbench Conservative attitudes to European integration', *The Political Quarterly*, vol 66, no 2, pp 221-33.

Baker, D., Gamble, A., Ludlam, S. and Seawright, D. (1996) 'Labour and Europe: a survey of MPs and MEPs', *The Political Quarterly*, vol 67, pp 353-71.

Baldwin, N.D.J. (1999) 'The membership and work of the House of Lords', in P. Carmichael and B. Dickson (eds) *The House of Lords: Its parliamentary and judicial roles*, Oxford: Hart.

Barnett, N. (2003) 'Local government, New Labour and 'active welfare': a case of "self responsiblisation"?', *Public Policy and Administration*, vol 18, no 3, pp 25-38.

Beer, S. H. (1965) *Modern British Politics*, London: Faber.

Beetham, D. (2003), 'Political participation, mass protest and representative democracy', *Parliamentary Affairs*, vol 56, no 4: pp 597-609.

Berrington, H. (1973) *Backbench opinion in the House of Commons, 1945-55*, Oxford: Pergamon Press.

Berrington, H. and Leece, J. (1977) 'Measurement of backbench attitudes by Guttman scaling of early day motions: a pilot study, Labour 1968-69', *British Journal of Political Science*, vol 7, no 4, pp 529-40.

Bochel, C. and Bochel, H. (2004) *The UK social policy process*, Basingstoke: Palgrave.

Bochel, C. and Briggs, J. (2000) 'Do women make a difference?', *Politics*, vol 20, no 2, pp 63-8.

Bochel, H. (1992) *Parliament and welfare policy*, Aldershot: Dartmouth Publishing.

Bogdanor, V. (1999) 'Reform of the House of Lords: a sceptical view', *The Political Quarterly*, vol 70, no 4, pp 375-82.

Bower, T. (2004) *Gordon Brown*, London: Harper Collins.

Brazier, A. (2000) *Systematic scrutiny: Reforming the Select Committees*, London: Hansard Society.

Brewer, M., Goodman, A., Shaw, J. and Shephard, A. (2005) *Poverty and inequality in Britain: 2005*, London: Institute for Fiscal Studies.

Brown, G. (2005) 'Make this a manifesto for children', *The Guardian*, 5 January.

Burke, E. (1808) *The works of Edmund Burke, Volume 3*, London: Rivington.

Cabinet Office (1998) *Modernising Parliament, reforming the House of Lords*, London: The Stationery Office.

Cabinet Office (1999a) *Professional policy making for the 21st century*, London: Cabinet Office.

Cabinet Office (1999b) *Modernising government*, London: The Stationery Office.

Childs, S. (2004) *New Labour's women MPs: Women representing women*, London: Routledge.

Childs, S. and Withey, J. (2004) 'Women representatives acting for women: sex and the signing of early day motions in the 1997 British Parliament', *Political Studies*, vol 52, no 3, pp 552-64.

Clarke, J. (2004) *Changing welfare, changing states*, London: Sage Publications.

Clarke, J., Gewirtz, S., Hughes, G. and Humphrey, J. (2002) 'Guarding the public interest?', in J. Clarke, S. Gewirtz and E. McLaughlin (eds) *New managerialism, new welfare?*, London: Sage Publications.

Commission to Strengthen Parliament (2000) *Strengthening Parliament*, London: Conservative Party.

Conservative Party (2005) *Are you thinking what we're thinking? It's time for action*, London: Conservative Party.

Cook, R. (2003) *The point of departure*, London: Simon and Schuster.

Cowley, P. (2001) 'The Commons: Mr Blair's lapdog?', *Parliamentary Affairs*, vol 54, no 4, pp 815-28.

Cowley, P. (2002) *Revolts and rebellions: Parliamentary voting under Blair*, London: Politico's.

Cowley, P. (2005) *The rebels: How Blair mislaid his majority*, London: Politico's.

Cowley, P. (2006) 'Making Parliament matter?', in P. Dunleavy, R. Heffernan, P. Cowley and C. Hay (eds) *Developments in British politics 8*, Basingstoke: Palgrave Macmillan.

Cowley, P. and Stuart, M. (2004) 'Parliament: more *Bleak House* than *Great Expectations*', *Parliamentary Affairs*, vol 57, no 2, pp 301-14.

Crewe, E. (2005) *Lords of Parliament*, Manchester: Manchester University Press.

Curtice, J. and Fisher, S. (2003) 'The power to persuade? A tale of two prime ministers', in A. Park, J. Curtice, K. Thomson, C. Bromley and M. Phillips (eds) *British Social Attitudes: The 20th report: Continuity and change over two decades*, London: Sage Publications.

DCA (Department for Constitutional Affairs) (2003) *Constitutional reform: Next steps for the House of Lords*, London: DCA.

DETR (Department of the Environment, Transport and the Regions) (1998a) *Modernising local government: Local democracy and community leadership*, London: The Stationery Office.

DETR (1998b) *Modern local government: In touch with the people*, London: The Stationery Office.

DETR (2000) *Quality and choice: A decent home for all: The way forward for housing*, London: DETR.

DfEE (Department for Education and Employment) (2001) *Schools: Building on success: Raising standards, promoting diversity, achieving results*, Cm 5050, London: The Stationery Office.

DfES (Department for Education and Skills) (2001) *Schools achieving success*, Annesley: DfES Publications.

DH (Department of Health) (1999) *Saving lives: Our healthier nation*, London: The Stationery Office.

DH (2002) *Government response to the House of Lords Select Committee Report on stem cell research*, London: The Stationery Office.

DSS (Department of Social Security) (1998) *A new contract for welfare: Partnership in pensions*, London: The Stationery Office.

DWP (Department for Work and Pensions) (2005) *Five year strategy: Opportunity and security throughout life*, London: The Stationery Office.

Economic Affairs Committee (2003) *Aspects of the economics of an ageing population*, London: House of Lords.

EU (European Union) Committee (2004a) *Ninth report: The European Working Time Directive: A response to the European Commission's review*, London: House of Lords.

EU Committee (2004b) *Twenty-seventh report: Sexual Equality in Access to Goods and Services*, London: House of Lords.

Finer, S.E., Berrington, H.B. and Bartholomew, D.S. (1961) *Backbench opinion in the House of Commons, 1955-59*, Oxford: Pergamon Press.

Fontana, A. and Frey, J.H. (2000) 'The interview: from structured questions to negotiated text', in N.K. Denzin and Y.S. Lincoln (eds) *Handbook of qualitative research*, London: Sage Publications, pp 645-72.

Gains, F. (2003) 'Surveying the landscape of modernisation: executive agencies under New Labour', *Public Policy and Administration*, vol 18, no 2, pp 4-20.

Game, C. (2002), 'Britain's "5 percent" local government revolution: the faltering impact of New Labour's modernization agenda', *International Review of Administrative Sciences*, vol 68, no 3, pp 405-17.

Garrett, J. (1992) *Westminster: Does Parliament work?*, London: Victor Gollancz.

Giddens, A. (2000) *The third way and its critics*, Cambridge: Polity Press.

Grant, W. (2004) 'Pressure politics: the changing world of pressure groups', *Parliamentary Affairs*, vol 57, no 2, pp 408-19.

Gregg, P., Waldfogel, J. and Washbrook, E. (2005) 'That's the way the money goes: expenditure patterns as real incomes rise for the poorest families with children', in J. Hills and K. Stewart (eds) *A more equal society? New Labour, poverty and social exclusion*, Bristol: The Policy Press, pp 251-75.

Hailsham, Lord (1976) *The elective dictatorship*, London: BBC.

Hansard Society (2001) *The challenge for Parliament: Making government accountable, Report of the Hansard Society Commission on Parliamentary Scrutiny*, London: Vacher Dod Publishing.

Hazell, R. (2006) 'Return of the constitution', *Prospect*, no 119, February.

Healey, J., Gill, M. and McHugh, D. (2005) *MPs and politics in our time*, London: Hansard Society.

Health Select Committee (2002) *The role of the private sector in the NHS*, London: The Stationery Office.

Hedges, A. (2005) *Perceptions of redistribution: Report on exploratory qualitative research*, CASE paper 96, London: Centre for Analysis of Social Exclusion, London School of Economics and Political Science.

Hennessy, P. (1995) *The hidden wiring: Unearthing the British constitution*, London: Victor Gollancz.

Hill, A. and Whichelow, A. (1964) *What's wrong with Parliament?*, London: Penguin Books.

Hills, J. and Lelkes, O. (1999) 'Social security, selective universalism and patchwork redistribution', in R. Jowell, J. Curtice, A. Park, K. Thomson, L. Jarvis, C. Bromley and N. Stratford (eds) *British Social Attitudes: The 16th report: Who shares New Labour values?*, Aldershot: Ashgate.

HM Treasury (2005) *Public expenditure statistical analyses 2005*, London: The Stationery Office.

Hollis, C. (1949) *Can Parliament survive?*, London: Hollis and Carter.

Home Office (2004) *Active communities: Headline findings from the 2003 Home Office Citizenship Survey*, London: Home Office.

Hood, C. (1991) 'A public management for all seasons', *Public Administration*, vol 69, no 1, pp 3-19.

House of Commons Information Office (2005) 'Early day motions', Factsheet P3, London: House of Commons.

House of Commons Library (2005) *Modernisation of the House of Commons 1997-2005*, House of Commons Research Paper 05/46, London: House of Commons.

House of Commons Library (2006) *House of Lords – Continuing debate*, House of Commons Research Note SN/PC/3895, London: House of Commons.

House of Lords (2004) 'The work of the House of Lords – its role, functions and powers', House of Lords Briefing, London: House of Lords.

House of Lords Information Office (2005) *The work of the House of Lords*, London: House of Lords.

Johnson, N. (1988) 'Departmental Select Committees', in M. Ryle and P.G. Richards (eds) *The Commons under scrutiny*, London: Routledge.

Joint Committee on House of Lords Reform (2002) *House of Lords reform: First report*, London: The Stationery Office.

Jowell, R., Curtice, J., Park, A. and Thomson, K. (eds) (1999) *British Social Attitudes: The 16th report: Who shares New Labour values?*, London: Ashgate/National Centre for Social Research.

Judge, D. (1990) *Parliament and industry*, Aldershot: Dartmouth Publishing.

Judge, D. (1999), *Representation: Theory and practice in Britain*, London: Routledge.

Kavanagh, D. (2004) 'Political parties', in B. Jones, D. Kavanagh, M. Moran and P. Norton (eds) *Politics UK* (5th edn), Harlow: Pearson, pp 263-90.

Kornberg, A. and Frasure, R.C. (1971) 'Policy differences in British parliamentary parties', *American Political Science Review*, vol 65, no 3, pp 694-703.

Labour Party, The (1997) *New Labour: Because Britain deserves better*, London: The Labour Party.

Labour Party, The (2005) *Britain forward not back*, London: The Labour Party.

Letwin, O. (2006) 'Why we have signed up to Labour's anti-poverty target', *The Guardian*, 11 April.

Liaison Committee (2000) *First report: Shifting the balance: Select Committees and the Executive*, London: The Stationery Office.

Liberal Democratic Party (1997) *Making the difference,* London: Liberal Democratic Party.

Lipsey, D. (1994) 'Do we really want more public spending?', in R. Jowell, J. Curtice, L. Brook, D. Ahrendt and A. Park (eds) *British Social Attitudes: The 11th report*, Aldershot: Dartmouth Publishing.

Lord Chancellor's Department (2001) *The House of Lords – Completing the reform*, London: Lord Chancellor's Department.

Lovenduski, J. and Norris, P. (2003) 'Westminster women: the politics of presence', *Political Studies*, vol 51, no 1, pp 84-102.

Lowe, R. (2005) *The welfare state in Britain since 1945*, Basingstoke: Palgrave.

Lund, B. (2002) *Understanding state welfare*, London: Sage Publications.

Major, J. (2003) *The erosion of parliamentary government*, London: Centre for Policy Studies.

Mandelson, P. and Liddle, R. (1996) *The Blair revolution: Can New Labour deliver?*, London: Faber and Faber.

Marsh, D., Smith, M.J. and Richards, D. (2001) *Changing patterns of governance: Reinventing Whitehall*, Basingstoke: Palgrave.

Marshall, P. and Laws, D. (eds) (2004) *The orange book: Reclaiming Liberalism*, London: Profiile Books.

May, T. (2001) *Social research: Issues, methods and process*, Buckingham: Open University Press.

Mitchell, A. (2005) 'The backbenchers lament', in N.D.J. Baldwin (ed) *Parliament in the 21st century*, London: Politico's.

Modernisation Committee (1997) *First report: The legislative process*, London: The Stationery Office.

Modernisation Committee (1998) *First report: The parliamentary calendar: Initial proposals*, London: The Stationery Office.

Modernisation Committee (2002a) *First report: Select Committees*, London, The Stationery Office.

Modernisation Committee (2002b) *Second report: Modernisation of the House of Commons: A reform programme*, London: The Stationery Office.

Modernisation Committee (2004) *First report: Connecting Parliament with the public*, London: The Stationery Office.

Mooney, G. and Scott, G. (eds) (2005) *Exploring social policy in the 'new' Scotland*, Bristol: The Policy Press.

NAO (National Audit Office) (2005) *Comptroller and Auditor General's standard report on the accounts of the Inland Revenue2004-05*, London: National Audit Office.

Newman, J. (2001) *Modernising governance: New Labour, policy and society*, London: Sage Publications.

Norris, P. and Lovenduski, J. (1995) *Political recruitment: Gender, race and class in the British Parliament*, Cambridge: Cambridge University Press.

Norton, P. (1975) *Dissension in the House of Commons, 1945-74*, London: Macmillan.

Norton, P. (1978) *Conservative dissidents*, London: Temple Smith.

Norton, P. (1980) *Dissension in the House of Commons, 1974-1979*, Oxford: Clarendon Press.

Norton, P. (2003) 'Cohesion without discipline: party voting in the House of Lords', *Journal of Legislative Studies*, vol 9, no 4, pp 57-72.

Norton, P. (2005) *Parliament in British politics*, Basingstoke: Palgrave Macmillan.

OECD (Organisation for Economic Co-operation and Development) (1993) *Public management developments: Survey*, Paris: OECD.

Packenham, R. (1970) 'Legislatures and political development', in A. Kornberg and L.D. Musolf (eds) *Legislatures in developmental perspective*, Durham, NC: Duke University Press.

Page, B. (2005) *Understanding public attitudes to tax and spend*, London: MORI Social Research Institute.

Park, A., Curtice, J., Thomson, K., Bromley, C., Phillips, M. and Johnson, M. (eds) (2005) *British Social Attitudes: The 22nd report: Two terms of New Labour: The public's reaction*, London: Sage Publications/ NATCEN.

Park, A., Curtice, J., Thomson, K., Bromley, C. and Phillips, M. (eds) (2004) *British Social Attitudes: The 21st report*, London: Sage Publications/NATCEN.

Park, A., Curtice, J., Thomson, K., Jarvis, L. and Bromley, C. (eds) (2003) *British Social Attitudes: The 20th report: Continuity and change over two decades*, London: Sage Publications/NATCEN.

Pensions Commission (2004) *Pensions challenges and choices: The first report of the Pensions Commission*, London: The Stationery Office.

Pensions Commission (2005) *A new pension settlement of the twenty-first century: The second report of the Pensions Commission*, London: The Stationery Office.

Pitkin, H.F. (1967) *The concept of representation*, Berkeley, CA: University of California Press.

Powell, M. (ed) (1999) *New Labour, new welfare state?*, Bristol: The Policy Press.

Public Accounts Committee (2005a) *Fourth report: Fraud and error in benefit expenditure*, London: The Stationery Office.

Public Accounts Committee (2005b) *Fifteenth report: Managing risks to improve public services*, London: The Stationery Office.

Public Administration Committee (2005) *Fourth report: Choice, voice and public services*, London: The Stationery Office.

Putnam, R.D. (1971) 'Studying elite political culture: the case of ideology', *American Political Science Review*, vol 65, no 3, pp 651-81.

Putnam, R.D. (1973) *The beliefs of politicians*, New Haven, CT: Yale University Press.

Puwar, N. (2004) 'Thinking about making a difference', *British Journal of Politics and International Relations*, vol 6, pp 65-80.

Pym, H. and Kochan, N. (1998) *Gordon Brown: The first year in power*, London: Bloomsbury.

Rawnsley, A. (2001) *Servants of the people: The inside story of New Labour*, London: Penguin.

RCLTC (Royal Commission on Long-term Care) (1999) *With respect to old age: Long-term care: Rights and responsibilities*, London: The Stationery Office.

Richards, D. and Smith, M.J. (2002) *Governance and public policy in the UK*, Oxford: Oxford University Press.

Riddell, P. (2000) *Parliament under Blair*, London: Politico's.

Riddell, P. (2004) 'Prime Ministers and Parliament', *Parliamentary Affairs*, vol 57, no 4, pp 814-29.

Rogers, R. and Walters, R. (2004) *How Parliament works*, Harlow: Pearson.

Rouse, J. and Smith, G. (2002) 'Evaluating New Labour's accountability reforms', in M. Powell (ed) *Evaluating New Labour's welfare reforms*, Bristol: The Policy Press, pp 39-60.

Rush, M. (1999) 'The House of Lords: the political context', in P. Carmichael and B. Dickson (eds) *The House of Lords: Its parliamentary and judicial roles*, Oxford: Hart.

Rush, M. (2001) *The role of the Member of Parliament since 1868*, Oxford: Oxford University Press.

Rush, M. (2005) *Parliament today*, Manchester: Manchester University Press.

Rush, M. and Ettinghausen, C. (2002) *Opening up the usual channels*, London: Hansard Society.

Russell, M. (2003) 'Is the House of Lords already reformed?', *The Political Quarterly*, vol 74, no 3, pp 311-18.

Russell, M. and Cornes, R. (2001) 'The Royal Commission on Reform of the House of Lords: a house for the future?', *The Modern Law Review*, vol 64, no 1, pp 82-99.

Russell, M. and Sciara, M. (2006a) 'Why does the government get defeated in the House of Lords?', Paper presented to the Political Studies Association Conference, University of Reading.

Russell, M. and Sciara, M. (2006b) 'Legitimacy and bicameral strength: a case study of the House of Lords', Paper presented at the PSA Parliaments and Legislatures Specialist Group Conference, 16 June, University of Sheffield.

Science and Technology Committee (2000) *Sixth report: Complementary and alternative medicine*, London: House of Lords.

Searing, D.D. (1994) *Westminster's world: Understanding political roles*, London: Harvard University Press.

Sefton, T. (2003) 'What we want from the welfare state', in A. Park, J. Curtice, K. Thomson, L. Jarvis and C. Bromley (eds) *British Social Attitudes: The 20th report: Continuity and change over two decades*, London: Sage Publications/NATCEN.

Seldon, A. and Snowdon, P. (2005) 'The Conservative Party', in A. Seldon and D. Kavanagh (eds) *The Blair effect 2001-5*, Cambridge: Cambridge University Press, pp 131-56.

Shell, D. (1992) *The House of Lords*, Hemel Hempstead: Harvester Wheatsheaf.

Sutton Trust (2005) *The educational backgrounds of Members of the House of Commons and the House of Lords*, London: Sutton Trust.

Taylor-Gooby, P. (2001) 'Welfare reform in the UK: the construction of a liberal consensus', in P. Taylor-Gooby (ed) *Welfare states under pressure*, London: Sage Publications.

Taylor-Gooby, P. (2004) 'The work-centred welfare state', in A. Park, J. Curtice, K. Thomson, C. Bromley and M. Phillips (eds) *British Social Attitudes: The 21st report*, London: Sage Publications/NATCEN.

Taylor-Gooby, P. (2005) 'Attitudes to social justice', in N. Pearce and W. Paxton (eds) *Social justice: Building a fairer Britain*, London: Politico's/IPPR.

Taylor-Gooby, P. and Bochel, H. (1988) 'Public opinion, party policy and MPs' attitudes to welfare', *Political Quarterly*, vol 59, no 2, pp 251-8.

Toynbee, P. and Walker, D. (2001) *Did things get better? An audit of Labour's successes and failures*, London: Penguin.

Toynbee, P. and Walker, D. (2005) *Better or worse? Has Labour delivered?*, London: Bloomsbury.

Tyrie, A. (2000) *Mr Blair's poodle: An agenda for reviving the House of Commons*, London: Centre for Policy Studies.

Wakeham, Lord (2000a) *A House for the future: Royal Commission on the Reform of the House of Lords*, London: The Stationery Office.

Wakeham, Lord (2000b) 'The Lords: building a house for the future', *The Political Quarterly*, vol 71, no 3, pp 277-81.

Wheeler-Booth, M. (2001) 'Procedure: a case study of the House of Lords', *Journal of Legislative Studies*, vol 7, no 1, pp 77-92.

Whiteley, P. (1983) *The Labour Party in crisis*, London: Methuen.

Whiteley, P. and Winyard, S. (1987) *Pressure for the poor*, London: Methuen.

Willetts, D. (2000) *Browned off: What's wrong with Gordon Brown's social policy?*, London: Politeia.

Willetts, D. (2005a) 'Compassionate Conservatism and the war on poverty', Speech to the Centre for Social Justice (www.davidwilletts.org.uk).

Willetts, D. (2005b) 'A new Conservatism for a new century', Speech to the Social Market Foundation (www.davidwilletts.org.uk).

Williams, M. (2000) *Crisis and consensus in British politics: From Bagehot to Blair*, London: Macmillan.

Wright, T. (1997) 'Does Parliament work?', *Talking Politics*, vol 9, no 3, pp 202-5.

Wright, T. (ed) (2000) *The British political process: An introduction*, London: Routledge.

Index